HURT *and* HEALED *by the* CHURCH

Redemption and Reconstruction
after Spiritual Abuse

RYAN GEORGE

ISBN Paperback: 978-1-955051-33-0
ISBN eBook: eBook: 978-1-955051-34-7

Design by Vanessa Mendozzi
Published by Punchline Publishers

CONTENTS

PART 1. SON OF A (DANGEROUS) PREACHER MAN

PART 2. SUPPLANTED PROPAGANDA

PART 3. LIFE IN GREENER PASTURES

AUTHOR'S NOTE

To respect the healing journeys of those my father abused, the names of his other victims have been changed.

Some female readers, having experienced great harm from despicable men, might bristle at the references to God in the gendered term "Father" in this book. On a few occasions, I've used this name of God because (1) Jesus did and (2) that word was redeemed for me in an unconventional way. In fact, that particular reframing proves central to the narrative arc of this book.

PART 1

SON OF A (DANGEROUS) PREACHER MAN

“All abuse is spiritual abuse”

— DIANE LANGBERG,
author and psychologist

01 BEATEN OUT OF SUBMISSION

Unsafe churches beat into me that God was a mercurial bully, but Jesus has wooed me to his always-available embrace.

I remember the dark pine paneling in my pastor's living room. I vaguely recall seeing my mom's moist eyes over the minister's shoulder as he berated me. Awkwardly sprawled on his couch, I had no way to escape. He had crawled on top of me. I tried to recline to get away, but the back of the couch wouldn't let me retreat. As I pressed into the cushions, he braced himself above me—bulging eyes and a red face just inches away from my nose. He yelled that I was going to hell and that he prayed every Sunday that I would walk the aisle toward his pulpit and repent of my sin.

This claim confused me. Fourteen years earlier, he had listened to me say the sinner's prayer in his bedroom and then watched me get baptized in a fiberglass tank behind a New York choir loft. He had wrapped his arm around my shoulders during middle school, when he guided me through "rededication" at a Tennessee summer camp. I was left to wonder why he now condemned me to hell.

I was a high school senior who didn't drink, smoke, do drugs, have sex, or hang out with people who did. I didn't watch R-rated movies or porn. Swear words weren't part of my vocabulary. I tithed my high school paychecks to his church and served Sunday mornings, Sunday nights, and Wednesday nights in his congregation. My sins? I didn't like being homeschooled; I debated with my parents; and I sneaked Shania Twain CDs into the Sony Discman between the bucket seats of the truck I drove to work.

I didn't push back against the raging pastor who was the same age then as I am now. Candidly, as a stick figure of a teenager in 1996, I couldn't have pushed back against the man who'd proven his physicality was stronger than my arguments. On previous occasions, he had tossed me through a door, thrown me into a wall hard enough to break the drywall, and—with only one arm—hung me off the ground with his hand around my throat while my feet dangled. He had threatened more violence, including punching me in the face so hard "you'll be picking your teeth off the floor." Our shared faith told me all this was a merciful reprieve on justice because the Old Testament penalty for rebelling against parents was death by public stoning.

• • •

At 11:18 a.m. on Wednesday, December 9, 2020, I hit send on an email to my sisters, divulging these and other abuses from that pastor—our dad. We had all learned stories of other victims whom he and others like him had abused, and we had rallied around them. After days and nights of writing and editing, I took a deep breath and released to my sisters my stories of commiseration with those other victims.

At 11:25 a.m. the next day, I finished reading that email to my counselor. I choked on tears through a couple of the final sentences and looked up to see Lindsey crying too. We both exhaled slowly; and then I blurted, "It's a wonder I still go to church."

Like a lot of teenagers in the United States, I didn't have a choice in where I went to church, or even *if* I went to church. The dysfunction I knew was all I knew. As the son of an "independent, fundamental, Bible-believing, KJV-only" Baptist pastor, I wasn't even allowed to be curious about my faith—let alone visit other churches. That ban even included the churches my grandparents attended. Not until the middle of high school (when I got a job and worked weeknights) did I get any reprieve from the four services a week my dad held in a local elementary school cafeteria. We never missed a Sunday. We couldn't. Depending on when you visited that church for most of its existence, my immediate family represented between 8 and 80 percent of the congregation.

Strangely, even as an independent fundamental Baptist (IFB) pastor beat on my will and my body, I proudly carried the fundamentalist flag. I left home not long after that episode on my parents' couch to attend an IFB college that required attending four church services, four chapel services, at least two Bible classes, and five late-night prayer groups—every week for thirty-two weeks each year—plus mandatory revival services and a three-day Bible conference in lieu of spring break.

For many who leave the fundamentalist movement, or even religion in general, college is where they get intellectually curious and subsequently leave the faith. That wasn't my story. Abusive theology was dyed into the fabric of who I was in college, even as I chafed under its rules. In fact, to help me ace my undergrad writing internship, my dad handed over his weekly newspaper column from which I bullhorned inflammatory, self-righteous proclamations to what I now hope was absolutely no readers. When I left college for my first career stop in Indiana, I searched only for IFB options for my Sunday mornings, Sunday nights, and Wednesday nights.

I did eventually leave fundamentalism. Unwittingly, fundamentalists helped me do it. So did a bevy of people whose jaws dropped when I've told them stories from the religious institutions of my first two decades in evangelical Christianity. In addition to those raised eyebrows, some have replied, "I don't even have a category for that." Sadly, I do. Despite these stories being so indelibly carved into my memory, what were normal practices and unquestioned assumptions for me in the 1980s and 1990s are thankfully growing more and more foreign to my current daily experience.

The ensuing two decades of distance weren't spent on demolition, though I understand why so many others have utterly torn down their faith after experiences similar to mine. For me, Jesus is still the hope of the world; and his church is how his grace gets distributed to all of humanity. At the same time, few cultural institutions have pushed as many people away from their Creator as has the church. A good number of those pushed-away souls were the kids who attended caustic Christian schools, Bible colleges, and summer camps like those I vividly remember.

I wrote this book for fellow refugees of legalism, victims of religious abuse, and survivors of bastardized orthodoxy. I want you to know you can salvage an active, intimate, and thriving relationship with Eternal Love regardless of what you've experienced in the North American church.

It's a long shot, but I hope current fundamentalists read this book too. If that's you, I have no doubt that you've watched so many friends and family members leave your way of life. One way humans cope with that loss is by denigrating the choices and voices of those who exit our community. I hope you'll be able to understand and accept that not everyone who abandons the IFB movement is chasing immorality or comfort or acceptance from secular culture. I pray you can offer grace to those of us who've immigrated to a different way of seeing the Gospel.

I wanted to document the waypoints of my journey and articulate an answer to the question I asked my wife, Crystal, a few months before I started writing this manuscript: "How am I still here?" What I meant with those words was actually a more specific enigma that I wanted to unpack: "Why did I leave an abusive faith system but not Jesus?" I had the same influences, the same experiences, and the same programming as both those who still cling to an extremist system and those who've long since let go of everything related to religion. In the computational language of faith, I've been pondering, "How did I end up neither a 1 nor a 0?"

This isn't the first time I've wrestled with splitting the difference in a seemingly binary system. In one of my college classes, we took a test to determine how left-brained or right-brained we were. Beyond an interesting way to spend some class time, we hoped to confirm that our respective career choices aligned with our cognitive wiring. If we scored a 50, we'd be adept at artistic, empathetic, or relational occupations. A 100 meant we would work well with numbers or science or rules.

I kid you not: I scored a 75.

It turns out that was the perfect score for God's sovereign plan for my life. I ended up in a profession where I ricochet in the space between the 50 and the 100 sides of the spectrum. All day every workday. Basically, my value is that I'm serviceably in the middle.

I feel like I somehow scored a 75 in the test that categorizes my relationship with abusive theology, too. I'm not AWOL from what early Christ followers called "The Way," but I'm also not law enforcement. I'm neither the cynical expat of a heavenly country nor the Pharisee who legislates and prosecutes its citizens. I don't jump back and forth between 50 and 100; I just revel in life at 75. I have found a sweet spot in my soul, a place where Jesus is living and active. I pinch myself, hearing my life experience in the lyrics that Abner Ramirez sings in one of my favorite JOHNNYSWIM songs: "While you pray for revival, I'm already living in one."

In between the deconstructed and the fundamentalists, I've continually watched the restoration of marriages and the blessing of surrender. I co-lead a serving incubator at my church and an outdoor faith community in which guys from a half dozen churches gather every week. With continual proximity to wounded hearts, I've had a front row seat to the eradication of addiction and the redemption of pain, the adoption of orphans and the astounding sacrifice of those who hear soul whispers. As a congregant, I've been formed by the vulnerability of teachers and the transparency of leadership. I've watched shepherds respond quickly and thoroughly to unhealthy situations in their churches rather than covering them up. As the husband of a missions director, I've seen international ministry evaluated while American and even Western centrality were sifted out and replaced by humble curiosity. In garages, on pool decks, next to traffic cones, and even at the Cracker Barrel, I've stood a few feet away from brothers and sisters in Christ who've relinquished their idols, bowed their egos, or yielded their long-held dreams for kingdom benefit.

After witnessing this ridiculously long streak of reclamation, it's difficult to argue with the results. It might be crazy, but what Jesus is doing is working. My friends, family members, and I have left religious ventilators to inhale and exhale Heaven's breath with our own lungs. When we've put ego, security, and comfort on the altar, God has raised us to new lives and new heights. We've traded the American Dream® for kingdom flourishing, and Jesus has responded with deeper friendship with him and others. Sovereignty has blessed us with serendipities we couldn't have dreamed for ourselves, when we've let go of superstitious mindsets. My faith life is as bright, colorful, and detailed as the sample videos on the TVs in the back of Best Buy.

I shouldn't have been surprised; but during my formative years, preachers didn't talk much about how Jesus claimed that he came to bring abundant life. Many of those preachers didn't portray a winsome or attractive life.

I've lived two decades in abusive faith systems and now two decades outside of them. I've seen a lot more life outside of the secrecy and façades. I've felt more joy beyond the myopia and caste system. I've watched humility replace arbitrary legalism. I've seen a holy curiosity supplant an insecure certainty. I've witnessed and personally experienced life change from the inside out rather than behavior modified by image management, forced compliance, and public shaming. I've noticed carrots outperform sticks. Jesus has proven time and time again that Romans 2:4 is true—that it is his kindness that leads us to repentance.

So, it is with kindness that I write both to those who consider me a defector and to those with very real wounds who dismiss my assertions about finding healing in the church as ridiculous fiction. Whether you've thrown it all away or you wouldn't relinquish a single pixel of your image of faith, I hope you'll pray the same prayer over the remaining pages that I've prayed over them: "Lord, would you reveal yourself in a way that I can't escape?" For those who continue reading or listening as an outsider of all of this religious milieu—even if you've never prayed in your life—I'd invite you to pray that very same prayer and see what happens.

02 BEHIND THE HEADLINES

Unsafe churches with dark secrets were all I knew and experienced, but Jesus has shown me an incredible life available out in the daylight.

In the first few days after my birth, my parents fought over my official religion. My mom, a Lutheran, wanted me to be sprinkled under the banner of her Protestant faith. My dad, named after the patron saint of his local Catholic parish, wanted his firstborn to be baptized in the church Martin Luther protested. My dad won the fight, though I didn't learn until four decades later that I had started my life as a Roman Catholic.

When I was two years old, my dad made that argument moot when he walked into the North Java, New York, church where he'd previously served as an altar boy and asked his former priest, "Why did you lie to me all of these years?" See, my parents had recently joined a cult led by men like Bill Gothard and Jack Hyles. Both of my parents jettisoned their former religions and went all-in on their new belief system.

Two years later, after a week of vacation Bible school that included a live sheep in the church foyer, I got dunked as an independent fundamental Baptist.

Twenty-five years later I escaped the cult, started the reconstruction of my spiritual life, and got baptized into my third version of Christianity. Don't worry: the last one stuck. I'm not going for a Guinness world record or anything. I now have a connection with the Divine that I never imagined in my first three decades of life. I experience Jesus of Nazareth in ways that have proven healing and challenging, authentic and serendipitous. I've been drawn into a paradox of nuance and simplicity. Now my encounters with the supernatural challenge my intellect even as they flirt with mysticism.

Despite spending the 1980s and 1990s in a caustic religious system, I somehow love the hope of what church can be—what Jesus can do in and through it. For me, church has the potential to do for a broken world what no other human endeavor can. Being part of a faith community brings me life, and my conversations with fellow believers fill some of my favorite hours of every week. I thoroughly enjoy serving at our local assembly, where I've been on the same volunteer squad since 2006.

I don't think my current church has the corner on God, and I appreciate that its leaders have never stopped experimenting with what "church" is and looks like in a changing culture. It has showcased different styles of ministry during my years there. My church isn't perfect. It's not even perfectly aligned with my beliefs. But my wife's on staff there. I've baptized friends and family members there. It lets me connect with the global church that keeps a fire stoked in my ribcage. My fellow parishioners have helped me stay in love with the Source of All Good Things.

I've given my life to the mission of the church, and a fire burns in my belly to eradicate the cancers that grow in it. I have financially supported the Roys Report, which investigates abuse in the American church. I follow Instagram accounts that give voice to victims of church violence or expose the hypocrisy of American faith leaders. I read books about what's behind the façades of the evangelical movement. Probably like you, I mainline podcasts like *Christianity Today*'s The Rise and Fall of Mars Hill and *Gangster Capitalism*'s series on the Falwell family. I applaud the work of reporters for publications such as the *Fort Worth Star-Telegram* who have exposed hundreds of sex offender pastors in the Southern Baptist Convention. I can rattle off the names of disgraced pastors, evangelists, and Christian celebrities as fast as I cycle through the gears on my motorcycle.

You'll find one of my former pastors on that list of names. My dad—my pastor for fifteen years—is one of the serial sex abusers in the spotlight. In fact, he was considered for inclusion in a documentary about abuse in the IFB movement. To make matters worse, my name is Ryan Timothy George, and my dad's name is Timothy Nicholas George. So, two-thirds of my name is tied to a reputation that—at the time of writing—I'm thankful doesn't yet come up in a ton of Google search results.

When I read headlines about Ravi Zacharias, Bill Hybels, Johnny Hunt, Jack Schaap, James MacDonald, and others, my mind probably goes to a place yours doesn't—and I'm glad it doesn't. Those news stories make me think about what it must be like for their kids. I hear my mom's voice again: "How many people know my shame?" I imagine the family meetings, the awkward explanations, and the silent stares out the window that I know too well. I wonder what their next family Christmas will look like or how they'll talk about everything but the elephant in the room at Thanksgiving tables. I picture the awkward moment after a grandkid or nephew asks an intuitive question. What's conjecture for many folks reading the news is nonfiction for me. What's temporary fodder of the American news cycle is written onto my heart in scars.

If the households behind the celebrity pastor headlines are anything like mine, each family member will respond in a slightly different way. In my immediate family there's been denial and anger, mourning and disgust, shock and a lack of surprise. Some have rooted for me to write this book. Others consider me unforgiving and un-Christlike. My mom called me a "monster" after a family gathering and reportedly has said several times that I retroactively deserve the abuse I endured as a teenager for telling my story thirty years later.

Sin of this magnitude and with my dad's level of coverup brings with it a thousand tiny deaths. The fallout forces dozens of decisions you never anticipated making. Even dumb stuff like, *With which of my half dozen different family text groups do I feel comfortable sharing this personal news?*

I've gotten accustomed to explaining my weird family situation in outdoor prayer huddles, Bible study circles, and even Zoom calls with publishing professionals. Most of the pain related to my parents has subsided through my retelling, leaving just socially awkward facts. I shrug my shoulders, but I've often found the person across the table with mouth agape or the person on the left side of my monitor slowly shaking their head. I can't tell you how many times I've heard, "I'm so sorry!" from someone who doesn't know what else to say.

• • •

What I mistakenly thought was the first piece of the puzzle arrived in the fall of 2012. I can still remember the sound of Crystal setting plates on the kitchen table after the doorbell rang. When I opened the door, I found my sixty-five-year-old pastor standing on our tiny front porch alone. Nan, his wife, wasn't behind him or waiting in the car. I shot a glance over to our kitchen, which held only three place settings, all on one end of the table.

I welcomed Woody inside our home, but my heart was racing. I wondered what sin or hypocrisy in my life could've necessitated an intervention. In the church we shared with Woody, we refer to these confrontations as "*Help me understand* conversations." I racked my brain to think of any lies I could've been called on.

My mind jumped there, because back in 1998 on our first date, I asked Crystal, "If you came with a warning label, what would it be?"

She replied, "Be real with me." Over our twenty-five years together, I don't know anyone who has pursued truth, and the health truth brings, more than Crystal has. For a decade, her only tattoo was the Japanese symbol for "truth." She's a walking lie detector, and she's called me on my spin more times than I can count. So, in the ten paces from our front door to our dinner table, I raced through a personal inventory.

Woody and Crystal must've seen those mental gymnastics playing out in my eyes. "You're not in trouble," Woody interjected. We took our seats at the table, prayed, and then it was Crystal—not our pastor—who did the talking.

Crystal is a missionary kid and the missions director at our church. She takes groups to Nicaragua each year to work with those whose lives have been marred by sex trafficking. Since more than a third of the women Crystal disciples in the States have endured sexual harassment or assault, she carefully prepares women for what might be triggering moments. Across our dinner table, my wife shared that in one of those pretrip planning meetings, Ruthie, one of my kid sister's friends, had confided in Crystal that my dad had sexually molested her while she had attended his church a decade earlier.

Crystal wanted Woody to be present when she told me, because she worried that I would have an irrational response. It was a gut punch, for sure. But I had more questions than exaggerated emotions. This young woman had gone from being one of my sister's friends to one of my friends in our now-shared adulthood. Crystal had helped her find her first two jobs when she moved to our area. Ruthie later came on staff at our church.

I hated this for Ruthie.

And I hated this for my mom. Roughly a decade earlier, my dad had admitted to cheating on her with a college coed. That revelation came just a year or two before the incidents I was now learning Ruthie had endured. For some reason—neither that night nor in the years afterward—the nickel didn't drop in my head that what my dad had called an affair could've been a series of sexual assaults. At the time of Ruthie's revelations, what my dad claimed as an affair sounded like a gateway drug to sexual deviancy that eventuated in pedophile behavior.

I have a mostly blank hard drive in regard to the weeks that followed that watershed dinner with Woody. I don't remember any of my conversations with Crystal, Ruthie, or anyone else about the revelations. What I do remember is that Ruthie asked me to drive up to my parents' house to confront her abuser. I felt so honored to be trusted with that role—especially as the son of that abuser. Pushing back against my dad had been physically and emotionally dangerous for me in high school and college, but I steeled myself for this showdown.

My dad agreed to talk to Ruthie in the privacy of his Ford Windstar, parked in his driveway. I joined them as both moral support for Ruthie and as a witness to my dad's reaction. As the sun rose over the recently harvested soybean field behind his house, Ruthie unburdened her heart. She didn't threaten legal ramifications. She didn't threaten to go public. She firmly reminded him of what he stole from her and why it wasn't a small matter.

In response, he worked some spiritual jujitsu in an attempt to absolve himself of consequences—grabbing tiny fragments of Bible verses that served him while ignoring the large swaths of Scripture that would've condemned him. He told Ruthie not to tell her family or anyone in my family, especially his wife. That went for me too. He insisted nothing good would come from that. He warned that freeing Ruthie's story would only bring pain to her family and to mine. He claimed God had forgiven him and that there was nothing else that needed to be done.

I knew my dad was misusing Scripture, but I was torn about what to do next. I wanted to honor Ruthie's privacy—but I also wanted my dad to face consequences for his actions. I knew his responses were sinister and self-serving, but I didn't feel the freedom to tell my mom, my siblings, or anyone in Ruthie's family. As my wife and I gathered with my parents, my siblings, their partners, and their kids every subsequent Christmas, the weight of that secret hung over me like an anvil swinging from bailing twine. I eventually grew so uncomfortable that I took a backpacking tent to family Christmas and slept outside in the cold.

During my last visit to my parents' house, my wife overheard my then-sixty-six-year-old dad talking to two elementary-aged girls my mom babysat. Crystal, who was painting at a nearby table, pulled out her earbuds in time to hear him tell these *children* how the woman in Song of Solomon was praised for her body parts. Internal alarm bells rang inside Crystal's ears and heart. The truth she and I had been silently carrying for years suddenly burned too hot to contain. My dad had a problem, not a few mistakes in his past. Innocent women and girls needed to be protected from him. Crystal informed the girls' parents, but they assumed Crystal misheard my dad or that some sort of context was missing. That didn't sound like the Pastor George they knew.

At communion a few weeks later, I couldn't partake. I wrestled with the warning not to take communion if you have an unaddressed relational rift in your life. After the service, I talked to one of my pastors. I no longer remember his advice or his exact prayer in that moment, but I walked out of the room knowing what I had to do.

I met with Ruthie for lunch. My sister joined us, having finally learned of her best friend's trauma. We agreed to fast and pray over the course of a month and then meet again to decide what to do. The subsequent gathering eventuated in Ruthie FaceTiming her family members to reveal her secret trauma. Ruthie's husband, my sister, Crystal, and I sat nearby as she relayed what my dad had done to her and what he had said to her in the years since. Several days later, I joined Ruthie and her husband on a drive to a riverside park where she told her story to my mom. After my mom left to process this news alone, the rest of us left from there to pick up an off-duty police officer and confront my dad one last time at a highway rest area.

My dad knew this conversation was coming. He had threatened Ruthie a few days prior in a condescending voice, bullying her not to tell my mom. I heard it in real time from Ruthie's speakerphone. Learning in the parking lot of that highway rest area that my mom and my kid sister now knew of his abusive and deviant behavior, my dad grew agitated. His eyes darkened. Like a trapped badger, he threw all kinds of excuses and invectives at me and at my friend. In a beautiful moment, Ruthie's strong husband stepped in front of her to shield her from the evil. I told my dad that Crystal and I were putting boundaries around him, especially in light of the teenage girl who'd just come to live with us a month earlier. I handed him a piece of paper with the prerequisite actions he would need to complete if he wanted us to allow him back into our lives.

These assignments weren't draconian. They included confessing his molestation to the pastors whose churches he served, apologizing to my friend's family members and to my immediate family, getting into a recovery group or therapy regimen, and staying out of the pulpit. I had wanted to stipulate that my dad had to confess his sins to his brothers, but one of my sisters and her husband asked me not to go that far.

My dad protested these stipulations in person and refused to do them. A week or so later, Ruthie and I got typed form letters saying he'd completed the full checklist already. He claimed that the pastors for whom he filled pulpits had all said he was okay. He insisted he was healthy and forgiven.

I didn't believe him. Neither did Ruthie. At the same time, it wouldn't have surprised either of us if Maryland's IFB pastors or his current pastor in Delaware did look the other way. We doubted his claims about attending therapy and distrusted his apologies. Members of my family accused me of holding a grudge. After we put boundaries around family gatherings with my dad in attendance, my oldest sister emailed Crystal and me, condescendingly asking us how we define forgiveness. Our perception of my dad's lack of contrition has been questioned ever since.

But two years after my sister first questioned our hearts, my family learned that my dad hadn't confessed to anyone who might be a mandatory reporter. Not a single pastor. Not a counselor. Not a recovery group. And the only thing that had kept him out of the pulpit was Maryland's pandemic precautions. Right before that, though, another bombshell dropped while Crystal and I were celebrating our anniversary in Belize. My youngest sister waited until we arrived home to tell us that a 112-minute podcast interview by one of my dad's victims had dropped.

I knew the voice immediately. Lisa was the teenager with whom my dad had claimed to have shared an affair. Lisa detailed despicable things he had done to her, and she had receipts and witnesses. In fact, she had a desperate coverup letter my dad had handwritten to her from the same yellow legal pad on which he normally transcribed his sermons. She revealed that not only did my mom know the acts weren't consensual and that they had started before Lisa turned eighteen, but also that my mom gave a curious initial response to the news. Witnesses to this conversation heard my mom say, "Oh, not again."

This had been a pattern for my dad, and my mom had known about it for decades.

I learned from the podcast that my dad hadn't stepped down from his church out of a sense of honor as he had told me but because Lisa's mom had told him to leave immediately or else she'd go public with his predatory behavior. I suddenly wondered if this explained why my parents—who were half of our tiny IFB school's collection of teachers—had pulled me out of a class pizza party in the middle of a school day and moved us from Pennsylvania's mountains to an island in Maryland in 1986. The church and school where my dad had previously worked (and some of their affiliated IFB churches) paid my dad's salary for a year or so while he got the new church started. *Was that "make the problem go away" money?* I didn't know. I still don't. All of a sudden, it made sense that after my dad slithered out of the pulpit my parents drove almost two hours each way to what they called "marriage counseling" with an IFB pastor out of state. My dad didn't want to take a chance that any licensed counselor in Maryland would report his crimes. And he wanted an IFB voice to coerce my mom into staying with him and giving him sex.

For two decades, my dad publicly got away with those crimes. As a brave teenager, Lisa had reported the abuse to her IFB college's administrators. They kicked the can to the pastors with whom my dad fraternized. None of them came to her aid. Instead, they circled the wagons around her abuser. By the time she told her story on the podcast, Lisa had been suffering for more than twenty years because these "men of God" found the reputations of Maryland's IFB churches and schools were more important than justice.

Somehow, I had never put the pieces together. I'm dumbfounded almost every time I look at it all in retrospect. *How did I not figure this out?* My dad was a college graduate who pursued my mom when she was a seventeen-year-old high school student. They married sixty-five days after my mom turned eighteen. He'd been preying on minors since before I was born.

And then came another bomb. In the podcast, Lisa suggested that I had probably covered for my dad for two decades—that I must have known. I was married, out of the house, and living six hundred miles away when her abuse happened; but she assumed my mom or dad must have told me. To make matters worse, this podcast had been shared on an alumni Facebook group of those who'd survived the same college I had. To this day, that accusation is out there on YouTube and anywhere podcasts are available. My inability to see through my dad's lies now seemed to thousands of people to be at least negligence and maybe even complicity.

That night, I found Lisa on Facebook. I wrote an impassioned letter and pasted it into Messenger. I apologized for her pain. I expressed my anguish over her suffering. I told her the story my dad had told us. I assured her she was not alone as a victim or in wanting justice. I told her I had reported two sex offenders during the course of serving at our current church, and that I'd do anything to help her pursue legal action against my dad.

After hours of writing and editing, with sweaty hands, I hit *Send*.

The next day, Lisa replied with gratitude. The ensuing conversation overwhelmed my office hours. She asked if I'd talk to her attorney. I immediately agreed. He called, and I answered every question I could to the best of my knowledge. This justice-seeker had been helping other women prosecute former pastors like my dad. But I didn't know enough to help. All I had were my dad's lies and now a sense that a large portion of my life had been subject to a series of sleight of hand tricks. The lawyer explained the two options still available within Maryland's legal system. Justice didn't have a lot of time left in what should've been a generous statute of limitations. There was still hope—if we could find more evidence.

Before he hung up, the dejected attorney said something I'll never forget: "Man. Your dad was slick. He covered his tracks well."

I wished like crazy that I had anything—anything at all—to help this lawyer put this predator behind bars for what he did to Lisa. I wanted that monster far away from my wife, the teenager who would later become my daughter, my sisters, their friends, and the elementary and middle school students who used Pastor and Mrs. George's pool during humid summers. I felt helpless. I can't imagine what Lisa felt.

I spent a lot of time after that in counseling sessions, on long hikes alone in the woods, and in profound conversations with Crystal. I wrestled not so much with the fact that Jesus hadn't protected all of these girls from my dad but with the reality that God hadn't let me know what my dad was up to so I could've intervened. I didn't want to be a hero. I just wished I could've prevented so much pain. I took solace in the fact that Lisa and Ruthie now knew my heart. They seemed assured that I was for them.

As a personal silver lining, Jesus had allowed me to disconnect from the abusive theology that fueled my dad and his peers before I learned he should be a registered sex offender. The Holy Spirit guided the reconstruction of my faith with thick concrete walls before darkness threw grenades into my life. My Heavenly Father let me find his heart and luxuriate in his embrace years before I had to put boundaries around my biological father. Sovereignty opened my eyes to the nonsexual abuses of my childhood faith system before they were opened to my dad's sexual predation.

So, these compounded revelations didn't shake my faith. If anything, they led to some of the most intimate prayers of my life. I took comfort that the Inventor of Justice didn't need more evidence and wasn't surprised by any of the revelations about my dad. Over and over again, I reminded myself that Jesus threatened a fate worse than a torturous death to anyone that harmed a child. Even better, I grew thankful that the apostle Paul didn't say to let the Lord handle only justice—but also vengeance.

Payback would be hell.

As the months and years tick by, I root less and less for that hell—in part because aspects of that hell are already burning in my dad's life. I long for him to face deserved consequences and any ramifications that would help his victims heal. I want their pain to be vindicated, their stories to be validated.

At the same time, I pray often that my dad's heart will soften, that it's not too late, that he might repent. I ask the Great Physician to heal my mom's oft-broken heart and pray that the Prince of Peace will somehow redeem all of the betrayal she's endured. Her pride and her corrupted theology told her to cover for my dad. The fear and bitterness that have held her hostage have covered her with brittle armor. Though she has blocked me on social media and avoids seeing me in person when she's in town, I ask Jesus to hug her into the kind of love he has lavished on me.

The same Jesus that promised recompense for child molesters asked me to pray for my enemies and those that curse me. The God that waited for me to return his love waits for my dad as well. He waits for the corrupt pastors in our news feeds, too—while he gently holds the hearts of their victims.

I don't understand how that works. I probably won't in this lifetime. An early church father commiserated with this sentiment when he admitted that in our human condition, we "see through a glass darkly."[1]

At the same time, the past few years of my life have given me courage to shine a light into the darkness that covers thousands of churches and millions of their attendees. Maybe I can help prevent potential victims from experiencing trauma and indignity by exposing the intentionality behind the IFB movement, institutionalized legalism, and church abuse in general.

Abuse isn't an unfortunate exception in many American churches. The enablement and coverup are baked into their theology. Evil is woven so well into the fabric of religion that the threads of heinous crimes can hide in plain sight. Maybe by describing the malignant signs and heretical defenses of abusive doctrine, I can do for you what I couldn't do for Lisa, Ruthie, and my dad's other victims. Maybe I can tune your radar for danger to be more sensitive. Maybe I can show you an escape hatch, so you don't have to frantically search for one later. Maybe, by sharing my stories of transformation and redemption, I can give you or someone you love the courage and determination to fight back.

If you could use any of those maybes, please keep reading.

1 1 Corinthians 13:12 KJV

03 A CONTINUOUS RECONSTRUCTION

Unsafe churches considered me a heretic, but Jesus has reminded me often that I'm a new creation.

Historians give Plutarch credit for a thought experiment—or at least for recording it: the enigmatic Greek legend of the Ship of Theseus. As Plutarch's story goes, Theseus and his crew rowed the *Argo* into their home harbor after defeating Crete. While the *Argo* sat in harbor as a tribute to their hero, the Athenians worked over many years to preserve it. As timber rotted, they replaced it, piece by piece. Over time, the entirety of the *Argo* would be composed completely of new wood that had never been part of the original. That's where the enigma came in:

At what point, if any, did the *Argo* stop being the *Argo*?

Was the new-wood version still the *Argo,* or was it a replacement?

If so, at what point did it become a replacement?

Or was the *Argo* defined by something other than its physical material?

Philosophers have debated the inherent questions of this puzzle for millennia. I'm not a philosopher, and I don't have an answer to any of these questions. But I've lived an *Argo*-like story for the past three decades.

My childhood faith was constructed for arbitrary culture wars by IFB leaders who indoctrinated me and hundreds of thousands of my peers. IFB leaders inculcated us with a very specific narrative of that battle. They force-fed us with a story of cultural oppression. We were stuffed with the virtues of a radical set of traditions we didn't realize were only decades old. Over time, though, parts of that warship fell into disrepair through skirmishes and decay. One by one, my untrustworthy boards were replaced with new timber. Truth replaced distortion. Scripture replaced heresy.

Grace displaced legalism.

And one day after years of these individual repairs, I looked up from the dock where my ship was moored and realized my faith and worldview were mostly composed of new materials. I'm not sure when exactly the *Argo* of my soul had been replaced. I just knew it had.

The word *deconstruction* is all over Christian social media, blog posts, and podcasts. Even former evangelical thought leaders and worship leaders are walking away from the Bible, from Jesus, and from major tenets of orthodox Christianity. So have non-famous people in my life. Rather than replace weathered pieces, they've disembarked and let their vessels sink where they left them. Or they've taken just the parts of their faith they liked with them and built personal canoes.

I don't blame them. Trauma, heresy, and blasphemy often don't leave much to redeem from our *Argos*. Refugees of these broken churches have washed up on the beach of my life, clutching pieces of splintered faith. They didn't care about rebuilding their boats, just getting on with their lives. All they knew is they were free from a vindictive, mercurial deity and his narcissistic shamans.

My story should've gone the same way. But despite taking on a lot of water, my *Argo* didn't sink.

A large part of the credit for that goes to new friends who came into my life to bail water and patch holes. I couldn't do it alone. I needed to rub shoulders with people whose lives were full of attractive vibrance—not just church busyness—people whose lives looked like Christ's yoke was actually easy. I heard seminary-trained pastors say, "I don't know," and ministry leaders say, "I used to think the Bible said this, but I've discovered I was wrong." Patient mentors gave me the gift of attuned listening as I tried to make sense of my story. I commiserated with others who had abandoned similar religious backgrounds. All of these people kept pointing me back to the actual words and example of Jesus—not a specific kind of church, not an accepted creed, and not narrowly selective slices of the Bible.

I don't know if this is descriptive or prescriptive, but I had to expand my religious experience. I researched my primary spiritual pathways and learned how I connect best to Jesus and how I sense the Holy Spirit's promised presence. I listened to people with different takes on faith topics and from multiple denominations. I got to experience church in different languages and cultures. When the Bible app arrived, I started reading and listening to the library of Scripture from multiple English translations. Eventually, I made a weekly habit of visiting a licensed professional counselor, who pushed against the lies I'd been told and the lies I've told myself. I spent a lot of time alone in the woods, whispering and crying and sighing as I talked to Jesus about my broken *Argo*.

In diverse and sovereign crucibles, my boat somehow didn't fall apart under the decay of bastardized theology. In hundreds of small moments, I found new wood, new ropes, and new sails at just the right time and in just the perfect shape to replace what was damaged or rotten in my soul. Benevolent interjections proved for me what the patriarch Joseph told his brothers: that evil's intent was foiled with a redemption meant not just for me, but also for those whose lives touch mine.

I choose the word *evil* on purpose. I think darkness uses unsafe churches. Hell's roaring lion salivates when religion dehumanizes those made in the image of God. I picture the enemy of Heaven rubbing his hands together in glee when the character of Jesus is distorted, and the work of the Holy Spirit is hijacked. An abandoned faith—especially in its modern, public scale—energizes the opponent of the One who defined himself as the source of all love and all good things.

Thankfully, redemption confounds those dark forces. Reconstruction shines a spotlight on Heaven's ongoing reclamation project. Renovated boats in the harbor bolster the hearts of the redeemed. New wood and ropes and fabric radiate with hope. Strong, seaworthy ships imbue us with the courage to leave the relative safety of land and explore new horizons.

The pervasiveness of past and present harm caused by unsafe churches can make the work of rebuilding spiritual boats—let alone a massive marina's worth—seem not only daunting but also hopeless, maybe even pointless. So, why start the process of repair? Why try the expensive and difficult undertaking of renovation? Why don't we just cut our losses, burn the ships, and build new lives in safe subdivisions or in verdant fields?

Because we were made for the sea. Because there's an ache inside us that asks if we're here for more than existence, subsistence, and self-indulgence. We've experienced altruism and realized survival of the fittest doesn't usually reward that. We've sensed wonder and serendipity and love that chance doesn't need and for which humanism has, at best, only excuses.

Maybe I shouldn't speak for you. Maybe you haven't seen a delicate beauty, a mind-boggling orderliness in nature, or an inescapable tenderness that stops you in your tracks. Maybe you've not attended a cookout or business mixer with someone of faith living an attractive life. Maybe your trust in others has been so frequently and thoroughly abused that you can't imagine giving a person associated with Jesus access to your heart.

First, know that you're not alone. Your experience might be unique, but it is not unknown. Many of us refugees commiserate with you about the repercussions of fleeing toxic or even abusive religion. We'd be the first to admit that the grind of refugee life is not where ballets are choreographed or standup comedy specials are written. Losing your religion can bring gray, lonely hopelessness.

What you've felt is legitimate. Your story deserves to be known and held with kindness. Leaving what you left is not an easy path to the rest of your life. Getting to your current camp may have been treacherous, but it's not where you're destined to finish out your precious life.

There's more.

There's better.

There's hope.

I can attest to those claims only because my unsafe belief system fell apart when I ran into haunting questions. *What if there's part of my relationship with Jesus that I've been missing? What if there's more intimacy and acceptance available than I currently experience? What if some of those who've defected from fundamentalism actually immigrated to a more fulfilling faith experience?* One by one, I learned those *what ifs* were whispers from my Creator—aches embedded in my chest.

As I've sought more intimacy with God, I've been convinced that life with Jesus can be vibrant. Asking those questions has led me to a more winsome faith, though not without consequences. I couldn't hold on to both my old beliefs and this newfound faith reality.

My unfulfilling certainty splintered on the reefs of mystery and enigma. Ever since, I've been exploring the kind of nuance inherent in the relationship between a finite human and the Infinite One. My assumptions and clichés keep breaking on the rocks of hard realities. Unconditional love regularly confronts my tendency to revert to self-righteousness. My brokenness has led to healing.

After leaving an unsafe belief system, I've had moments with the Holy Spirit where he almost tangibly wrapped his arms around me as he whispered "I see you" into my soul. I couldn't keep that to myself. I don't own whatever *it* is, anyway. And I didn't need to keep it a secret to make what I own more valuable. There's plenty to go around, and it can't be hoarded. All that to say: I hope you can experience it for yourself.

I don't mean to imply that I've reached the mountaintop and have everything figured out. My faith is still evolving, still growing, still course-correcting. Following Jesus has caused my GPS to interject "Recalculating!" over and over again. I'll probably look back on this book—even though it has been bathed in prayer—with some critiques a decade from now. I hold a sneaking suspicion that's healthy and good.

I don't yet have answers to all of my questions. What I do have are personal discoveries that might serve as compass headings for you to try. I hope they lead you to the freedom, adventure, and fulfillment I've known—and a reconstructed *Argo* of your own.

04 ACCEPTING THE CULT LABEL

Unsafe churches declared that I was one of a chosen few, but Jesus has convinced me he wishes everyone would surrender to him.

A couple weeks ago, my buddy and his wife joined us for tacos. After we transitioned from the dining room to the living room, the conversation made its way from wakeboarding to parenting and then to our backstories. I've co-led two faith communities with this friend for a decade, and we've shared a lot of vulnerable moments with each other. But I'd never heard some of the tales of his and his wife's past that they shared that Thursday night.

My ministry partner and his wife took turns telling stories about when they started dating—when she still lived in a cult compound. Her church's parishioners all lived on the same street as the church, and they'd built each other's houses—the only houses in the subdivision. Their pastor lived in a mansion behind the gate at the back of the property. The commune flourished—until it didn't. The youth pastor murdered his wife, while other men of the church traded theirs. Some of the details of this faith community matched those of the different documentary series my wife loves to watch on Netflix.

I'm tempted to look at the cult of my youth as an entry-level one. My specific corner of fundamentalism didn't include communes, though I was told my fundamentalist college had barbed wire and infrared sensors on the walls of our campus where cameras monitored our movement. One of my buddies on the campus security team claimed that all but sixty square feet of the outdoor space on our campus was covered by cameras—in 1996.

(That's how most colleges would respond to a couple sneaking forbidden sex under the solar panels next to the campus pool, right?) Our leaders didn't make the news like David Koresh. Nobody bought matching Nikes and drank poison together like the Heaven's Gate members. We didn't even have a cool name like that, though my dad suggested that all alien encounters were interactions with demons who could travel at the speed of light. Jim Jones' followers drank lethally laced Flavor Aid at his command. We were forced to drink a figurative Kool-Aid filled with relational and spiritual toxins that choked humanity and individuality out of us.

I felt that insecurity about my cult again yesterday. I was talking to a publishing specialist about my life story, and she asked, "What was the name of your cult? Or are you saying the cult is just fundamentalism?" Those are legitimate, pragmatic questions; but I heard, "Were you *really* in a cult?" It resonated with a question I had asked myself multiple times over the past year: "Are you making a bigger deal out of your spiritual past than it is?" In that moment, as her questions hung in the air, I wished my cult had another name other than fundamentalism. I regretted that the subculture of my youth wasn't weird and salacious enough for outsiders—at least until the *Shiny Happy People* documentary dropped.

I've known since middle school that I wasn't a normal person, but I thought my first two decades on the planet were normal-adjacent. In my mind, my eccentric beliefs and practices weren't any odder than those of costumed attendees at Comic-Con or a Renaissance Faire. I was just some version of a Bible nerd. It took time and distance to realize what I actually experienced was cult life.

Cult as a word and concept is having a moment. As more of us Westerners are connected online and comparing our experiences, we're realizing some of our formative ecosystems were not normal within the culture at large. That has led to a burgeoning genre of both fiction and nonfiction entertainment exploring these rabbit holes. For those that get out, there are also Instagram accounts and memes about subcultural anomalies that we survived. We discovered our former cult status by exposure to the larger world, or at least to healthier churches.

At the same time, that enlarged connectedness allows people to find each other, speak in their communal shorthand, and prioritize their lives around their shared passions. This happens so frequently memes about cults like CrossFit, Apple, and essential oils fill our social media streams. It's not just lifestyle products. Our political landscape has moved from partisan platforms to cultish camps. You have to be ride-or-die for your team; you have to defend the hypocrisy of your demagogues and support whatever company line is determined for your red hat or light blue tie.

Turns out, humans are adept at putting the *cult* in *culture.*

But that's not what I mean by *cult* in this book. While those dynamics can be true of many faith systems, that label in the following pages refers to a religious sect that (1) worships in an unorthodox way, (2) holds an extreme stance on a tertiary belief, or (3) has an elevated susceptibility to authoritarianism. Your dictionary or Google search will have a different definition, but those realities have been both my observation and lived experience.

If you've been bristling at me using the word *cult* to describe a large segment of evangelical faith, I feel you. It took me more than a decade outside of the faith system of my youth to use that word in describing it.

After leaving the clutches of abusive theology, I first framed its orthopraxy (prescribed behavior) and orthodoxy (prescribed beliefs) as simply more conservative than what other churchgoers experienced. Then, I moved to calling it more legalistic. Eventually, though, as do many who wrestle with the packaging of their former faith, I realized almost everything about the milieu of my church experience had been malignant—if not dangerous. Over time, as I read more books about abuse, trauma, mental health, and church history, I realized that the movement that swallowed the first half of my life was a system intentionally designed, managed, and protected to create the realities I'd known.

The more I witnessed healthy leadership, humble shepherding, and empathetic mentoring, the more I realized that the guardians of my previous faith weren't well-intentioned-but-misdirected sales reps. No, they were vengeful, arrogant, insecure shamans who leveraged corrupted theology for their own gain. It wasn't just my dad. That group of deceived and deceiving leaders included a large collection of the preachers, missionaries, and educators in a movement with tentacles reaching around the globe.

Part of the success of the IFB movement's subterfuge emerged from the inability to define our cult outside of our beliefs and codes of conduct. While some of the more extreme sects within the cult no doubt looked more like the subjects of documentary exposés and podcast journalism, a lot of it was only in the vicinity of that stuff. We weren't hiding on a ranch or back in some remote valley. We were on Main Street. We were your plumber or police officer, your daycare worker or the guy cleaning your carpet.

We held loose connections with the grossest predators and the most egregious dehumanizers. My dad got the *Sword of the Lord* newspaper with the cult's latest talking points—the same paper that other ironfisted pastors read before yelling invectives at their congregations. We trained under Bill Gothard's curriculum, which among other cultish tenets included indoctrination for victims of sexual assault by church leaders. (Gothard's materials told victims to accept their abuse as a gift from God to show off his grace and mercy for the Lord's anointed and to prove their own dedication to the Gospel.) We used the same homeschool curriculum as parents in the Quiverfull movement that spawned families such as the Duggars. We distributed the same fear-based Chick Tracts that men from more extreme sects left atop urinals and pay phones. We read the same Scofield and Thompson Chain-reference Bibles that decades of predators and narcissists used to defend their unchecked power.

Fundamentalist almost always arrived in a sentence with *independent* when describing our brand of Baptist faith. In the IFB movement, nobody could tell a pastor what to do with his congregation or what to say to it. That included the people who attended his church. So, while abuse and heresy ran rampant in the unchecked individualism of our churches, none of us could see a bigger picture. We didn't know our experiences were abnormal. Abusers rubbed shoulders at "preacher fellowships," but their respective secrecy didn't allow most IFB pastors to see their abuses as widespread, let alone systemic. As with our Southern Baptist Convention counterparts, any potential reform would look like Whac-A-Mole. That independence protected despots and dictators ruling their fiefdoms in their own image.

In this way, fundamentalism has proven to be both a cult and a cult incubator. Each IFB church could create its own cult within the framework of ideology of the movement at large. Preachers often made up their own definitions of orthodoxy to which they held their congregations accountable.

To be fair, religion in general has been fraught with grift and abuse since the beginning of spirituality as a social construct. Faith systems have protected patriarchy and racism since they first appeared on the planet. Historians have documented how religious zealotry has overlapped with jingoist nationalism so often and so much that the Venn diagram is almost a single circle, particularly in the United States. Powerful men have exploited the church for earthly gain at the cost of eternal consequences since long before Jesus arrived to rebuke it. White Christian men have weaponized Scripture against people of color, women, children, opponents, and outsiders ever since the Bible was canonized. Where that more universal hijacking of the Gospel becomes a cult is in the way it's packaged and defended. At the time of writing, IFB preachers are still quoting Paul's letter to the Galatians to claim protection over their bastardized Gospel: "But though we, or an angel from heaven, preach any other gospel unto you than that which we have preached unto you, let him be accursed."[2] Even though each of them preach something that arrived more than eighteen hundred years after Paul's Gospel, they claim theirs as the original intent of the Creator. They don't just claim that their denomination or Christianity is exclusive; many bark that their "fundamentals" are the only, narrow path to heaven and God's approval.

Each of these preachers makes up their own parameters around that gospel. Then they declare that every other religious person in the world who doesn't ascribe to their full slate of standards is bound for hell—or barely making it into heaven on a Romans Road technicality. They decide everything they want their gospel to include and then challenge congregants to accept everything as a package deal or spend eternity in torment. These yelling, sweating preachers fume about non-IFB churches as though they are led by Satanic operatives. Inside their walls, everyone who kisses the ring of the flamethrower gets eternal life. These demagogues-in-miniature reward the sycophants who stay under their specific brand of brimstone with affirmation, promotion, and sometimes even physical gifts. Any who don't bow to these preachers' egos can be subjected to public rebuke, excommunication, and even extreme shunning.

Not all IFB or unsafe churches are that extreme, and some of the healthier congregations aren't even close to the middle of the cult spectrum. But they often use the same hymnals, Sunday school materials, or Christian school curriculum as the churches represented in this book. They occasionally send their kids to the same summer camps or colleges as do the extremist churches, and they often ascribe to the same talking points.

---

2 Galatians 1:8 KJV

You might hear words like *cult* and *fundamentalist* and *extremist* in the news and picture brainwashed rural simpletons—backwoods mouth breathers with low IQs. Those assumptions might even make you feel smug for not buying into the construct of a religious faith at all. Even if what you see in a cable news scroll is the far end of a continuum, I don't fault you for avoiding the whole spectrum—though I would vouch for an alternative option for relating with the supernatural than either extremism or avoidance.

Malignant people will always take advantage of humanity's primal desires and good intentions. The most cunning can build fiefdoms and even small empires with these tactics. People with our same insecurities and longings can be deceived and manipulated just like anyone else. I want to believe that's the case with most folks in IFB churches.

Even in a seemingly problematic library of ancient texts, the Jesus I've met isn't the problem. He didn't design the church as we see it in the news. He called his followers to the opposite of the dogma and behavior that fundamentalists practice daily. His exact words—those printed in red ink throughout the New Testament—condemn the hate and vitriol many fundamentalists spew over the souls embodied around them. Christ's recorded example demonstrates a way of living and a worldview 180° opposed to what I experienced growing up and what you might've seen in documentaries or social media clips. The teachings and patterns of Jesus compose a light that reveal the cracks in dark and wicked façades. The way people around Jesus responded to his message and example reveal that the movement he started has been hijacked by connivers—just like almost every other human institution on the planet.

If you and I are growing more like Jesus, then people will respond to our empathy and authenticity the same way. As I've pursued that impact, I've needed to constantly listen to diverse voices in my life, to regularly evaluate my opinion silos, and to consistently pursue humility with everything I have.

Any secular or sacred belief system can become a cult in one shape or another, and all of us are susceptible in varying degrees to the temptations inherent in these harmful ecosystems. The first step in confronting these distortions and robbing them of more victims is shining light into their shadows. Rescue follows the unmasking of perpetrators and the naming of their crimes—legal ones and otherwise. I don't use a lot of names in this book because these pages aren't a prosecution. I'm not trying to litigate any specific case, because that's not my role in what I hope is a reformation. I'm not trying to drive a cancel mob, though a loss of platform could be the best thing to happen to fundamentalism's shamans, let alone for their congregations.

No, I hope you'll gain filters through which to absorb news stories, personal anecdotes, and even your own experience. I hope there's enough of an attractive real thing to make any counterfeits obvious, because Jesus and his Way have been the truest thing about the last two decades of my life.

05 A LAUGHABLE IRONY

Unsafe churches coached me on how to look for loopholes in a legalist system, but Jesus has proven that there are no holes in his love.

The biggest irony of my experience in IFB churches has been that fundamentalism isn't about the fundamentals. You can't have more essentials than the rest of your religion and call yourself a minimalist. You can't have more blocks in your foundation and claim a smaller footprint. You can't be a fundamentalist with more requirements than the founder of your faith had.

Jesus didn't have rules about what styles of music his followers could listen to or what kind of clothes they should wear to church. He didn't tell the women in his entourage or in the surrounding crowds where their hemlines should be. In red letters or even black ones, Jesus didn't tell us how many church services a week people should attend. English wouldn't be a language until half a millennium after he left Jerusalem for the last time. So he definitely didn't require anyone to read any specific English translation of the words he spoke or the stories from his life that his biographers would someday transcribe.

Rebuffing a religious lawyer (arguably a fundamentalist of his day), Jesus reduced the 613 laws of the *mitzvoth* in the Jewish Torah to two: love God with all your heart and love your neighbor as yourself. He didn't just say these were the most important, though that was the question he was answering. Jesus proclaimed that all of the law and the prophets hung on those two commands. He would know. He's the reason we have Leviticus and Deuteronomy. He carved the first tablets Moses carried down Mount

Sinai. According to his brother, James, Jesus is the source of all good gifts. Those gifts include beneficial boundaries. If hundreds of rules were better for those of us who come to him through the New Testament version of the Gospel, he'd have given us hundreds of laws while he was here.

He didn't.

He came to earth because he loved us, because he wanted to give us a way to live in love together for eternity. This isn't a hippie version of Jesus, a watered-down dose of God. Love isn't just an aspect of who Jesus is. He was the walking embodiment of it. We know this because Jesus said if we've seen him, we've seen the Father. No matter which translation of the Bible you read, you can't escape a God of love.

"God is love."[3]

"For God so loved the world."[4]

"See how very much our Father loves us!"[5]

"We love him, because he first loved us."[6]

"And may you have the power to understand, as all God's people should, how wide, how long, how high, and how deep his love is. May you experience the love of Christ."[7]

While true love often needs boundaries, it doesn't need a lot of rules. In fact, in romantic relationships like the one between Jesus and his bride (the church), rules and trust are inversely proportional. In requited, fervent, selfless love, each half of the relationship can luxuriate in mutual trust. And trust doesn't need rules. Even outside of romantic partnerships, relationships based on love need fewer rules than those based on transactions.

In his book *Better Decisions, Fewer Regrets*, Andy Stanley tells the story of a conversation with a young lady he and his wife fostered for a season. The teenager wanted to know the house rules. If she was like me, she wanted to find the loopholes, the technicalities, the unwritten gap in the fence about which she could later say, "But that's not what you *said*." Andy knew this but still obliged her. He grabbed a note card and wrote "HONOR"

---

3 1 John 4:8 CEV

4 John 3:16 KJV

5 1 John 3:1 NLT

6 1 John 4:19 KJV

7 Ephesians 3:18–19 NLT

on it. He spun the card toward his foster child and slid it in front of her. He explained that honoring his wife, Sandra, was the couple's full list of rules. The young lady protested this. Over her time in their home, she chafed under it. That one rule couldn't be gamed. There was no "letter of the law" to exploit —just the inescapable spirit of one. On that law hung all of Sandra's law and Andy's prophets.

Jesus' list of fundamentals was shockingly short for someone laying the foundation of an entire religious system. Most corporate mission statements have more stated objectives than the short list Jesus gave. He wanted a relationship that followed his whispers, a connection that pulsed in time with his heartbeat. Simple, unfettered love is the most beautiful kind of love. It doesn't have to be earned, maintained, or proven. It's just known. And that pervasive connection is what Jesus wanted us to fully know.

So, the list of requirements and the web of restrictions that define unsafe churches aren't from Jesus. The arbitrary regulations aren't omniscient or sovereign. They can't be. They're myopic. They're artificial. They're human.

As fundamentalists claim to spurn the traditions of mainline denominations and other faith systems in favor of a supposedly personal relationship with God, they form idols out of their traditions, their sacred cows, and their extra-biblical yard sticks. They try to build and maintain a romance with Jesus with noncanonical rules instead of intimate love. Having been a fundamentalist from 1982 until 2002, I can tell you that the marriage a fundamentalist shares with Jesus looks less like a honeymoon and more like Stockholm syndrome.

Love is work, sometimes difficult work. But true love can't be earned. No amount or severity of fundamentals will lead to a thriving love, an abundant life, or an attractive existence. Just as with the Tower of Babel, none of us can stack enough fundamentals—enough steps—to shorten the distance between Heaven and our imperfection. If anything, that baked clay creates barriers to an intimate relationship with our Creator. Our towers of self-righteousness lead to confusion and division and people moving away.

One of the other analogies of our relationship with God is that of father and child. As with parenting, Jesus demonstrated that a trajectory toward spiritual maturity should evolve from the training wheels of rules to the impetus of love. That's not a movement from difficulty to ease. If anything, the more I try to be "guided by the Spirit"[8], the tougher my spiritual assignments have grown. It's more difficult to wear authenticity to church than a suit. It's harder to listen to inconvenient prompts from the Holy Spirit than music performed in prairie dresses. It's more uncomfortable to bring my sins and dysfunction into the light than to avoid the dance floor at a coworker's wedding. Reading eighteenth-century English is less taxing than managing the tensions of justice and mercy, accountability and grace, public worship and private piety.

I've learned that a faith based on affection rather than fear isn't easy. It's just a different kind of hard. In his song, "Surely We Can Change," David Crowder describes the challenge of following love instead of rules: "And I don't know what to do with a love like that. And I don't know how to be a love like that."

A simpler faith proves harder to measure, to quantify, to gain an edge in comparison with the people in our caste. Our security in where we are with Jesus can't be based on superficial criteria, and that's frustrating to someone—especially a bootstrap American—who wants to control our place on the org chart. Within the country that invented broadcast television and Photoshop, Facebook, and Instagram, it's particularly frustrating to be called to personal surrender instead of public image management.

Whether the comparison is marriage or parenting, we can't escape the individualism of each other's relationship with Jesus. My favorite vacation locations and activities with Crystal look different from those in your marriage. The things that convince her and me of each other's love might not move the love meter for my friends. Different children with different personalities—even within the same family—require different relational dynamics to nurture them to their truest maturity and fullest potential. Our respective relationships with Jesus grow from nuanced intimacy, tailored love, and bespoke encounters. Following Christ's heart instead of rigid tradition frustrates Pharisees who want to standardize what it means to look like Jesus.

Jesus told some people not to tell of his miracles and others to go tell of his resurrection. He healed some people with spoken words and others with a touch and at least one other through a passive connection to his robe. He

---

8 Galatians 5:16 CEV

turned down a disciple in Decapolis yet invited disciples in Galilee. Jesus told Peter to stay in his boat and cast a net into the same lake where he also told him to leave the boat and walk on water. He told one man he healed to take up his mat and walk away, and he asked others to go show themselves to a priest. He made a donkey speak for a day and a high priest mute for months. He told the rich young ruler to go sell all he had for the poor but praised the woman who washed his feet with extravagantly expensive perfume rather than sell it for the poor. In back-to-back *sentences*, he told a woman who'd just been pulled out from under her adultery partner (1) that she wasn't condemned but (2) that she should "go and sin no more."[9]

It's not that Jesus is trying to be ambiguous. He's clear on his instructions, but he's also personal. Unity around his love and mission doesn't require conformity. In fact, it thrives in diversity. That's why he gives different gifts, different personalities, different burdens, and different assignments. When Peter asked about John's assignment, Jesus asked, "What does that matter to you?"[10] No matter what Jesus wanted from John, he wanted Peter to feed his sheep.

That diversity thrives when there are fewer rules, fewer universal parameters. The Gospel was designed for both glossy Monaco and arid Morocco. Jesus wants to reveal himself amidst Kansas corn fields and Hollywood production sets. We can follow Jesus behind iron curtains and across Bible Belts. But that requires flexibility and pragmatism, both of which were frowned upon in the unsafe churches I endured. Freedom and autonomy were threats to institutional conformity and pastoral control. Individual expressions of faith jeopardized the levers pastors could pull and the switches administrators could toggle to keep their organizations in their image. My experience in IFB institutions proved that the fundamentals were human, not divine. The standards purported as basic and foundational were enforced with more detail and complication than what Jesus actually said.

To preserve a 1950s version of American asceticism, churches and schools were drowned in a metaphoric formaldehyde. That's why they needed so many revival services. Only dead organisms need resuscitation.

---

9 John 8:11 NLT

10 John 21:22 NIRV

Fire and brimstone didn't bring life to the plains that Lot and his family fled, and the sulfuric sermons yelled at me stirred at best the temporary energy that fear can generate. Fear and shame make poor substitutes for the sustaining power of love. Few, if any, things set on fire by arsonists look alive, let alone stay alive. In legalistic ecosystems, I was covered in a suit of self-righteous matchsticks, living a superstitious existence that was far from a vibrant faith.

Abundant life intimidates the stationary nature of religious traditions. That shouldn't surprise anyone. Jesus was almost always walking when he called out, "Follow me."

06 HIJACKING SCRIPTURE

Unsafe churches forbade me from asking questions, but Jesus has often assured me that truth isn't afraid of inspection.

In second grade, I could pass comprehension tests while reading on a machine set to scroll my assigned reading at two hundred words per minute. That school year, I completed all of the curriculum for second grade, all of advanced placement second grade, and part of third grade. Five years later during my last year in an IFB day school, I tied with a classmate for valedictorian with a 98.6 GPA.

I couldn't tell you what my GPA was in high school—and not just because I listened to Rush Limbaugh for three hours during every school day. I was homeschooled and didn't care. I hated not being able to compete, even though I had been consistently bullied at my old school. I failed all but one science class and only got a passing D in physics—and that was only thanks to a technicality. Thankfully, Maryland required only one passing science grade to get a high school diploma.

In college, my grades shot back up. Once I got to my sophomore year, I really turned it on. I minored in both graphic design and advertising/public relations. Almost every art project at my alma mater was publicly critiqued, and professors hung all A-graded projects on the walls for weeks in our art labs. By my junior year, I was competing in the same classes as graphic design majors and saw my design work on the wall at least as many weeks as I didn't. My senior year, I got the first perfect score that the dean of education ever awarded to a senior writing portfolio. I graduated with academic honors, the senior writing award, and a national marketing manager job waiting for me.

So, if you're looking at my academic life as an ice cream sandwich, you see cookies at or near the top of my class squishing a lackluster time of insufficient drive during my homeschool years. My dad shamed that creamy middle effort, even though I saved enough from my high school paychecks to pay cash for a year and a half of college. He said I should've been motivated by glorifying God, not by competing with other students.

That cloud rained on my first semester of college grade reports. At the end of the semester, I registered to take eighteen credit hours for the pending spring semester, including a junior-level Bible class and catamaran sailing. If you've never had to write an eight-page paper on church discipline while also learning how to tie nautical knots, you're missing out. But that effort wasn't the biggest response to my dad's shaming. No, my primary rebuttal came from the English 102 research paper that loomed over a semester full of note cards, bibliographies, and mandatory rough drafts. I manipulated the parameters of the assignment to pick a topic not on the recommended subject list. I wanted to prove the thesis that Jesus was competitive. Obviously, no books in our six-story campus library addressed that topic. So, I had to take phrases out of context from books about Jesus' life. I don't have a copy of this paper, but I assume I handled Scripture with equal disregard for context.

What I actually proved had nothing to do with whether or not Jesus wanted to win anything. In retrospect, my greatest demonstration wouldn't hit me until I started writing this book twenty-five years later. That paper illustrated how I approached Scripture. As a high school graduation gift, my church gave me a huge black Thompson Chain-Reference Bible. That heavy King James unfolded as a leather-bound Rorschach test of sorts. I came to it with an idea of what I expected it to mean. I used fragments of Scripture to affirm what fundamentalists had taught me. On the micro level, I wanted a Jesus who competed for souls. On the macro level, I wanted a Christ who was a fundamentalist—instead of a Messiah framed by fundamentalists. My Jesus agreed with me, and I could prove it.

Back in 1984, Prego began airing a series of TV commercials you can still watch thanks to YouTube. They featured Italian Americans (or actors who fit the part) to give credence to their store-bought spaghetti sauce. In every commercial, one character would ask if the sauce could possibly include the same onions, garlic, herbs, and "homemade taste" as sauce that didn't come in a jar. The hosts of the meals just kept repeating the same replies to the interrogation: "It's in there." Those commercials complemented my freshman research paper a decade later. Was Jesus competitive? "It's in there." Did Jesus have realistic opponents? "It's in there." Did Jesus *win* souls? "It's in there."

I came by this approach honestly. When IFB preachers wanted to defend some arbitrary regulation, they'd say some version of "It's in there." Should you dress as though for a funeral to attend church? "It's in there." Did Jesus say the King James Bible is the only accurate English translation? "It's in there." Should women have to give their husbands sex whenever asked? "It's in there." Is black skin or brown skin a curse? "It's in there." Did Jesus make promises to the United States of America? "It's in there." Why should American men not wear beards when Jesus was quite notably bearded? "It's in there."

Actually, their version of the Prego slogan took the form of "It's biblical."

This practice wasn't new to my Baptist faith, either. Prooftexting is probably as old as the Gutenberg Bible. Plantation owners reminded their slaves that the apostle Paul commanded slaves to be subject to their masters. I wouldn't be surprised if they exploited the story of Onesimus to validate sending runaway slaves back to their plantations. Throughout history, political leaders have used Scripture to justify Crusades and other genocides. As I write this, Vladimir Putin has recently quoted Bible verses to elicit support for his invasion of Ukraine. Throughout the Middle Ages, religious leaders found approval from their holy book to torture and murder anyone who disagreed with their views. Even in our country, white men wielding big Bibles punished New England "witches" with horrible deaths. Abraham Lincoln noted in his second inaugural address that the North and the South "read the same Bible." And both, no doubt, had verses to support their respective causes.

Prooftexting isn't exclusive to IFB churches. All of Western Christianity and even its detractors like to weaponize phrases or sentences from the Bible to support their agendas. On the week I'm writing this chapter, I saw an Instagram post by a Christian author with a painting of bannered trucks from the Canadian Freedom Convoy driving through puddles—notably not dry land—as if between a parted Red Sea. Underneath the illustration sat a Bible verse: a quote from Jeremiah's rebuke of King Zedekiah nine hundred years after the Red Sea crossing followed with a declaration very much not used in the Old Testament: "You are free in Christ!" This regular guest on Christian talk shows was 100 percent sure Jeremiah's confrontation of an evil ancient king proved that Jesus was against a representative democracy's mask mandates, vaccine requirements, and travel restrictions.

Something tells me even a competitive Jesus wouldn't have signed off on that thesis.

Part of this inappropriate treatment of Scripture comes from an ignorance of cultural contexts that we can't escape. We don't understand the social dynamics at play in a lot of stories transcribed in the Bible. Another part comes from attributing descriptive narratives with prescriptive connotation. Just because someone had multiple wives, for instance, doesn't mean that God condoned the practice. Enigmatic tensions in any holy book make us uncomfortable. Nuance and mystery push us toward selective reading. And confirmation bias turns any tweetable line into a biblical "mandate." Thus, we transform the Bible into a legal document we use for bludgeoning others or making ourselves feel better about our beliefs.

I like how theologian and author Kaitlyn Schiess addressed this malignant approach to Scripture:

> This is a pretty common way, especially among American evangelicals, of thinking about the Bible where we sort of treat it like a guidebook or a dictionary. You look up your question, find the right answer. That doesn't treat Scripture in the way that it is, the way it describes itself, the way the church has traditionally thought about it. It doesn't treat Scripture like the sprawling, cosmic story of God's redemptive work in creation. It instead treats it like a phone book or a dictionary where I just look up the answers to the problems I have in my life. I don't think that's helpful, and I think it causes us to miss some really important things. It causes us to flatten all of the wild, interesting stories and applications and history into "What do I do?"[11]

Fundamentalism takes this one step further by contending the library of the Bible affirms perspectives opposite of what it actually does. And on

---

11 Shared as an Instagram story.

top of this misuse of Scripture sits a belligerent condescension of any other approach to reading the poetry, saved letters, biographies, and historical archives that compose the biblical canon. Even when there's no clear canonical language about a topic—like hem lengths, syncopated rhythm, or vintages of English Bible translations—fundamentalists will go to the mat over what is "biblical."

I've actually heard a few "men of God" admit "I can't show you any Scripture on that" about some random, personal pet peeve yet nevertheless insist that the Bible still aligns with their opinion. Pastor Tony Hutson complained in a sermon posted online: "I'm so tired of this generation saying, 'Well, give me a verse for that.' " These "men of God" claim free authority to declare these hot takes because they use enough "Thus saith the Lord" references in their sermons before and after their rants. It's as if their Prego commercial ended with a disclaimer: "It's not in there, but it doesn't have to be in there for us to be right."

I've seen fundamentalists telling their congregations that men who take selfies are gay and that women don't need to get college degrees because their highest calling is to be a stay-at-home mom. One IFB preacher I heard claimed that those who attend three church services a week get their prayers answered faster. I heard another IFB preacher lionize one of his mentors for condemning open-toed shoes and shopping at Walmart. I watched an evangelist admit that he had previously preached against putting a protective cover on Bibles while exalting his IFB hero who preached against candy bars. My sister told me I missed out on hearing my preacher dad call Crystal's tiny Japanese-symbol tattoo "the mark of a whore."

That brashness comes from spooked fragility. Like the Wizard of Oz, the loud bravado covers a frailty. I can't speak for everyone else, but every one of the moments of arrogance in my life has been rooted in compensation for my insecurities. Bestselling author Adam Grant wasn't speaking specifically about the ecosystems of my youth, but he described them well: "In cultures of arrogance, people get rewarded for expressing certainty and conviction. The most confident speaker claims the most status. In cultures of humility, people are applauded for admitting ignorance and asking questions. The most complex thinker earns the most respect."[12]

---

12 March 10, 2022, post on Instagram (@adamgrant)

It's as if the "man of God" is playing poker. He knows most of his audience doesn't know if he has real, Jesus-breathed words to back up his claim. He's counting on his "man of God" card and his "obey them that have the rule over you"[13] card to prevent anyone from calling his bluff. If that doesn't work, he can always pull out the story of Elisha and the "she bears."

My dad wasn't the only pastor I've heard invoke the story of Elisha and the "she bears." If you haven't heard the story, know that Hebrew scholars disagree on the translation of the original language's narrative into English, which leads to two very different morals of the story. The Hebrew word, *na'ar*, translated as "young boy" also translates as "servant" more than fifty times in the Old Testament—including for men with children and for men who oversaw other servants. Because these *na'ar* were in Bethel, they're probably the same idolatrous Levites who taunted Elisha earlier in the chapter about him losing his spiritual head, Elijah. Theology writer and campus minister Derek Rishmawy contends that the chiastic structure—a common Hebrew literary device—of the chapter supports this interpretation.[14] So, Elisha was retaliating but probably against an intimidating group of men. Thus, this is more of a David-and-Goliath kind of tale than it is a "Respect your elders" story.

Anyway, the version I was taught included forty-two boys who made fun of the ancient Hebrew prophet for being bald. Elisha bristled at this and cursed the kids. Then two female bears lumbered out of the forest and mauled them. Repeated throughout my youth—especially by my bald dad—the church used this version to remind parishioners that no criticism of the "man of God" was tolerable.

That never sat right with me. Frustrated by spiritual authorities whose spaghetti sauce didn't have all of the ingredients promised in the commercial, I chafed under their arbitrary standards—all while being labeled rebellious for it. That shaming pushed me to spend the rest of my life exploring what was actually "in there."

Since writing that freshman research paper, I've refrained from publishing blog posts and I've backspaced paragraphs when I couldn't

---

13 Hebrews 13:17 KJV

14 "Really Elisha? Bears Attacking Children? This is Why We Can't Have Nice Things," December 5, 2015, Reformedish.com

find evidence to support my claim. That process is part of why writing is how I figure out what I believe—and why those beliefs have changed so much since I started writing essays in college. I've found so many untenable positions that I've needed to surrender.

That happens outside of writing for me too, usually when listening to theology books while I hike or during conversations with profound people. A dozen years or so ago, two of my pastors invited me to join the teaching team for an environment our church called TruthWorks. I taught only once, but I got to be in the "room where it happened" every week as a group of us prepared by reading the next week's passage, unpacking it together, and developing application questions. Because of my upbringing, I tended to see what I wanted to see while we were whiteboarding our takeaways. That regularly led to a question from Dave or Jeremy: "Does it *say* that anywhere?" or "Where do you see that?" or "What does it actually *say*?" I had to unlearn Scripture as I learned it.

The following week on TruthWorks night, Dave or Jeremy would ask the tables of congregants what they had seen, what that truth meant to them, and what they were taking home to apply. On a lot of those nights, the big thing circled on the whiteboard at the end of table time wasn't something we had wrestled with in the conference room a week earlier. Even while prayerfully trying to extricate our agenda from the passage, we teaching team members sometimes didn't unearth what some humble, curious parishioners did.

By the time Dave and Jeremy shuttered TruthWorks, I had participated in somewhere around fifteen exegetical series, excavating either a character study or a book of the Bible. I learned a lot but maybe nothing more important than the question, "What does it actually *say*?"

A couple years after TruthWorks ended, I started a book discussion group that grew into a spiritual adventure community. After a year or so, we transitioned to include group Bible study almost every week—usually outdoors, often around a fire. One of the major differences between TruthWorks and what we now call "Dude Group" is that there is no conference room meeting the week before. Nobody decides the emphasis of the night in advance. There is no predetermined takeaway toward which to steer the conversation. Everyone disciples each other, and every prospector has equal claim to publicly dig with everyone else. Even with the advantage of egalitarian discovery, though, we still battle the human propensity to confirm our biases. Every so often, one of us will have to ask another, "Where did you see that?" or "Does it actually *say* that anywhere?" It's not a chide or a reprimand. It's benevolent accountability, and we all need it.

The reality is that just about every Christian will wrestle with the temptation to carve our Bibles into our own respective images. That goes for conservatives and liberals. That's a gravitational pull for those within fundamentalism and those within mainline denominations. It's an insidious allure for a screaming "man of God" or a pleasant female minister. Religious refugees and Christian extremists both can make the Bible say what they want it to say.

So can authors. One of the temptations of writing this book was in resorting to the same weaponization of selective Bible quotes that I endured for decades of my life. That's why the folder labeled "Cutting Room Floor" in my book-writing software is filled with pages upon pages of sentences, paragraphs, and trains of thought I couldn't include in this book if I wanted to represent the heart of Jesus well. Over the past two decades, I've replaced theology built on slivers of out-of-cultural-context Scripture with theology anchored in the words and example of Jesus. And that will be the pattern you see in the following chapters.

A Bible that only supports our politics, our tendencies, or our philosophy isn't the Word of God. If our God doesn't confront our suppositions, either he isn't God, or we're gods. Even the English translators hired by King James would tell you neither of those are tenable positions. No matter what our GPA was in Bible class, none of us owns a sovereign view of original context, full intent, or historical understanding. That should humble us enough to approach Scripture with a bowed posture, open hands, and curious pragmatism. That humility is a key mark of a safe church and a safe pastor. God told us through an Old Testament prophet that our thoughts aren't as high as his thoughts.

I still can't prove that Jesus is competitive; but I know he doesn't compete with us or our finite understanding. If God would even let the race between us start, the disparity would be laughable. And if that race were a sailing regatta, here's a pro tip: you wouldn't want me tying the knots on your lines.

07 UNTOUCHABLE DEMAGOGUES

Unsafe churches told me I needed an insecure shaman to know God, but Jesus has often proven himself a Good Shepherd who feeds and protects his sheep.

The closest IFB school to where we lived was in a different state. So, during the years before my parents started homeschooling us, we were part of a carpool group that included one or two vehicle changes as we picked up more students over the hour-long journey to school. Every weekday, from 6:50 to 7:00, one of my parents drove my oldest sister and I down Bloomingdale Road to the first handoff point. On the mornings when that driver was my dad, we rode in an army-green station wagon. During those short drives, he spoke a specific prayer over us so many times I could've recited it for him.

"Lord, if you will, would you please call Ryan and [my oldest sister] into full-time service? May they be vessels for you—a pastor or pastor's wife, a missionary or a missionary's wife!"

We all assumed Jesus knew which gendered request went to which gendered child. I have to mention that, because I eventually became the husband of a woman who makes her living performing pastoral duties. And there's no way a fundamentalist would ask God for his daughter to be a prophet or a pastor. In a world where the Southern Baptist Convention excommunicates churches who ordain women yet not those who harbor child molesters, a woman becoming a pastor is that much of an anathema. Despite the apostle Peter proclaiming that female prophets would be part of the work of the Holy Spirit, all of us in IFB churches knew the highest calling of a fundamentalist woman was to support a "man of God" and bear his children.

While parents might pray for their kids to grow up to be doctors or engineers or lawyers, most of us would think it odd if they prayed that aloud over their elementary school-age kids in a captive environment on a regular basis. I would rather my dad had prayed that I would make my living as an architect or car designer or writer for *Car and Driver*, but even ten-year-old Ryan knew his dad shouldn't pray for that. I assumed my dad wanted what was best for me. So, of course he would beseech Jesus to select me for the highest possible caste. Any good father would lobby a capricious deity to choose me to be the one who pulled the "man of God" sword out of the stone.

In IFB churches, you don't choose to be a professional minister. It's chosen for you by an indisputable fate. At least that's how the process is sold to congregations. If God called a man to be a pastor, who could argue with God as to whether or not he should hold the position? And if he was "God's anointed," who but another "man of God" could argue with anything the man said from his pulpit, his desk, or your living room couch? He could go back and forth from reading Scripture to spouting absurd opinions—and demand the same respect for both. When yelling, sweating, and spitting (all signs of a "powerful" or "anointed" preacher in the cult of my youth), the red-faced preacher could constantly cash the blank check of "Thus saith the Lord." I once even heard an IFB pastor tell his audience, "The Holy Spirit told me twice to tell you this joke about two Italians." He meant it tongue in cheek, but more insidious obfuscation happens every Sunday in our country.

The line between what Scripture actually says and what the "man of God" declares gets intentionally blurred. You can imagine the kind of men attracted to that kind of systemic confusion. And you can now watch them on Facebook, Instagram, TikTok, and YouTube. I've yet to be surprised seeing these guys bark about topics far outside of biblical priority—or even biblical mention at all—because I witnessed so much of that in my twenty years in IFB churches. Just during my college years, I endured between fifteen and twenty-five different pastors and evangelists each semester from the fundamentalist movement.

On the local church level, proximity to this "man of God" is doled out as reward for obedience, loyalty, and pretty much anything obsequious. Behind or beside the fomenting orator on stage at many IFB churches, you'll notice this man's posse of "yes men"—sometimes in chairs, sometimes on miniature thrones. In a video from a leading church in the IFB cult, I've even seen these men wear matching outfits identical to what the pastor was wearing—right down to the stripe pattern on their ties. There was a memo, and the second-level caste all got it. I've even heard of a pastor in this cancerous sect who sporadically commanded his men on stage to drop down and do pushups during the service.

The drill instructors have to show the congregation who the alpha male is, who the "man of God" is around these parts. Chain of command is pounded into parishioners almost as much as it is into teenagers on Parris Island. Just tonight, I saw a clip of one of these arrogant preachers telling his congregation they should be content shining the shoes of the "man of God," because Elisha served Elijah until it was his turn to be the "man of God."

There is never any doubt who is in charge. Just as with a Shi'a imam or a sub-Saharan witch doctor, one man's mercurial word trumps all others. Anyone who would dare contradict the assertions of the "man of God" risks shunning and excommunication. I've watched videos of IFB pastors publicly shaming specific members of their congregation for not complying with the pastor's edict or opinion. Religious historian Molly Worthen documented this proclivity: "There's the tendency of evangelical culture to produce pastor-warlords who are used to operating with no particular checks and balances and create their own systems with very little accountability."[15] (In chapter 23, we'll explore how IFB preachers are fascinated with violence and especially the war motif.) I found this warlord language fitting to what I experienced growing up. Church worked like the mafia with an unassailable godfather in each congregation.

Seemingly invincible, abusive pastors can run through anyone and any criticism. They can dismiss people who don't comply with their whims or theology as heretics, because any unsubmissive congregants aren't obeying their spiritual authority. They can deny all allegations of abuse, because the "man of God" wouldn't do such a thing, and his word trumps the word of anyone beneath him. They can force sexual assault victims into silence because the oracle can't be sullied. They and their enablers ask, "What would happen to the Gospel if you told people what just happened!?" A

15 "Can anyone lead the Southern Baptist Convention forward?," October 19, 2021, Bob Smietana, Religion News Service

victim's physical and mental health are expendable resources, sometimes pilfered as gifts to support the abuser's public work.

For the record, I'm not saying that all IFB pastors are predators or that they all abuse their power. That said, the language and beliefs of the cult make it frighteningly easy for depraved men to get away with their crimes. W. Edwards Deming said it best: "Every system is perfectly designed to get the result that it does." For ambitious, narcissistic, and self-righteous men, the "man of God" mantle comes with the perks of a fiefdom. With this malignant doctrine, any man—it's always a man—can claim his own kingdom. He can put in his time to take over one; or if he has enough charisma and drive, he can start his own. He can even start it in another IFB pastor's town, because IFB congregants like to shop for the flamethrowers that aim their ire at the exact same things they hate. Since these pastors see their small congregations as proof of their exclusivity, it doesn't matter that fundamentalists are splitting the customer base. Besides, smaller congregations are easier to dominate than larger ones.

To be sure, a similar dynamic can and does sprout up in other denominations and non-fundamentalist churches; but it's not baked into the church's core beliefs and reinforced with the same gusto from the stage. Celebrity culture rewards affable narcissists, especially in megachurches. In those situations, the idol of church growth and the cult of personality replace the heavy-handed self-reinforcement of the "man of God" trope. Abusive men will always gaslight. Proud and insecure people in power will always manipulate. You can even watch sermons posted online of fundamentalists beating their chests about their untouchable position and even leaving the pulpit to physically chase a detractor from the room.

No matter how many times I heard my dad entreat God for me to receive the commission to become a "man of God," I didn't want that job. As a kid, it seemed like a prison sentence—forced, mostly joyless labor. My dad wasn't happy. He was just sacrificing himself on the stone from which he pulled his Excalibur.

The perks of that power don't offset the pressure inherent in protecting your walled city. I remember when my dad told me that he couldn't confess his sins to anyone in his church, or else he'd lose his spiritual authority. That was a huge red flag to me, because the early church father, James, said confession is how we are healed. (Secular therapists and biblical counselors would agree with that first-century assertion.) So, someone committed not to confessing but instead to maintaining an air of superiority can't be healthy. The unhealed wounds and grievous secrets these men carry must be so heavy! No wonder the primary emotion these men project from their pulpits is angst.

When was the last time you saw a convincingly joyful dictator?

IFB churches teach people that they need a shaman to truly know God. They combine two Old Testament models of the shaman: (1) the prophets who claimed to speak new revelations from God not in the Torah, and (2) high priests born into a system in which they stood as liaisons between Yahweh and his people. Thus, an IFB "man of God" could make his own "Thus saith the Lord" and then proclaim punishment on those who didn't submit to his authority.

Those old holy-man roles became obsolete a couple millennia ago on the day Jesus died. The veil of the caste-layered Jewish temple ripped from top to bottom. Jesus' close friend, Peter, later declared that all believers are royal priests. We are all invited to approach God now as equals. Whoever wrote the book of Hebrews declared that all who follow Jesus have equal access to the throne of grace. The Holy Spirit becomes a counselor to everyone who hosts him in their souls.

After Jesus' resurrection, *all* of his disciples were assigned the Great Commission. At Jesus' ascension, *every* believer was deputized to be a minister of the Gospel. We were *all* told to make disciples and teach. The apostle Paul said *everyone* who has the Holy Spirit in their life has a gift of ministry; none of those gifts is touted as more important, more valuable, or more favored.

If these spiritually abusive preachers were truly following Jesus, you'd think Jesus would be their model for the role of the "man of God." Jesus surrendered his infinity to fit in a human body. The Source of All Wisdom hung a towel over his arm and humbly washed the dirty, smelly, gnarled feet of those he taught. The Origin of All Life laid his life down for everyone who ever lived. The One Who Holds the Universe Together let men beat him, mock him, spit on him, yank out his beard hair—and crucify him. The King of Righteousness only yelled at one kind of sinner: the fundamentalists of his day. His biographers take note of Jesus weeping and having compassion more often than they give accounts of his anger.

When we do see the risen Christ discipling Peter as a future leader of the church, Jesus doesn't talk about how to motivate sheep, how to force sheep to conform, how to scare people into becoming sheep, or how to build any power structures. He asks Peter to feed his lambs. For emphasis, Jesus asks him a second time to feed his sheep. In between those two requests—depending on which translation of the Bible you read—Jesus asked Peter to tend his sheep, take care of his sheep, shepherd his sheep, or simply feed his sheep.

It's important to note that Jesus never said "your sheep." Those sheep didn't belong to Peter, even though they were in his care. Those followers belonged to Jesus, not any human shepherds. Just as critically, Jesus says that if Peter loves him, the way to prove that affection is to nurture and provide for his sheep. None of us—pastors included—prove how close we are to Jesus by what we yell, what we demand, or what we criticize. We don't show people the heart of God with medals we earned in a culture war.

Shepherds don't feed sheep from a podium. They don't throw food at neat rows of sheep from a platform. They hike with sheep—often on uneven ground—guiding them to nourishing places. Pastoral care is a lifestyle of walking with people where they are. The markers of a good shepherd aren't oratory at all. Going by Luke's accounts in the Book of Acts, early followers of the Way of Jesus spent at least as much time being discipled around tables in homes as absorbing sermons at synagogues.

The converted fundamentalist, Paul, admonished mature men and women to invest in younger people in their faith community. What he described sounds more like a mentorship program than scheduled times for someone to bark insults and invectives. Over the past seventeen years, I've found a relational capital model true of my own spiritual growth. As I've pursued the goal of being a more mature disciple and a better disciple-maker, I've probably learned more from my pastors offstage than I have from their time on an auditorium platform.

• • •

I left my last IFB church in the summer of 2002 when we moved to Virginia. For the next three and a half years, my wife and I served in a Spanish-speaking Baptist congregation that primarily served immigrants from Central and South America but also from Africa and Asia. Our diverse assembly bonded over a shared sense of being far from home. I speak very little

Spanish, and by the time we left that church I was drifting spiritually. My brother-in-law recommended a faith community very different from both the IFB churches of my youth and the culture of our Hispanic church. I gave it a try, despite assuming it would be uncomfortable.

My assumption was correct. It seemed like almost everything about the atmosphere and the services was different from anything I'd experienced in a church. So, I signed up for a midweek gathering they advertised as a study of the question: "What should a believer's experience in a New Testament church look like?" I attended every week to wrestle with the assertions from the videos on the big screens and to go over my homework with the table leaders. At the end of that eight-week course, they offered us a four-week seminar on what should be true of healthy church small groups. At the end of that seminar, my table decided I should be the organizer for a new in-home community group.

Having attended this church for only six or eight months, I felt under-qualified for my assignment. So, I invited one of the pastors out to lunch. I asked Dave why he or any other leaders of the church would trust me with leadership without having vetted my knowledge of the Bible.

I still remember how the bustle of our local Panera Bread faded into silence as Dave answered my question. I've never forgotten his response. Dave told me that the criteria he used wasn't how much of the Bible I knew. "We look at how long it takes you to respond to the Holy Spirit's prompting. If the time between your prompting and obedience is growing shorter and shorter, we trust the Holy Spirit to guide you." He pointed out that the early church leaders often had to address incorrect theology and malignant behavior in their exploding movement. That correction was an expected part of discipleship in a growing church, but a soft heart made that coaching and correction easier.

Neither Dave nor my church ever asked if I was called into ministry. They didn't have to. We'd all read the Great Commission. Two thousand years ago, we were all called to the one-another life. That decentralized model doesn't reward the self-appointed "man of God" like his bully pulpit does. Sheep of different maturity levels can disciple *each other* in egalitarian circles—the mature contributing wisdom and perspective and the young contributing wonder and passion. The people in the faith circles I've enjoyed have different strengths and weaknesses than mine, and we challenge and encourage each other. The discipleship flows in both directions. Some of those circles have included people on a ministry's payroll, but most of those truth-sayers have been tradesmen and engineers, teachers and entrepreneurs, truck drivers and medical professionals.

When the first COVID lockdowns hit, it was the IFB streams of my social media feed that flouted government mandates the loudest. Thanks to Facebook live streaming, I even watched the defiant "man of God" from a friend's church tear up government orders at his massive pulpit. "Church is essential!" these dethroned zealots yelled or wrote in ALL CAPS. I agreed with the extremists on the importance of a faith community, but I noticed that they defined it differently. They didn't have a category for the church to be anything other than someone hurling brimstone at rows of pews.

Interestingly enough, it was churches who followed Romans 13's call to submit to authority that saw church change in a positive way. A year after the shutdown, I heard and read stories of churches that saw *more* people come to Christ during the COVID lockdowns. One church documented more baptisms than in any other year of its existence. A wave of people wrestling with economic hardships, relational challenges, racial tension, and the politicization of everything sought camaraderie in their neighbors' backyard Bible studies and prayer groups. The hosts may not have had all of the answers, but they didn't feel the need to pretend they did to maintain some aura of a holier, higher-called caste. They just fed the sheep that wandered into their care or that they invited into their field. Eventually the immutable hope of Jesus led to surrenders, and thousands of people made public declarations of faith in makeshift backyard baptisms. Those churches weren't outliers. My spiritual adventure community gained new guys during the pandemic. Crystal's circles welcomed fresh faces too.

That's how this whole thing is supposed to work. Every follower of Jesus is charged with the assignment and equipped with assistance to welcome more sheep to the fold.

While writing this chapter, it dawned on me that maybe Jesus *did* answer my dad's prayers. I've led Bible studies and other faith environments for more than fifteen years, either as the primary organizer or as a table host. What I've found is that whatever authority I might have comes not from how much Scripture I've read and memorized, how many Bible classes I've taken, or the books I've written. No, my influence as a shepherd of souls has grown as I've intentionally worked to demonstrate humility and authenticity, surrender and empathy. My guys have heard me confess sins before peccadilloes spiraled into big regrets. Strong, capable men and women have watched me sacrifice my comfort for obedience, replacing my plan with God's. I've fed them with encouragement and example, and that's louder than anything a fundamentalist has ever yelled from stage.

Sheep go where they're fed, where they're cared for. I'm a sheep, and I gravitate to the leaders who feed the souls around them instead of their own egos. I'm also a sheep feeder, and I look to a Good Shepherd who gave up his privileges to tend to his sheep. When he was offered lower-case-k kingdoms, he declined. When he was offered fake and fading glory, he passed. He didn't ask anyone to dress like him or do pushups in front of a crowd. He didn't take advantage of his position and rack up victims. He didn't have to protect his turf with angry rants about what he didn't like.

He just fed his sheep.

08 AN INSIDIOUS CASTE SYSTEM

Unsafe churches ingrained in me a hierarchy of religion—not just in my denomination—but Jesus' documented words have reminded me that we're all equals and all valuable.

I learned to drive in a 1978 Datsun 510. I remember that first session like it was yesterday. It was 1987. I was nine years old. My dad pulled over on a ribbon of dirt between farm fields off John Brown Road. After some lurching starts, I shifted through the gears working my way up to fifty-some miles an hour, kicking up dust around a long, slow bend between row crops. My dad calmly told me that was fast enough and that I should slow down and pull over for my sister's turn. I couldn't figure out the downshifting thing. So he told me to push in the clutch and just brake to a stop. At the end of the coast, the Datsun stalled and lurched to an abrupt halt.

I didn't learn how to stop correctly that day. So, I'm not sure if what I was doing counts as driving. Either way, I was hooked—and not just with driving in general. Since 2001, my daily drivers have been exclusively vehicles with a manual transmission.

Around the same time as that dirt road lesson, my dad taught me something else in that Japanese station wagon that influenced the next few decades of my life. See, that was the same car in which my dad offered those loving-but-uncomfortable benedictions I mentioned in the last chapter. It was in those vinyl seats where I first came to realize I lived in a caste system.

I extend grace to my dad for those driver-seat intercessions. He was trained to want that for us. His former pastors and professors had ingrained in him the idea that those top ladder rungs offered a unique closeness to God and an enviable personal fulfillment. Also, if my sister and I ended up on a ministry payroll, we would affirm his parenting influence and his example. In more fairness to my dad, I heard that same prayer again and again from other pastors in schools, churches, and summer camps throughout my youth.

This caste system was rarely referenced directly—mostly implied. So I've never seen it officially transcribed. In general, though, here is the approximate order of that hierarchy for men:

- Martyr
- Foreign missionary
- Inner city missionary
- Evangelist
- Pastor
- Youth pastor
- Camp director
- Teacher or administrator in an IFB school or college
- Church staff
- Deacon
- Sunday school teacher
- Song leader
- Usher
- All other church volunteers
- Anyone else who reads out of a KJV Bible
- The lost

For women, the list started and ended the same but with different strata in the middle:

- Martyr
- Foreign missionary
- Wife of a "man of God"
- IFB school or college teacher
- Church secretary
- Camp employee
- Sunday school teacher
- Pianist or organist

- Homeschooling mother
- Nursery attendant
- Choir member
- Homemaker
- All other church volunteers
- Nurse
- Anyone else who reads out of a KJV Bible
- Woman who works outside the home other than in ministries
- The lost

You could climb certain of these ladder rungs on your own through volunteering or through your choice of career. The rest of the rungs required a (self-described) epiphany moment where you were definitely, unequivocally, sovereignly called by God to accept your position in the hierarchy. The top three scared most of us guys, and maybe they still should. I don't know. Anyway, most of us aimed our goals no higher than the second tier. That explains why the most populated school at my alma mater was the School of Ministry. In case you didn't already assume as much: young women could take Bible classes, but they couldn't pursue the same degrees. After looking at the lists above, you won't be surprised that the school within my alma mater that held the most female students by far was the School of Education.

My fundamentalist college only reinforced this caste system, despite offering education to the lower castes. The guest pastors at our mandatory Sunday night services typically taught our Monday and Tuesday chapel sessions. Our guest preachers for the required Wednesday night services usually gave the sermons at our Thursday and Friday chapel sessions. Time and again, these men charged us to follow the Lord's call to be pastors or missionaries, Christian schoolteachers or nurses. The list almost always ended there or not long after that with the suffix, "or whatever you might be."

As a commercial writing major with minors in graphic design and advertising/public relations, I always fell into the mumbled catchall disclaimer of "or whatever you might be." This dynamic was pervasive enough that at one stretch during my undergrad years—despite the fifty-five programs available in our course catalog—all three of my roommates were youth ministry majors. During the college's annual missions emphasis week, surrounded by the flags of our international students' home countries, the administration put on a hard press. They pulled out all of the emotional stops in the grand finale moment to get hundreds of students to walk the aisles and commit to change their majors and ensuing careers to be foreign missionaries.

I don't think they really wanted us all to keep our heads bowed. You couldn't, anyway. Too many of the students in your row needed you to back up as they side-shuffled between your knees and the hymnal rack. And there was always a straggler—a student finally surrendering during the fourth or fifth time through the chorus. "Can you sing those lyrics honestly!?" the pacing suit would interject from stage.

This intended career flip happened in more subtle ways, too. I remember getting in a debate with the academic dean who presided over both my major and my minors. During my last semester of my senior year, we were discussing job placement or a job fair or something, and he told me, "We're really hoping you get a job with a mission board or on staff at a church. Our goal is not to send you into the secular workforce."

I found this particularly puzzling for my field. Outside of the entertainment industry, you'd be hard pressed to find a long list of more godless careers than advertising. It's our job to make people discontented and envious—to make them want more and different from what they have. Many of us are tasked with appealing to greed and lust, insecurity and ambition, pride and peer pressure. It's in the best interest of our clients to promote items under the disguised promise that the material item will fill a void or heal an ache that only God's love can remedy. Advertising doesn't have to operate this way, but that's the default setting of my industry. Your light doesn't have to be very bright to be noticed there.

If the goal of the Christian life is to be "a light to a dying world," wouldn't it make sense to send your most-trained, most-ingrained zealots out into the darkest places? According to my academic dean, no. My alma mater would not measure success by well-dispersed professional achievements or a diversity of personal ministry. No, the administrators aimed to launch students into the highest cumulative IFB caste strata possible.

I have dear friends who've leveraged their skill, ambition, and innovation for religious organizations. They bring a taste of Heaven's excellence and the Creator's originality to their ministry employers or clients. But those same friends would be the first to tell you that's not the only way to honor Jesus with our careers, let alone our lives.

Social caste systems are nothing but artificial constructs, but they stand as impenetrable walls that have prevented millions of people from reaching their full potential. In every society where these hierarchies form, they start as protection from adulteration for the rich or powerful. The founders craft exclusive levels to share their relational, financial, governmental, or spiritual capital only with the people they prefer. I'm not enough of a historian to know who gets the credit for creating the caste system in which I was reared. I just know I bumped up against it externally enough that it became a low-grade internal shame.

I had chosen the bottom rungs of the ladder. I wondered if God had called me to be a "man of God," and I had just been too stubborn to step up to that mantle.

One of the early cracks in that worldview came when I was trying to move back to the East Coast from my first career stop in Indiana. If my memory serves me, I had submitted my résumé for more than forty positions. I distinctly remember that—however many there were—I had struck out on every single one of them. I walked out into the cornfield east of our townhouse complex and lay prostrate between the brittle stalks of recently harvested corn. "God, you gave me these talents," I blurted before my prayer requests.

That was a record-scratch on the narrative I'd been sold. Why would Sovereignty dole out talents and proficiencies that would anchor someone at the bottom of the ladder? Was he a cruel deity who gave you things only for you to sacrifice? In the story of Abraham and Isaac at Mount Moriah, that call to sacrifice was just a test. For me, there was no ram in the thicket surrounding my job search. I didn't think I was entitled to a job, let alone a dream job; but I preferred the weight of a corporate ladder to a spiritual one.

Certainly, Jesus asks us all to lay our idols on his altar, and sometimes those idols are careers, wealth, or notoriety. But those callings are tied to a specific individual's formation. They're not a universal prescription for the history of humanity.

Four years later in a watershed moment, that crack in my worldview turned into irreparable damage to the caste system of my childhood cult. It happened in front of a screen playing Louie Giglio's "Songs in the Key of Life" sermon from his *Soundtracks* series. Giglio opened his Bible to the apostle Paul's letter to the Colossians and read, "And whatever you do, whether in word or deed, do it all in the name of the Lord Jesus, giving thanks to God the Father through him."[16] Giglio went onto explain that whether we're a hairstylist or a bond trader, we're all called to use our profession to shine a light on the heart and character of Jesus. He contended that we're all part of the soundtrack to the story God is writing in our world. Giglio passionately explained that no matter where we live or what we do for a living, our calling is to serve Jesus. He emphasized *whatever* each time he said it, and he didn't mumble it like a perfunctory disclaimer. For the first time in my life, being part of *whatever* felt like a divine calling, not a holy junk drawer.

Under a bright screen in that dark room, I realized that Jesus doesn't have favorite kids. We're all equal heirs. We're all royal priests.

There. Is. No. Ladder.

A ladder implies that we can climb—that we can achieve our way to a higher position. But we don't need a ladder if we're all equally loved and valued by our Father. And that's just it. Across my two decades in IFB institutions, I was taught ways to earn God's favor. I endured these lectures despite all of the verses that were quoted about universal grace and unmerited forgiveness. I absorbed these implied statements despite hearing, "not of works, lest any man should boast" literally *hundreds* of times.[17]

From my experience inside the walls of fundamentalism, our god used grace and love as giveaways in a bait and switch scheme. What was sufficient to get you out of hell wasn't sufficient to keep you close to the heart of Jesus.

Since the Tower of Babel, humans have been trying to manage the distance between heaven and earth. Fundamentalism just puts a different spin on that. Its preachers and parishioners alike forget that the Holy Spirit is—or at least can be—as close as our own soul. I forgot that. Or maybe I never fully knew it during those twenty years.

We don't have to yearn for a different caste position, because there are no castes. Our professions and church positions don't earn us any more or any less love. I've had friends from multiple denominations or lack thereof transition from the marketplace onto a ministry's payroll. I've probably had just as many friends, though, leave nonprofit organizations to use their God-given instincts and Spirit-blessed talents in the secular workforce. That

16 Colossians 3:16-18 NIV

17 Ephesians 2:9 KJV

fluidity makes sense in a kingdom that doesn't ask for spiritual résumés, let alone uses them to determine our worth.

There is no divide between the sacred and the secular when all of life is sacred. The apostle Paul told his friends in the Corinthian church that even the acts of eating and drinking offer a chance to bring glory to their rightful recipient. Holy moments and sovereign encounters await all who are looking for them everywhere—not just in a church house, a ministry position, or a specific sect of a solitary denomination.

All of life is part of our calling. Anywhere and everywhere we go is a section of our mission field. Everyone we meet is a character in the story of God's redemptive work in our lives. Our worth doesn't come from our striving or our place on an arbitrary list. It comes from the One who imbued us with life and who laid down his life to prove the value of ours.

I still have the rearview mirror from that Datsun 510 wagon. Every time I look in it, I see someone God called to represent him as an ambassador. That's why my first prayer in the morning—sometimes before I even roll out of bed—includes this request: "Help me represent you well today." Whether I'm heading to my office or the rock climbing gym, my church's parking lots or a bonfire with my buddies . . . *whatever* I do can be part of what I was placed on this planet to do.

09 WORSHIPPING THE PAST

Unsafe churches educated me on how to worship the past, but Jesus has often invited me to celebrate his current redemption available to everyone.

My friend, Will, had been following Jesus for about a year. He met once a week for breakfast with two other new believers and their shared mentor, Woody. Eventually, that group grew to five, then six, then seven. They pushed tables together in the back of Carol's Place restaurant for their weekly gatherings. They didn't follow a curriculum. They talked about their past week and then investigated what the Bible said about whatever was front-and-center in their respective lives.

I was guy number eight. Will had gotten excited about what was happening around those tables and invited me—without asking the group. After I left that first breakfast, Woody approached Will about my participation. In the end, they allowed me to continue participating—on one condition: I had to act like a new believer. I had just been baptized, but I came with baggage: four years of Bible college after thirteen years of Christian school, a published devotional book, and decades as the son of a minister. That type of résumé set off warning lights on the group's dashboard, and I would soon learn why.

I held up my end of the bargain, though it wasn't work. Everything about Jesus was new again as I explored an upside-down kingdom. I sat around tables with former gang members, recovered addicts, and fellow religious refugees. Guys who'd lost jobs and marriages and assumptions had found a Jesus they'd never known. And they invited their buddies to experience what they had just discovered. As the group grew to a dozen and then two dozen and then more, it grew easy to spot the "old" Christians. When we asked each other where we had seen God move in our lives recently, they always went back to some past religious experience. They had said a prayer in Sunday school or walked an aisle at summer camp. They had gotten baptized after a week of revival services or after witnessing the miraculous birth of their child.

"No, like recently. What is Jesus doing in your life right now?"

"Well, I've believed in Jesus for years, and I've just been on a journey ever since."

"Cool. Okay. What has he been showing you over the past few weeks?"

"I just need to keep my eyes on him, you know—stay faithful, probably be in the Word more."

No doubt, these historians harkened from churches that claimed "it's not about religion but a relationship." I wouldn't be surprised if some of these dudes fully believed that too. But I shudder to imagine how their other friendships functioned with this definition of relationship. It was like asking a guy about his marriage and having him tell me about his wedding.

Seventeen years ago.

"Just been a honeymoon ever since, you know?"

No, I didn't know.

Crystal is not the woman I married, and I'm not the man to whom she said "I do." Today we relate to the world and to each other in ways quite different than did those barefoot kids holding hands on Conquest Beach during the first September of the twenty-first century. Voracious readers mentored by insightful souls, we've become students of ourselves and of each other. We've had sporadic bouts of doubting each other and sitting in disillusionment. We've also had beautiful moments of convergence and contentment. In different seasons, the themes ring familiar. But in almost every week over the past few years, we would've offered a fresh answer to the questions, "What's happening in your relationship right now?" or "What are you and your wife talking about the most right now?"

The dynamic nature of any close friendship is very much true of marriage, the relationship Jesus uses so much to explain his relationship with us. For me, it's also true of my relationship with the world. Just this morning, I told my counselor how it seems like since I started therapy, my weeks seem to throw more at me to process with her. When my buddies ask what they can pray for me, it's not hard for me to have a different answer than

I had the previous Wednesday night or Sunday morning. If you're leaning into life, you're leaning into change. And change brings friction and heat, uncertainty and surrender.

The men at Will and Woody's group who didn't have stories of recent encounters with Jesus, new assignments from the Holy Spirit, or wrestling matches with surrender eventually washed out of our group or congregated with each other at a table where they'd be less likely to get asked. As we table leaders compared notes after meetings, it became clear that the "old" Christians were the anchors in the room, creating drag for those running after Jesus. Maybe that's part of why that environment eventually took on the name Engage. The branding warned invitees of a core cultural value that would be present with their eggs over easy or French toast.

The weekly challenge from both Scripture and those living it out pressed uncomfortably into my habits and idols, my autonomy and assumptions. But I looked at the vibrance of the lives of guys chasing after Jesus in contrast to the lethargy of those with stories only in the past. As difficult as the path would be, I wanted to always be a new believer.

Fundamentalism's primary focus is on preserving old things, holding onto old practices, and measuring with old yardsticks. Proudly on the conservative extreme of conservative evangelicalism, anything new is at least an enemy if not anathema. On the congregational level, progress gets labeled as heresy. So, it's not surprising that there's no expectation of personal progress. Once you're on the checklist system of extra-biblical dos and don'ts, you're good.

If your adherence to the same beliefs is what makes you a good Christian, why would you ever want to change—let alone attempt to change? (We'll explore this question more in chapter 22.)

My two decades in fundamentalist churches used an EKG to measure my spiritual heart. The goal was no irregularities. We all just wanted to see a consistent rhythm, a predictable pattern. Since leaving the IFB movement, I've learned to use a different graphing paradigm. Now, I chart my spiritual life like a stock chart—always looking for growth, hopefully pressing up and to the right. Just as with the EKG, there are blips in both directions; but the average trajectory angles upward.

That uphill climb requires risk and sweat and accountability. Instead of measuring holiness by conformity to noncanonical criteria that others can verify, I'm left to tend an internal garden of surrender. So are you. If there is a chart, it's measuring quiet, private fruit. Eventually, those small obediences lead to more selfless choices and more public relinquishing. As beautiful things grow within us, they supplant weeds. Eventually, we come to realize that fruit doesn't need measuring. It's just sweet or savory enough that others want a taste.

Going back to that indelible conversation with my friend Dave in Panera Bread, I remember saying something along the lines of "You guys don't really know me."

Dave smiled. "We know enough." He and other church leaders saw what I couldn't. Back then—before I participated in journaling, therapy, and intentional self-regulation—I didn't have a mirror-type mechanism to recognize deep changes in my soul or its expressions. While I was reconsidering everything I had ever believed, these mentors observed my response to that truth. While I was learning a new way to relate to God, they witnessed an engagement with new things—even uncomfortable things.

I don't know if it's the adrenaline junkie in me, but now the warning lights in my heart start blinking when I haven't crossed paths with a difficult surrender in a while. I love the steadfast sameness of Jesus, but I long for fresh encounters with him that burn new pathways into my brain.

That mindset developed from watching shepherds for whom new is normative. I've seen my spiritual mentors wrestle through uncertainty and difficult choices with candor. I've heard them explain changes of heart—not just around a table but also from a stage. They've invited others into the kind of prayer that seeks to change the person praying more than to change the heart of God. I regularly hear my big brothers in the faith talk about their new ways of being and doing, thinking and praying.

In my last decade in the IFB movement I genuinely thought I was following God, but there was no scenery change. Even if I were actually walking in the steps of Jesus, I was at best following him around a four-hundred-meter track—probably in the same lane. For the most strident members of the IFB movement, those monotonous circles develop deep grooves. Neuroscientists tell us that these patterns of thought cut literal pathways into our physical brains that make changing our thoughts and perceptions more and more difficult.

It makes sense, then, that the last time a past-worshipping Christian remembers something new in their relationship with Jesus is from that first lap. As someone who has followed Jesus into remote canyons and scary precipices, I pity them for what they've never explored. There's only so much you can see and experience of the kingdom of heaven on a quarter-mile loop.

Jesus physically led his disciples to boats and beaches, villages and cities, mountains and lowlands, verdant fields and dusty roads. He visited the holiest places in his culture's religion and the forbidden places most Jews walked days around to avoid. He spent time next to saltwater and fresh. He discipled around campfires and in gardens, around tables and in front of megachurch-size crowds. He healed people with his words, his touch, and even mud made out of his spit.

Following Jesus showed you a multifaceted Messiah, a creative Christ. His disciples asked him lots of questions because he kept putting them in interesting situations.

Why would he operate any differently today?

I've followed multiple wilderness guides to remote, jaw-dropping places. They've shown me aspects of creation and anthropology that've blown my mind. My most frequent guide over the years holds a degree in experiential education. Woody was trained to take people into nature, challenge them physically, and then leverage their accomplishment for introspection. "You just did something difficult—something you'd never done before and may not have thought you could do. What's something in your life back home that's intimidating? What's something you haven't thought you could conquer that maybe now you might consider that you can?"

It makes sense that Woody took that same mode of teaching into the faith space—including into the back rooms of Carol's Place restaurant. He has leveraged the stress tests and the intimidating giants in the lives around him to ask, "What does God have to say about that?" and "What are you learning from God in that?" and "How has this changed the way you look at God?"

Along those lines, I regularly ask friends in my spiritual circles, "What do your conversations with Jesus look like right now?" Or I ask them to rate where they are in their relationship with Jesus on a scale of one to ten. After they answer, I ask what would move that number higher and then what would be one small step they could take before our next meeting to move in that direction.

Across my two decades in fundamentalism, no spiritual leader asked me questions like those. Learning about God wasn't tailored to my current lived experience. Solutions (or at least clichés) were one-size-fits-all. Instead of handing me questions, fundamentalism shoveled regurgitated answers that applied to lap one or lap forty-seven.

Education researchers will tell you that learning information as needed in different situations makes those lessons stickier than linear lessons. For the most indelible discoveries, humans need context. That's why we remember the relational and cultural lessons from college far more than we remember what was broadcast to us as we sat silently in rows of desks.

Moments of need breed comprehension. Those of us who learned how to drive with a manual transmission had to absorb the instruction, or our car was useless to us. If you've learned how to operate a parachute, it's because your life quite literally has hung in the balance. I learned Facebook's intimidating advertising system because the trajectory of my livelihood in traditional media was dropping significantly.

Our uptake of new knowledge is proportional to our dependence on it. Thankfully, the Source of All Wisdom teaches experientially. In his sovereignty, Omniscience brings situations into our lives in the order we need them to absorb the linked revelation of his character. Sometimes those lessons are rooted in sorrow and loss, hardship and puzzles. Other times, they are delivered through moments of beauty, wonder, and serendipity.

No two of us have the exact same curriculum. The course outlines in our respective syllabi have different bold headings, or maybe the same ones but in different orders. That's probably why more life changes occur in circles than in rows. We're all on different journeys with and toward Jesus.

That's just one reason the constant inundation of the same IFB talking points didn't practically improve my life. I've yet to hit one of those crucible moments where what got me through were defenses of the King James Bible, listening to music without a beat, or gender-separated swimming. In the moments when the kayak of my life is upside down in a tumultuous river, what Eternal Love reveals about himself is not patriarchy or tradition or political affiliation.

No, I default to muscle memory rooted in what I've seen in the Father's heart during past rapids. After a loved one's words wound me, I recall the verses that comforted me in past painful moments. When I'm unsure at a crossroads, I claim promises that have proven themselves true in my past. I pull out a journal entry or blog post or unwritten memory of a similar moment. I may need a different map, but it uses the same key to decipher distances, elevation, and resting places.

Even a map of an Olympic track helps little during a marathon, let alone a mountain trail race. Likewise, a peek at someone else's old course catalog only hints at what our next semester might include. Whoever wrote Hebrews told us that God's Word is living and active. It only makes sense that the application of his truth would be too.

If the last time God's engagement with your life felt new was in a calendar with a different number (or two) in the year, maybe what you have is a college degree instead of a thriving relationship. If nothing has changed in your spiritual journey since the last presidential administration, maybe it's time to drive yourself to a trail you've never walked.

A safe church will give you space, freedom, and even encouragement to go to new places. A safe pastor knows an infinite God has a lot more to show him and to show us. The One "who makes all things new" uses our pasts, but he doesn't stay there. If we're following him, neither should we.

10 RELEGATED HOLINESS

Unsafe churches told me God's presence is confined to arbitrary places and times, but Jesus has demonstrated he's always with me everywhere—on all seven continents.

It's weird. I can still remember the diagonal rays pouring through the blinds in our efficiency kitchen on a Saturday morning. But I can't even tell you what time of year it was, let alone the date. With a phone rubbing the cartilage of my right ear, I paced the cheap carpet and cheaper linoleum of our townhouse with the lights off. I sat on the stairs and then paced some more. Crystal and I had not been married long. Our 750-square-foot home sat next to an Indiana corn field more than six hundred miles from Conquest Beach, where my dad had officiated our barefoot wedding.

On the other end of the line, my dad revealed that he had cheated on my mom with someone four or five years younger than me. (As I mentioned in chapter 2, we would learn twenty years later that this was a nonconsensual relationship that had turned sexually abusive well before her eighteenth birthday.) After assigning partial blame to the teenage girl and then to my mom, my dad finally blamed exhaustion: "I was just tired." He explained that he had grown too depleted to resist the temptation.

I'm embarrassed now that I thought a teenager could have been complicit in my dad's gross sin. I regret that I didn't challenge his excuses, push back on his deflected blame, or ask more questions in general.

But my dad didn't have to explain how he got so tired. Everybody in my family knew he had been exhausted for years on end. He taught Sunday school along with services on Sunday morning, Sunday evening, and Wednesday night. Not brief Bible studies—full lectures four times a week.

He spent Thursday nights going door-to-door to "win souls," and he wrote a weekly religion column in the *Record-Observer*, our county newspaper. On top of that, he ran a dirty, physical business that offered a slight reprieve from the dirtier and more physical job he held before I left for college. Four of his kids still lived at home, and all of them were homeschooled.

Dad wrote his sermons by hand on yellow legal pads. I spent two hundred services each year of my youth counting down the pages as he slid the used pieces of paper onto the top shelf inside his pulpit. Even now as a professional writer with a laptop, I couldn't write four sermons and a newspaper article per week in only three nights and a Saturday, let alone every week for a decade and a half. Dad had no lieutenant to take services off his plate. He mopped the floors of the elementary school cafeteria, wheeled in a rack of chairs, set them out in optimistic rows, and then pushed and pulled the upright piano into place. He unpacked the church's former U-Haul truck every Sunday morning and repacked it all every Sunday night and Wednesday night. And I don't need any of the fingers on one hand to count the vacations he took during my twelve years living in Maryland, other than to take church kids to an IFB summer camp.

I don't know how he managed it all, let alone for as long as he did.

The saddest part of it all wasn't that his sexual assault of a teenager cost what little he had worked so hard to build or even that most of that work wasn't necessary to advance the kingdom. No, I aim my pity at the bad theology he inherited from his IFB mentors that gave him no other options.

The cult that reared me failed to notice that no church building got a mention in Acts or the Epistles. From the sounds of it, church often happened in homes and outdoor gatherings in a wide range of sizes. Syncretizing Old Testament reverence for the tabernacle and temple, my childhood religion adhered to the language that the church building was where you went to meet Jesus.

It made sense to me as a kid. If Jesus was Lord, then of course he lived at "the Lord's House." Fundamentalists co-opted the beauty of a Sabbath filled with rest, withdrawal, and reflection and transformed it into a litmus test of church attendance. For them, if Sunday was the Lord's Day, the way to spend our waking hours with him was to spend them in rows of chairs or pews. They arbitrarily chose three Sunday services and a Wednesday night gathering despite no biblical precedent. Then they judged those who couldn't hack the weekly gauntlet. The oft-quoted standard was that a good Christian was "there every time the doors were open."

I remember the only time my dad criticized me in person for my post-IFB church attendance. (Usually, he distributes his criticisms behind my back.) I asked him to show me where the Bible directed Christians to attend Sunday night church. He mentioned the incident in Acts 20 when Paul preached a goodbye sermon that went late into a Sunday night—a sermon so long that a kid fell asleep and tumbled out of a third-story window to his death. Paul revived him to life and then preached until dawn. If a nine-hour service is *prescriptive* (not just *descriptive*), why would the rest of the scheduling details of that meeting become orthopraxy? Why don't all Sunday night services last until Monday morning?

When I then asked my dad about the necessity of Wednesday night services, his legalistic criteria anchored itself to the verses in Acts where Luke recorded that the early church believers met every day in each other's houses or the closest Jewish synagogue. "Then why don't you have services every day?" I asked. He replied that it would be unfeasible. "So, if you can arbitrarily pick and choose days, why can't I?" I replied.

The irony is that my nondenominational church's doors stay unlocked for gatherings way more often than those of any IFB church I ever attended. Before COVID shutdowns, we had groups meeting there several daytimes and at least five evenings a week for people to gather in topical, life-stage, needs-based, and gender-specific groups. And you'd need more than your fingers and toes to count all the doors at restaurants, coffee shops, outreach centers, and private homes that are open for discipleship gatherings of our church community throughout the week.

And that doesn't count the spontaneous worship sessions I've experienced on top of mountains and in backyards with other people chasing after Jesus. If Jesus joins with two or three gathered in his name (as he promised to do in the red letters of the Bible), then church happens anywhere saints gather in his name.

In my life, that moment of church happens at least as much outside of programmed services as in them, and I tend to remember those moments at least as much as the official Sunday ones. One recent moment will stick with me for years. A few Friday mornings ago, my friend Nate pulled into the gravel lot of a brand-new disc golf course we wanted to try. He had all four of his windows rolled down. The six a.m. birdsongs faded behind music so loud that his Nissan's speakers crackled with distortion and vibrated his doors. It wasn't rock and roll. It was just loud. Nate pulled up next to my MINI without saying a word. No "Good morning!" No "Hello." He just started singing along with the worship music while standing in the open door of his SUV. As he did this, he looked in my eyes in one of the most intense, intimate ways two straight guys could experience. Because we spend a weeknight with each other and our Bible apps around a fire pit most weeks, I knew how a section of those lyrics (1) had been Nate's prayer ten days prior and (2) were now a grateful reflection on Jesus' omnipotence. As Nate's eyes softened with tears, I joined him in singing. After the song ended and he turned off his ignition, I knelt in the dew of the first tee box and prayed over us.

Nobody had to prepare a sermon. Nobody had to put on a suit. Nobody had to set out chairs. But we worshipped. We connected to the Creator of Our Souls and to each other. We shared stories of God's provision and talked about what we were learning on our journeys.

We had church.

It wasn't Sunday, but it didn't have to be. Every day is the Lord's Day. There wasn't a building, but there didn't have to be. God is at home in our hearts. The Most High dwells in temples made without hands.

That's the first problem with the IFB preoccupation with "the house of the Lord." Jesus doesn't live in a building. There isn't a place to which you must walk or drive to be in his presence. Jesus said his father does have a home, but it's in heaven. When God is on earth, he dwells in us—the men and women who've surrendered control of their soul to him. When believers gather in any capacity in Jesus' name, he doesn't need to welcomed. He's already there. I've been in the Lord's presence while circling for prayer before whitewater rafting, mountain hiking, and helicopter expeditions. I've shared tear-punctuated worship communally around backcountry campsites, in the corner of a South American airport, and in parking lots. I've watched Jesus change lives through informal gatherings of souls in a Cracker Barrel, in a hostel bunk room, and in my buddy's garage. My friend Jeremy gave his life to Christ after a group time of Bible study and prayer—on a fire-engine-red wake boarding boat.

A church building is not imbued with an exclusive presence of the divine. How inadequate would any man-made edifice be if it were? We actually know. God told Isaiah that all of heaven and earth is his throne and rhetorically asked, "Could you build me a temple as good as that?[18] Stephen, one of the first deacons of the Christian church, quoted that exchange between Isaiah and the Almighty in a rigged trial conducted by the fundamentalist leaders of his day. They liked that reminder so much that they murdered him within the hour.

Despite this reinforced precedence spanning more than seven hundred years of the Bible's transcription, the Pharisees of my youth thought men could build thrones or homes for the Most High. It treated the church building (whether a dedicated property or a rented cafeteria) as God's royal residence—like the White House, the Vatican, or Buckingham Palace.

That belief doesn't exist in a vacuum. It's not just wrong by itself. That line of thinking leads to more unbiblical suppositions like "your Sunday best." Nowhere in the Bible do Jesus, the apostles, or any other early church leaders suggest that congregants should dress up to go to church. Not a single verse. In fact, the only verses about clothes and the assembling of believers admonish people *not* to give preference to those dressed in a way to show off their wealth.

Besides, "Sunday best" is ambiguous. Is *best* most fashionable? Fundamentalists would emphatically say no. Is *best* most expensive? In that case, my ice climbing boots cost more than all of my wedding and funeral shoes combined. Is *best* the most formal? If so, tuxes and ball gowns would be the standard. I've heard one "man of God" say *best* is a form of asceticism, a matter of sacrificing comfort—but he wasn't wearing burlap.

It's.

All.

Arbitrary.

And that's the point. Man-made standards allow people to craft a manageable menu of self-righteous acts. They create artificial criteria for holiness and reinforce false castes.

Multiple times during my decades in fundamentalism, a "man of God" would defend the legalism around Sunday attire with something like, "You wouldn't wear that to visit the president, would you?" This question always seemed weird to me. If the Holy Spirit is always with me seven days a week,

---

18 Isaiah 66:1 NLT

why would what I wear Monday through Saturday suddenly offend his sensibilities? Also, in this scenario, God is my father. I'm an adopted child. What do the president's *kids* wear to hang out with their dad? And actually, as a dad, I'm more concerned with what my daughter wears outside my house than in it. I'm grateful she doesn't feel she needs to impress me with anything in our shared home. Nothing she could wear would make me love her more. And nothing any of us might wear could impress Jesus, let alone convince him to love us. That's not how love works. Thankfully, the Gospel and its free benefits aren't contingent on any of our efforts.

The lyrics of the song Nate was playing when he pulled up at dawn that morning explain this reality well:

> I'll never be more loved than I am right now.[19]
> Wasn't holding You up.
> So there's nothing I can do to let You down.
> It doesn't take a trophy to make You proud.
> I'll never be more loved than I am right now.

The construct of "the House of the Lord" creates a more dangerous system than do the days and times we worship and what we have to wear during those times. The construct forms a malignant framework of thinking about God. It erects an artificial wall between the sacred and the secular. It assumes there is a time and a place to be, along with a wardrobe to wear, to draw us near to our Father—and then we go home. In this heresy, there's a location where we go to impress God or impress others or both. In this worldview, there's a place where we expect the presence of the Almighty, and there's a place that looks different and holds different expectations.

For hundreds of thousands of people in IFB environments, this pattern leads to a double life. When you talk to those who've walked away from this abusive theology, and sometimes the faith altogether, you'll hear them talk about the hypocrisy of their parents and their friends' parents. So much could be hidden by suits and ties and perfect attendance. In just my house, my dad hid verbal, physical, and sexual abuse. In other houses, the façade covered addiction or infidelity or even just pain and depression. In

---

19 "Jireh," from *Old Church Basement*, 2021, by Maverick City & Elevation Worship

this dichotomy-framed lifestyle, you don't have to be truly seen or known. Someone more trained in trauma-informed counseling could probably make the case that the system fights against those who try.

This House of God system serves those trying to hide the things in their life that don't align with Jesus' teachings. That's why fundamentalism as a religious sect attracts those who want to harm women and children. But it also serves the Arthurs who pull their "man of God" swords out of their respective stones. See, a House of God requires an attendant—a "man of God." If the divine must funnel through a specific place at a specific time, then someone has to open and close the valves of that conduit. It's a lot of work to create content for three or four services a week, but that work comes with a lot of unchecked and uncheckable power.

Unfortunately, power corrupts even those who start with good intentions. And tired people break. That's not an excuse for grotesque sin, but it does explain why congregants lose hope for a safe church. Broken people walk away, even when they have to lose friends and family to do it. Separated from the House of God, they can feel abandoned by the God of that house. If a specific type of meeting in a specific type of place controlled by a specific type of man is how and where access to God is achieved, it makes sense that for many, a relationship with God isn't worth it. In this way, constructs like the Lord's Day and the Lord's House can become barriers to authentic faith—both for those who stay and for those who leave.

That breaks my heart. An inundation of stories like this drove me to write this book. I imagine Jesus weeps over these wounded hearts far more than I do. The modern IFB movement isn't how he designed his church to operate. Jesus preached on mountainsides in the middle of the week. He discipled next to wells and fields, on boats and on beaches. He taught while he walked. He mentored over dinner. He distributed both truth and healing in standing crowds on dusty streets. He read Scripture in the synagogue, too. As a boy he spent three days in the temple, engaging with rabbis. But he wasn't constrained by those religious walls or the voices within them.

It's been decades since I attended four services a week in "the Lord's House," and my heart has learned how to make its home in my Creator. I've found it more challenging to follow a God who says he overlooks my exterior to scan my heart, but I've found a freedom to be more candid with him and his other kids. I've felt seen and known and accepted on the soul level. So, while life can be weary at times, my faith doesn't contribute to the exhaustion. If anything, a safe church in all the various forms I experience it throughout my week energizes me for the intervals in between.

Something tells me that's how it's meant to be.

PART 2

SUPPLANTED PROPAGANDA

“The true greatness of a man’s power is the measure of his surrender.”

— WILLIAM BOOTH,
founder of the Salvation Army

11 A DENIAL OF DIGNITY

Unsafe churches demonstrated how to demonize people who disagreed with them, but Jesus' biographies show he treated everyone as though they were made in his image.

You'd think the most memorable learning moment of my college career would've been in one of those specialized classes required only for the handful of people who shared my commercial writing major, but I couldn't tell you more than a few things my professors taught us in those mostly empty classrooms.

In contrast, the most indelible assertion I can recall from a college instructor came in a large, senior-level class I shared with—of all departments—criminal justice majors.

PR411—Social Ethics.

It didn't dawn on me until writing this book how fitting it was that IFB college administrators framed ethics as a public relations topic.

Anyway, in that windowless, beige room, the instructor declared that the only women who got pregnant from rape were those who enjoyed being raped.

I left that space to allow that fundamentalist's statement to fully land on you. But you read it correctly. In my *ethics* class, a male assistant dean of the college told us that a woman's uterus will accept sperm only when she is enjoying sex. Yes—that means he implied that some women liked to be violently assaulted—that pregnancy is irrefutable proof of enjoyment.

He offered no counterargument.

He gave no citations of scientific evidence.

He referenced no medical experts.

He quoted no women, let alone did he bring a woman to the lectern.

Nobody referenced the peer-reviewed scientific studies or firsthand accounts that prove that male and female bodies often respond to sexual stimuli against their will. A human biological system—even during a violent assault—often follows its natural progression against the volition of these victims. These perplexing physical responses have long left survivors feeling confused, some even feeling betrayed by their own bodies.

The nuance of this incredibly sensitive subject was too dangerous for the dean-turned-professor to address. In a senior-level undergraduate class, he made the case with a straight face that a woman could have consensual conception from nonconsensual sex. He needed that preposterous premise to support his claim that all but an infinitesimally small number of pregnancies are the result of a woman's will and, thus, all abortions are of intentional, wanted pregnancies. In the mind of my IFB college's brain trust, our curriculum needed a hard-and-fast rule with no exemptions. Not empathy, not an invitation to spend a class period in a crisis pregnancy shelter, not a list of foster organizations and adoption charities we could support. Just judgmental dogmatism.

Conversations about rape and abortion should always lead with empathy and compassion instead of judgment. For abortions that aren't part of rape or incest, I've rarely heard a fundamentalist offer practical solutions to the situations that led to an abortion seeming like the better alternative. For abortions following rape and incest, fundamentalists somehow blame the victim for her predicament. After a woman is sexually assaulted, self-righteous people ask what she was wearing or drinking, where she was walking, or with whom she was socializing. I've yet to hear an IFB preacher question why the *assailant* was in the same wrong place, why he was at that same party, why he felt entitled to take advantage of someone in a compromised situation—let alone why he didn't transport the woman to a safe place.

I struggle with regret on that last indictment. In high school, I spent my summers working at both a gorgeous waterfront golf course and a stately public library on Maryland's Eastern Shore. I can still smell both places from 240 miles and twenty-eight years away. And I can still remember the low-hanging clouds and the thick, humid air from an occasion where my mowing partner, a DIII college football lineman, told me that one of the teenagers who drove the concessions cart was wasted up in the loft of the cart barn. (My coworkers had a saying: "The shorter the shorts, the bigger the tips." By that measurement system, the concessions cart gals pocketed great gratuities.) He bragged that he had taken sexual liberties with her, and he left me with the impression that either others had too or that they could. As one of the guys who mocked my virginity, he suggested that I should go rape her. I rebuffed his invitation but never went to her aid. I never asked more questions. I never alerted golf course management. I felt horrible for her, but my formative culture told me that her predicament was the fault of her choices. Maybe I thought honoring her meant not making matters worse? Regardless, like the religious travelers in the story of the good Samaritan, I didn't assist her in a time of great vulnerability.

I will never forget the next time I saw her. When she walked into the library with her mom, she avoided eye contact. She didn't know that I knew about her rape. I tried to give her the most empathetic face a seventeen-year-old could muster. I didn't know how to do that, having not acted nobly on the information I was given by her pig-nosed rapist. In that moment, though, something changed in me—softened in me. She had made some bad choices, but she didn't deserve what happened to her.

If you have endured physical, sexual, or verbal assault, it's not your fault. If someone stole dignity, autonomy, and security from you, you didn't deserve it. If a "man of God" abused his position and trapped you in yours, you did *nothing* to invite that. You are neither dirty nor unworthy of love. You are not damaged goods or "an unclean offering," as voices of purity culture might've told you. No, God created you in his likeness. You are a beloved child, a rightful heir to anything and everything the Father holds for his children—especially innocence.

Jesus weeps with and for you. In his goodness, he let us know that vengeance is in his sovereign, omnipotent hands. The Inventor of Justice said it's better to be cast into the sea with a millstone around your neck than to endure the fate prepared for those who hurt a child. A fire burns in Jesus for those who rob the vulnerable of innocence. What has been stolen from you is priceless, and your assailant thankfully will pay a hefty eternal debt for his crimes. Remembering that helps me unclench my jaw and my involuntary fists.

I know too many victims of abuse. Any is too many, but the quantity of my friends and extended family members with stories of physical and sexual trauma is jaw-dropping. Almost all those stories are from within the church, and most of those are from IFB churches. The weight of those stories motivates me to tell mine. As more and more IFB predators are caught, I find myself more and more zealous to confront the system that enables and hides these moral monsters.

I've watched multiple holders of the "man of God" title demand instant and permanent mercy for their felonies, while showing no mercy for those with different religious beliefs, different musical preferences, and different sexual sins. In front of his congregation, my dad excommunicated a man for a pattern of consensual sex outside of marriage. My dad, that same "man of God," also quietly resigned from that same church without explanation to its congregants after a mother confronted him for repeatedly sexually assaulting her teenage daughter. One matriarch in my dad's congregation blamed the teenager for the crimes she endured, punctuating her indictment with "What did you expect!?" In her mind, the teenage victim invited the advances of a pastor more than twice her age—a predator with two kids older than her.

In most conversations within fundamentalism around sexuality, women receive more blame than empathy, more skepticism than security, more condemnation than compassion. And in most of those conversations, the tenor doesn't connote a mourning for the loss of innocence or a focus on holistic healing.

At the time of this writing, you can still watch a prime example of this online. A thorough sample of the inappropriate theology of my childhood takes less than a minute of playback. In the sermon clip, Jack Hyles barks, "Women in shorts . . . caused boys to get so stirred up passionately that they'll rape a girl. Brother, you listen to me. For every single man who goes to prison for rape, there ought to be right there beside him a half-naked girl in the next cell."[20]

In the video, the cheers from this IFB leader's audience are loud and rowdy—and damning. Can you find any sentence Jesus said that would even hint at a tacit approval of such sexism and insensitivity? Do any of the Bible's authors document him mistreating or demeaning a woman? Can you imagine the Messiah saying anything remotely close to this chauvinistic diatribe? Apparently, many of the men from IFB churches have and still do.

---

20 https://x.com/IFBSermons/status/1360763612965519363

What I've come to realize in my years since leaving the clutches of a pervasive cult is that the way we have these conversations about life, trauma, sin, and sexuality reflects on what we believe about the Gospel. Where the discussions start and what they focus on reveals whether the beat of our heart aligns with the pulse of Christ's heart. Jesus' biographers noted that he had compassion on crowds and even on those who would reject him. Before the Messiah told the rich young ruler to sacrifice his wealth, we're told that Jesus first held compassion for him. I mentioned earlier how Jesus gave a woman caught in extramarital sex two vastly different statements, but I want to bring them up again to point out their order. *Before* Jesus told the woman, "Go, and sin no more," he assured her. "Neither do I condemn you."[21]

The posture of the "man of sorrows, acquainted with grief"[22] was neither stiff nor aloof. Over and again, Jesus first affirmed his love and then prescribed his remedy. Jesus was open with his lament, generous with his mercy, and sacrificial with his solutions. He leveled shame not on victims but on perpetrators, not on the contrite but on the arrogant. Nobody in human history has understood all that is lost when someone sins against another as much as the Creator who remembers life before sin. Nobody feels that brokenness more than he does or as deeply as he does.

You wouldn't know that from the significant time I spent in fundamentalist churches. I sat through more than five thousand IFB sermons, chapel services, Bible classes, and mandatory devotional presentations but I don't remember hearing that grieving gentleness expressed once. And I can't count the number of times I was reminded of God's wrath and punishment. The men who waved big black Bibles seemed to take pleasure in reminding their audiences about a God waiting to punish sinners. Some delivered those lines and other caustic declarations with a smirk. They came by it honestly, as veneration for fire-breathing preachers and evangelists of bygone days has been passing from one generation to the next since Billy Sunday.

The truth of the matter is that Jesus loves children more than any of us do. He loves the women carrying them and the medical professionals who serve them just as fiercely. Having created life, he roots for alive-ness. The

---

21 John 8:11 LEB

22 Isaiah 53:3 KJV

beauty of life itself should be enough reason for humanity to preserve the unborn. Whether inside or outside the womb, we carry the image of God. Birth doesn't suddenly or magically imbue us with that dignity.

I might have assumptions about Jesus' view on abortion, but I know he's pro-life. That goes for the lives of the unborn and the lives of refugees, the lives of the poor and the lives of the imprisoned, the lives of orphans and the lives of the trafficked, the lives of unarmed Black men in traffic stops and the lives of police officers hunted by drug cartels. He cares about the lives of teenage women in golf course barns and the lives of high schoolers trapped by a pastor with his pants down.

Jesus said he came to give us life—abundant life. As agents of his mission to bring heaven to earth, we are to be conduits and dispensers of life. Being a life-giver means more than voting for elephants in hopes of stacking the Supreme Court with a specific persuasion of judges. Dispensing and defending life has to go further than bumper stickers and protest signs. As conduits of life, churches should comprise a higher percentage of foster and adoptive parents than their communities at large. Followers of Jesus should lead the charge in advocacy for education and mentoring as well as access to healthcare, affordable housing, and attainable childcare. Children of God should seek solutions that make keeping a pregnancy easier.

Christ's apprentices should work to address root causes instead of culture warring over the downline consequences. For those of us who want God's life to permeate our culture, we should advocate for a legal system that gives hope and confidence to victims that reporting their assaults will lead to appropriate legal consequences.Our friends and coworkers need to see their Rescuer's heart. Our culture needs to know they are pursued—not prejudged—by the God of our Bible. Jesus claimed he is the Way, the Truth, and the Life. He lived out that claim. He proved that compassion is the way Sovereignty operates. He illustrated that love is the truest thing about God. He proved that life holds dignity when he breathed his own breath into us.

You and I have never looked into the eyes of a woman, child, or man who Jesus didn't love, didn't die for, didn't make in his image. When that reality permeates our lives, how we talk to and about others changes. People—especially the ostracized, the wounded, and the grieving—will take notice of our sensitivity. When people of faith take this approach, that grace reflects on its source. Observers find courage to unburden their hearts, to embrace their humanity. With those courageous steps comes the bravery to surrender fears and pride and even dreams that aren't big enough.

The softer and more careful I've let my heart grow, the more it seems to break. As empathy has become more and more my default setting, hurting people have either asked to meet with me alone or have trusted our shared circles. Around those tables and campfires, pain from my past is redeemed and pressure in my present finds relief. The symbiosis of these safe places has rewarded me far more often than it has cost me, and the other voices in those circles echo that same sentiment. Somehow one life plus one life equals more than two existences.

Who doesn't want to hold more life than they have days to contain it? Who wouldn't want their faith community to be the place where they feel most alive and most worthy of love? Who wouldn't want conversations about our mistakes, our trauma, and our poor choices to flow from grace? Who, other than religious dictators and despots, abusers and shamans?

12 THE WRONG KIND OF DIFFERENT

Unsafe churches created artificial walls between me and other bearers of the image of God, but Jesus continues to call me to an attractive life only he can provide.

I'm so embarrassed by this story, which is why I have to tell it.

My Aunt Sandi is just the best. When I was in second grade, she took me to Toys "R" Us to buy my first LEGO set. When I was in college, she let me stay at her house and watch the movies I kept hearing quoted: *Dumb and Dumber*, *The Princess Bride*, and *Tommy Boy*. For thirty years, Aunt Sandi drove hundreds of miles every December to celebrate Christmas with my immediate family. (That streak has stopped only because we no longer gather everyone in my family for Christmas.) More than her gifts, we George kids craved her attuned listening, her scatological humor, and her exaggerated hugs.

As a gift for one of my high school Christmases, Aunt Sandi bought me a Michael W. Smith CD to play on my new stereo. If you've not heard of this artist, he's been the Phil Collins of Christian radio for decades. His hit single, "Friends," was the song many Christian teenagers played as they drove away from graduations or summer camps in the nineties. But Michael W. Smith music was contraband in an IFB home. He had collaborated with Amy Grant—who, as we were falsely told, did a TV interview in her underwear. And his music featured drums.

I sneaked some album spins up in my attic bedroom while Aunt Sandi was in town. After she returned to New York, I did what I knew must be done. My parents had submitted all their secular vinyl except the Statler Brothers and the Carpenters to a church bonfire years earlier, and it was my turn to prove my commitment to the IFB cult. So, I took the shiny plastic out to our woodpile, grabbed the axe, and smashed the CD into pieces. At once, I felt both ashamed of my ungrateful act and self-righteous for my sacrifice. More important than my feelings was the fact that I had earned a stripe for my "separated" designation.

• • •

Outside of church walls, the Bible verse most Americans see referenced is probably John 3:16. "For this is how God loved the world: He gave his one and only Son, so that everyone who believes in him will not perish but have eternal life." Inside the sanctuaries of IFB churches, though, one of the most quoted Scripture verses is the King James Version's rendering of 2 Corinthians 6:17: "Come out from among them, and be ye separate, saith the Lord."

This verse without context could make you think Jesus prefers his followers in communes, and we've all seen enough documentaries to know that's exactly what cults do. But several sentences before this imperative, the apostle Paul told the church that they couldn't conjoin their temples with the idols and practices of pagan religions. In a pantheistic culture, he wanted them to worship only the God represented by Christ. In a culture that tended to yes-and gods, Paul exhorted them to take an approach of "Yeah, no."

A theologian could extend this command today in terms of the gods offered in various religions. They could probably even make an application to the pantheism inherent in the American Dream®. We're all drawn to one or more of the gods of wealth, fame, comfort, political power, and sexual conquest. We can make idols of romantic partners and children. We can also carve idols out of jobs, sports, social media, travel, comfort, denominations, traditions, and socioeconomic status.

Jimmy Needham catches all of our misdirected worship with his "Clear the Stage" lyrics: "Anything I want with all my heart is an idol. Anything I can't stop thinking of is an idol. And anything that I give all my love is an idol." (For all of fundamentalism's declarations of modern worship being doctrine-less anathema, I'd put the spiritual stakes of this song up against any lyrics I sang from a hymnbook.)

If it's true that we can't serve two masters, following Jesus requires us to leave our modern version of pantheism to "be guided by the Spirit."[23] The interrogations of what we worship and how to bring that under submission to Jesus deserve frequent inspection. The rich soil of this introspection could lead to deep conversations and then crucibles of surrender, but that's not where fundamentalism takes that verse. Instead of evaluating where we mix our faith with the belief systems of our surrounding culture, they bang a drum of pulling away from "the world."

As you can probably imagine, a literal translation of 2 Corinthians 6:17 leads to an Amish-like withdrawal from culture. I wouldn't be surprised if the extreme end of fundamentalism takes the train of separation that far. Most of the sect, though, chooses a weird "neither" from the options above. IFB preachers make this verse the basis for the oft-referenced "doctrine of separation." With that elevated status of doctrine comes an adjective you'll often see on IFB church websites, parishioners' social media bios, and blogger's "about me" pages.

Separated.

You can court a Christian girl, "but is she *separated*?" You can join a Baptist church, "but are they *separated*?" *Separated* is the gold standard. *Separated* is a dog whistle that acts as a shorthand for everything inherent in the cult: KJV-only, hymns-only, women only in long dresses, men only with hair off the collar, church only in rows, and only men in leadership (with only one man in charge), and only silent victims. Okay, I added that last one; but it typically goes without saying in these congregations.

Often *separated* includes no television in the home and even, in some cases, no Internet. At a Walmart in Columbia City, Indiana, I heard a fundamentalist woman ream a Walmart employee who included a CD of her photos for online sharing in addition to her prints. The customer angrily barked about the unholy dangers of the Internet that no one should allow in their house.

The big goal of doctrine-level separation is to be as different as possible from culture. And each church gets to decide what that looks like. More specifically, each church's "man of God" draws the lines for his congregants. It works similarly to the Amish hierarchal system. In many Amish

23 Galatians 5:16 CEB

communities, the local elders determine whether they can use tractors or not (with rubber tires or not), axles with bearings or only with grease, and buggies with coverings or not. IFB separatists vary on the maximum age of male students a woman can teach, whether her skirt has to be knee- or ankle-length, and whether women can sing on stage. Each church sets the limit as far as how new the music in the hymnal can be. I was told that my alma mater was looked down upon by some from Bob Jones University (BJU) because our vocalists were allowed to hold their microphones—even though our campus church made them hold the mics at their waists (to avoid holding a mic like a secular singer). It all reminds me of the exasperation in Jesus' words when he proclaimed, "Blind guides! You strain your water so you won't accidentally swallow a gnat, but you swallow a camel!"[24]

Separated creates a checklist of external, verifiable proofs that you are different from "the world." You can get away with the same hate as a drug dealer in your heart, as long as you wear a suit and tie on Sunday. You can justify bitterness or jealousy, as long as you sing old enough religious songs. You can rationalize lust for a minor, as long as your wife and daughter are covered in prairie dresses. You can feel better about your addiction to porn than someone else's premarital sex because you study the right translation of the Bible. You can feel righteous in condemning Democrats, Hollywood actors, and news anchors to hell as long as you go to church four services a week and don't shop on Sundays.

It's no wonder that Jesus called the *separated* men of his day "white-washed tombs."[25] They dotted their public i's and crossed their external t's while forgoing common decencies like taking care of elderly parents. They strained a lot of water to wash down huge portions of camel meat.

Candidly, I was one of those camel eaters. I remember bragging to my workmates in high school and college about all the things I didn't do. I wanted them to know I wasn't like them. I thought I was showing them a better way to live, but I was just showing them I was a self-righteous jerk. To be fair, I don't think fundamentalists always do this out of intentional condescension. I didn't. Back then, though, I never stopped to ponder the ramifications of pointing out someone else's otherness. I never analyzed

---

24 Matthew 23:24 NLT

25 Matthew 23:27 NLT

how I assuaged my own insecurities by looking down my long nose at someone else's. I never considered that I added obstacles to someone's path to new life.

Separated is a two-sided coin of pride and insecurity. Instead of resting in the acceptance of Jesus, IFB separatists must inventory how many of their sect's boxes they can check. If not enough boxes are checked, they hold a list of very clear actions to help them feel better about their relationship with their Eternal Groom. If most of their boxes are checked, that supernatural marriage is safe. If all of them are checked, they have permission to feel like they've lived a better life than their peers. As an added perk, they can then discount the choices, opinions, and confrontations of those with fewer boxes checked.

Fortunately, our security in Jesus doesn't come from what we do or even can do. No amount of asceticism can impress a Son who gave up heaven and infinite dignity to suffer in nakedness on a cross. No number of religious bricks can make our respective Towers of Babel tall enough to deserve heaven. Our dresses can't be long enough to cover our inadequacies. Our music can't be quiet enough nor slow enough to hear a Holy Spirit whose revelations we reject if they don't agree with the king of our local fiefdom.

We can't earn more love, more affection, more approval, or more acceptance from Jesus. All of those are built into the gift of the Gospel. They're not prizes we earn for beating different levels in a spiritual video game. Even if our efforts could win these prizes, the criteria that would determine them wouldn't have been crafted by IFB forefathers two thousand years after Jesus' resurrection.

Undeterred, IFB preachers go to their *separated* whip often to beat a dead horse. If it weren't dead, why would they need so many revival services? These loud, angry preachers must keep verbally slapping their audiences, because it's easier than quietly shepherding their flocks in what would be a real countercultural lifestyle.

Ironically, the one thing fundamentalists prove they're separated from is the example of Jesus. For sure, Jesus said difficult things. All of his biographers document him repeating uncomfortable standards. But none of those standards were about gathering places, clothing, music, political affiliation, the subjugation of women, or specific translations of the library of Scripture.

No, Jesus rebuked proud people.

Jesus made his disciples walk with him on the wrong side of the tracks. He told people the first will be last and that greatness is measured by meekness. He made things awkward by being the rabbi—the honored guest—who washed guests' feet while on his knees. He taught that those who lay down their lives keep them. He asked fundamentalists riddles to catch them in their hypocrisy. He wasn't a hippie full of moral relativity; but he wasn't a red-faced policeman, either.

Jesus demonstrated an authentic, unconditional love. He fully saw shame and guilt but offered forgiveness and admonition. He appealed to both ends of multiple continuums.

- The humble and the proud were drawn to him.
- The sinner and the religious leader wanted to talk with him.
- Jews and Gentiles appealed to him for miracles.
- Blue-collar tradesmen and academic elites wanted to engage with him.
- Patriotic zealots and turncoat tax collectors followed him.
- Men and women felt seen and known by him.
- Children and adults found themselves worthy to be close to him.
- The rich and poor brought their needs to him.

I don't know of many pulpit pounders who have this reputation. Somehow, IFB preachers consider the lived example of Jesus as less important than their artificial standards. Fundamentalists are taught to pull sentences out of context rather than to put highly parsed verses into the context of Christ's actions and primary teaching themes. How did Jesus treat those who were not like him? How did the Messiah relate to women? How did the Son of God relate to his culture? Who in the religious milieu drew his compassion, and who drew his reprimand?

Jesus and the early church fathers said his disciples would be known for their love and their unity. What would make them different was how they responded to wrongs, offenses, and oppression. The guy who started the Thessalonian church told its congregants that believers have a different hope, that we can grieve differently. In the Great Commission, we have a purpose and a calling that surpasses the siren calls of hedonism, humanism, and the American Dream®. A mentor for the Galatian church said those who host the Holy Spirit will produce the fruit of love, joy, peace, patience, kindness, goodness, faithfulness, gentleness, and self-control.

All it takes is a quick skim of news headlines to see why that fruit would be so different from what secular culture produces. What separates those within the universal church from those outside it should be how we respond to hardship and delays, betrayal and disappointment, accolades and accomplishment. When pressed, our fruit should create a countercultural juice. Selflessness will stand out from the crowd more than self-righteousness will. Quiet surrender will contrast the deafening selfishness that surrounds us. The dignity we give to all who are made in the image of God will demand notice in a world that looks to dehumanize opponents and the less fortunate.

A noticeably different life doesn't start on the outside. In fact, a countercultural life vulnerably *connects* our inner world with our outer one. A holistic spirituality removes the separation between our unhealthy motives and our malignant behaviors. With courage and curiosity, we can find healing by looking at the thing behind the thing—the root pathways in which our trauma, training, and dysfunction become sin. An actually separated life removes masks and reveals secrets; it separates our fig-leaf façades from our nakedness and shame. If we want to look different from a world whose prince is a liar, we must allow integrity to remove the walls, filters, and compensations we use to hide our brokenness. We must not wait for Toto to pull back the curtain on our wizardry, and we must not circle the wagons around #metoo monsters when they are unveiled.

This authenticity attracts people to the universal church and to our Jesus. This vulnerable-but-contagious healing happens at tables, around campfires, on road trips, and in other circles a thousand times more than sitting silently in rows—especially the rows berated by proud men. Those domineering voices aren't that *separated* from those on cable "news" and sports channels or those of abusive parents in the homes of the self-medicated. In contrast, a "set apart" congregation will separate the concept of church from church buildings; they will be the church rather than go to church.

A truly separated life showcases another contrast too: the contrast between who we used to be and who we are becoming. Recently, my wife, my siblings, and my closest friends have all told me I'm different than I was just half a decade ago—in a good way. A better different. As much as it hurts to hear their specific examples of my former attitudes, personas, and behaviors, there's relief that those traits are no longer my default settings. The changes they acknowledge aren't that my church attire better matches funeral standards or that the verses I quote sound more like seventeenth-century poetry. No, one friend said my heart has grown softer. Others have noticed less striving, more intentionality, and greater generosity. Crystal said I no longer remind her of my caustic dad.

The more I've brought my dysfunction into the light, the healthier I've grown. The more I've said yes to the Holy Spirit and no to my plans, the further I've gotten from where my momentum was taking me. The more separated I've become from sin management and religious externalism, the more attractive my faith has become to others. I don't have to take a fun CD to the woodpile when I'm taking an axe to my ego and entitlement instead.

The distance I've created between me and a caste-based ladder has created a safe place for other people to find acceptance, healing, encouragement, challenge, and counsel. This redefined separation for me has worked like an equilateral triangle: the more I've worked to separate myself from the abusive theology of my youth, the more separated I've also grown from what people outside the church expect from a hypocritical Christian.

13 A DEHUMANIZING SILENCE

Unsafe churches insisted that women must be subjugated and silenced, but Jesus demonstrated how to elevate women above the limits that patriarchal cultures place on their status.

All students of my alma mater who weren't interning at IFB ministries were required to attend its on-campus church. Jim, the campus pastor, knew well that he spoke to a captive audience every Sunday. So, he tried to liven up his sermons with surprising props. I remember Jim walking along the front row with a shockingly long cow tongue in butcher paper during a sermon about guarding our tongue and blowing a ram's horn in connection with some Old Testament story. But the sermon garnish I will remember most wasn't one he planned.

Two or three times a semester, the wife of the college's vice president leveraged her professional opera background during our Sunday services. In my rough memory, she performed in makeup so thick and exaggerated that she looked like she had a dress rehearsal for the *Mikado* immediately following the service. I don't know who thought the hearts of college students would be quickened by the warbling of a soprano uncomfortably close to cultural appropriation. Anyway, immediately after enduring one of her Sunday morning "specials" from the balcony, one of the most fascinating moments of my forty years of church experience launched a couple sections to my right.

As Mrs. Vice President walked off the stage, Jim bounded up toward the podium. In the silence of that brief transition, a man stood at the front of the balcony and shouted, "WOMEN SHALL KEEP SILENT IN THE CHURCH!" a couple of times. Due to his placement and his timing, my first thought was that he was a plant—one of Jim's attention grabbers. But then he started shouting Scripture passages while the preacher grimaced and stammered. Ushers in suits with matching red ties and Secret Service earpieces rushed from the back doors down the stairs like it was a matter of national security. The heckler bolted, weaving his way through the congregation to an unattended door, escaping the stiffs more accustomed to synchronized steps with offering plates than chasing bad actors. Campus security was alerted. They closed the gates to our campus and monitored the fences with cameras. They detained the intruder as he was trying to scale the outer walls of our IFB compound.

The rumor on campus was that the perpetrator belonged to the Ruckmanite cult, a competing IFB sub-sect headquartered at a Bible institute in the same city. Their extremism considered everyone at our far-right college to be weak-minded liberals. Our student body included people of color, and their leader was a documented segregationist. On most weekends, Peter Ruckman's disciples could be found in our beach town, yelling cringy invectives at motorists while their wives in prairie dresses held doomsday-message signs. We were told that they weren't hoping to get sinners to repent but, instead, they were practicing rejection acclimation—since the world would reject them for any number of their tenets.

To this day, I tip my hat to that extremist heckler. He shot his shot. He took one of fundamentalism's favorite pastimes—out-fundamentalizing other fundamentalists—and turned the dial up to eleven. He personally delivered the explosive argument behind enemy lines. While I vehemently disagree with his mission and his dehumanization of women, I applaud the chutzpah of his protest.

And I give him credit for taking his literalism to its proper end. If women are to keep silent in the church, that would include singing—especially on stage. (Oh, sorry—on the *platform*. IFB churches don't have *stages*.) While the Ruckmanite heckler clearly expressed that in a disruptive manner, he was at least intellectually consistent.

Almost every church I've ever visited parsed out what women could and couldn't do in a church so much that a female's place in the body of Christ looks like one of those gerrymandered voting districts after a census. And that parsing was done almost exclusively by men.

When we first started attending our current church seventeen years ago, women freely sang, prayed, read Scripture, and performed spoken-word pieces on stage, but they weren't allowed to expound on a single line of the Bible. Women were applauded for telling stories of what Jesus has done in their lives and for baptizing other women or children, but they weren't permitted to baptize a husband or adult son they had led to Jesus. Women couldn't preach or teach from stage, but our church took dozens of men to conferences where women did. Ladies took up seats on organizational leadership teams, but a woman taking an issue—including abuse or assault—to their elders wouldn't have been able to look into even a single set of understanding female eyes.

And at the time, our church sat on the contemporary end of the spectrum in a metro area whose phone book held more than two hundred churches under its bolded Baptist heading. Compared to the churches I attended in my first two decades of life, that assembly was a liberal outpost. Because of the churches we had previously attended, the gender situation was such an improvement that we didn't press into the issue. Frankly, in the early years of our attendance, I was weirded out when I heard a woman praying.

Crystal and I talk more about gender equality in the church these days. We both officiate weddings as civil ceremonies, and ordination could come in handy. When people have asked if I've considered getting ordained, I tell people I might someday—but only after my wife does. Because we aren't part of a denomination, ordination is administered by our church's elders. That collection of men currently wouldn't consider bestowing that honor on my wife. They have, however, hosted conversations with Crystal and our church's other female leaders about how their ministry can be supported, how their discipleship work can be honored, and how their rightful place in the kingdom can be recognized. While we don't have women teachers on the platform on Sundays, they are on the teaching team that determines what is talked about on Sundays; and they are welcomed to teach in smaller environments.

I can't speak for others in our church, but the whole gender equality deal feels more like a "not yet" than a "not ever." I don't think my church has treated women with the equality worthy of joint holders of God's image; but I respect our elder's humility and I have seen movement on the issue in the right direction. Crystal, who currently serves on staff in a shepherd's role without the title of pastor, is content with the posture and momentum of our elders' hearts. So, there's nuance to my real life engagement with this topic, and that nuanced position is far better than that of any IFB church I ever attended.

I don't know that I can point to a big, watershed moment in my journey from participating in structural misogyny to being an advocate for women's voices. Part of the process for me has been being married to a gifted shepherd who studies the Bible with fervor and nurtures hearts better than any male pastor I've ever met. Part of it has been all of the times I cringed at weddings after hearing brides vow to always obey their husbands just hours before their honeymoons. This might sound weird, but I think one of the cracks started when I learned what the term "Stockholm syndrome" meant. The fissure broke wide open after I read books by experts in Greek and Hebrew translation, cultural context, and church history. Nijay Gupta's book *Tell Her Story* stretched that canyon into a sprawling valley.

For some reason, I never noticed during all of my trips through the KJV's creation mythology that the writer of Genesis said both men and women were created in the image of God. I hadn't paid attention to the fact that when forbidden fruit brought death and darkness into our world, Eve didn't get more blame from God than Adam did.

When God warned Eve about the forthcoming pain in childbirth and her future subjugation to men, his words comprised a prophesy, not his plan. Eden was his plan. Eve's Creator foresaw the patriarchy the same way he foresaw sweat, thorns, callouses, and sunburns for men. I've never heard a sermon aimed at men about how they don't sweat or bleed enough. But I've heard an IFB pastor yell from his bully pulpit that because of Eve, he will never get his theology from a woman—in front of an audience that probably held hundreds of women.

Christine Caine, the founder of A21, an anti-trafficking organization, was the first voice I heard point out that the fruit of the Spirit is not gendered, and neither are the gifts of the Spirit. Why would the truth of what a woman teaches change when the gender or age of her audience changes? For a religion that hangs its hat on absolute and immutable truth, I find that inconsistency fascinating.

While we're talking about selective literalism, in the same letter to Timothy where the apostle Paul says women in Timothy's church shouldn't lead or teach, the elder pastor also says women will be saved through childbirth.[26] I've not met a single IFB pastor who would preach that full context. I can probably count on one hand—two at the most—the times I've heard that verse read aloud in an IFB environment, and I took a full semester of a junior-level college class on just the books of 1 and 2 Timothy and Titus.

As Beth Allison Barr documents in *The Making of Biblical Womanhood,* conservative faith leaders have worked throughout the centuries to change the gender of the named female church leaders who Paul greeted and exhorted in his letters and to make excuses for the ones they couldn't explain away. During my decades inside the IFB patriarchy, I never heard anyone even hint that there might be nuance in one early church father's advice to scattered churches with different local cultural contexts. Frankly, I doubt I ever heard the word *nuance* at all.

Pastors told me about rabbis and their pupils—usually in discussions of Saul of Tarsus and his esteemed mentor, Gamaliel. But not one of the pastors in front of me ever pointed out the implications of the rabbi-training inherent in the story in which Jesus commended Mary of Bethany for sitting and listening to her teacher at his feet. In fact, the Messiah told her busy sister that Mary had chosen the better pursuit in what would've been a controversial mentoring. Quite possibly, even just Mary's physical proximity to Jesus might have raised eyebrows. The fundamentalists of Jesus' day would not have entertained the possibility of a rabbi welcoming a female pupil.

I love Sovereignty's subversiveness in assigning women as the first proclaimers of the Gospel message of Jesus' resurrection. Who taught Jesus' inner circle of disciples that their Savior was alive? (Hint: it wasn't another dude.) God has a long history of using people of lower status in their patriarchal, racist, and religious systems to proclaim eternal truth. Sovereignty seems to love leveraging the lives of people considered unreliable narrators by their dominant cultures. God still does, by the way. An early church father asserted that the Omniscient One uses the weak of the world to confound the wise, and Jesus' Great Commission wasn't limited to those with a penis.

Fundamentalists selectively quote the Bible, forgo an Eastern approach to the library of Scripture, and ignore cultural nuances on purpose. IFB

26 1 Timothy 2:15

demagogues like Bill Gothard and Jack Hyles used their platforms to twist their theology around the silencing of women. Thousands of sexual predators and insecure pastors gladly cosigned on all of that. And that's no accident. As Dr. Wade Mullen says in *Something's Not Right,* his fantastic book on church abuse, "Nothing stays hidden without help."

IFB preachers repeatedly tell women they're second-class citizens for a reason. For one thing, if a woman can't teach a man—let alone a "man of God"—that means the cult leader in question now has less than half as many people who can hold him accountable. (Pew Research found that there are more women than men in IFB churches.) Secondly, when you verbally beat into a woman over and again that her will must be subjugated to a man's will, men don't have to worry about consent.

The church should be the champion of consent. Men wearing the name of Christ should be the absolute *last* people who would perpetrate verbal, physical, or sexual abuse. Women should feel the most honored, most cherished, and most respected around followers of Jesus—more than anywhere else on this planet.

Church should be the safest place a woman can go.

Before my dad and his best friend, Kent, became IFB pastors, the man my dad prompted me to call "Uncle Kent" lived in a mobile home up the hill from us. His daughter and I got baptized together. Anyway, I remember being intrigued that sometimes he spanked his kids with a wooden spoon instead of always using a belt. But even more indelibly, I remember him yelling to his wife, "Don't make me get out my submission stick!" I don't know if he ever wielded such a stick on "Aunt Lori," but if he had, he wouldn't have been the only pastor in my life to have stolen the autonomy and dignity of his wife.

The stick most IFB "men of God" wield as a weapon against a woman's personhood comes from a distorted reading of Paul's first letter to the debauched and dysfunctional church in Corinth. "The husband should fulfill his wife's sexual needs, and the wife should fulfill her husband's needs. The wife gives authority over her body to her husband, and the husband gives authority over his body to his wife."[27] IFB pastors and their wives have told women this pair of verses means that wives must allow their husbands to use their bodies and specifically their sexual organs at will. Some go so far

---

27 1 Corinthians 7:3–4 NLT

as to tell women to fake pleasure and endure pain to live within the spirit of this verse. But that's not the spirit of that verse.

It wasn't until after my honeymoon that I paid attention to the facts that (1) this coupling of verses has two halves, and (2) the second half says men aren't the masters of their own bodies, either. The first verse starts with a wife's sexual fulfillment, and I've never heard an IFB preacher talk about making sure a wife's sexual needs are met as a priority. The verse after the ones quoted above continues the theme of equality by insisting on consensual agreement on the scheduling of sex.

Fundamentalists will then use a letter Paul wrote to a different church to imply that these verses are meant more for women to read and heed than for men. I've watched this happen: a "man of God" will pound the apostle Paul's call for wives to submit to their husbands in Ephesians 5:22 without even reading or referencing the verse—immediately before it—the verse that calls spouses to submit to *each other*. In other words, Paul's charge to wives is that mutual submission applies to them too. While the charge to men in this passage covers 64 percent more verses and 75 percent more English words, you'll have to sit through thousands of IFB sermons before you'll hear the man's self-sacrifice emphasized in that proportion. Actually, you might never hear it, especially in mixed company.

One prominent California IFB preacher recently posted a video reinforcing this hijacking of that Ephesians prooftext. With an arrogant smirk he looked into the camera and declared, "The husband is the savior of the body that the husband and wife have in marriage. He's the savior. Take that in your female, anti-male pipe and smoke it." Neither the 1787 King James Bible nor the 1611 original King James Bible use the word *savior*—and neither do the original Greek transcripts. Still, this IFB preacher reveals the underlying belief of these misogynists: that women owe them for their spiritual condition. As you can imagine that debt must be continually repaid, and the terms of that repayment are decided by each little-s savior.

I've read accounts of women whose husbands have stretched the sexual-submission narrative to include the husband's sexual fantasies, not just his sexual release. They treat their wives as chattel—like they are owned rather than loved. They demand their privileges as rights, exploiting out-of-context lines from their holy book as the violence necessary to get sex—and sex their way. If they were using any other weapon but the Bible, everyone reading this would call it rape.

Because it *is* rape.

This submission-and-silence theology imprisons women in abusive relationships. IFB preachers in Sunday pulpits and their wives at women's retreats sell Stockholm syndrome as a divine solution. That goes for women married to monsters, single women assaulted by perverts, and children molested by deviants. From an early age, girls in IFB churches know that total submission is their future. And the notion is ingrained in both genders that submission to spiritual authority is the only way to stay in God's will. So, is it any surprise that when a "man of God" does anything untoward he finds compliance? Women are told their voices are neither equal nor welcomed in church, so why would we expect victims to come forward?

Satan salivates over this institutional grooming for sexual assault. The roaring lion uses the façade of religion to steal innocence, devastate lives, and bring death to personal faith. Often, the only viable option for finding justice or even just freedom and safety requires leaving your IFB church. If you've been sheltered in your church, that's pretty much your whole interpersonal ecosystem. Whether the church excommunicates and shuns you or not, you're left on the outside of your bubble looking in. So, your choice is to endure pain and debauched indignities or leave the only semblance of love that you've ever known.

I've never read anything in the red letters of the Bible that would make me think that dynamic aligns with God's heart. Nothing about Christ's behavior across his biographies would lead one to assume that's how women should be treated.

It gets worse. This cult makes women scapegoats by labeling them as the culprits—or at least as the triggers for these wolves' uncheckable, malignant behavior. It's sickeningly ironic to me that so many preachers treat women as the dangerous gender. The IFB patriarchy uses its legalism to protect men from women and especially from the female form. The rules are framed at least as much to safeguard men from themselves as women from the unstoppable inertia of their lust. I don't know how many times I heard a "man of God" implore ladies with a line like, "Ladies! You've got to help your brothers out!"

One high-ranking "preacher boy" at my alma mater contended that women with skirt hems higher than their ankles were tempting men to sin.

(He explained that visible shins and knees lead male eyes to travel north.) He wasn't alone. There was no place on the planet with more women in ankle-length khaki skirts.

This defensive approach explains the rules at the above-ground pool in my parents' backyard. My dad requires every female swimmer to wear a T-shirt over their swimsuits at all times. (To make it fair, guys must wear shirts too.) Many fundamentalists would find my dad's rule a compromise, as many IFB preachers still point their flamethrowers at the danger of males and females swimming together at all.

At this point in the chapter, you might be sensing a theme: women in IFB churches—much like their counterparts in Islam—are strong-armed into silence, submission, and shame. Trifecta.

Now, it's true that not all men in this cult actively mistreat women. Some let their pastor's sermons do the dirty work for them, and others don't abide by the worst of the implications in their home or daily lives. But this isn't just a "Well, there will always be a few bad apples" situation. Fundamentalism incentivizes the rotting of apples. Again, the words of W. Edwards Deming apply: "Every system is perfectly designed to get the result that it does."

Dysfunctional theology leads to systemic messaging that fuels a disgusting sexual ethic. Just as when the apostle Paul told the debauched Corinthians that what was going on in sexual relationships in their church shouldn't even be named outside the church,[28] so it is with the IFB treatment of women. The double-edged sword of silence and submission needs to be beaten into plowshares. The unnecessary weight of shame needs to be thrown into the sea—maybe around the necks of abusers like the millstone that Jesus promised?

I long for these women to be free!

Despite what fundamentalists will tell you, I will not stand before God in the afterlife responsible for Crystal or anyone else. Neither will any man reading this book. (I just spent $29.95 for in-flight Internet access to verify that with Google searches for IFB prooftexts.) There is no marriage in heaven. Ultimately, we'll all be responsible for either (A) our own decision to reject Jesus or (B) the legitimacy of our personal fruit after surrendering

---

28 1 Corinthians 5:1 KJV

our lives to Christ. For those of us in group B, the coming evaluation is not a matter of indictment for sin but of recognition for good works. My works and yours will be weighed by fire to determine whether they were for Christ and his kingdom or for my selfish ambitions.

Even if—without any Bible reference to foretell it—I am measured by the spiritual flourishing of my wife and daughter, God's pattern is grace. He rewards the posture of the heart. He will know there was a two-thousand-year gap between my culture and a series of Paul's conflicting opinions about women in leadership, the example of Jesus, and the Holy Spirit's voice. If I don't weed perfectly though all of that, I won't have to live with a scarlet letter or a blinking ankle monitor in heaven.

So, then, I have to ask myself if in that final reckoning I'd rather afford the women in my life more or less voice, more or less autonomy, more or less honor. The safer bet is with more. I won't be punished for going with the *more* option, because the afterlife evaluation of believers is not about punishment anyway.

Every man reading this book could benefit from inviting Christian women to more honor and more voice. The men of IFB and other patriarchal churches rob themselves of a vital resource in their sanctification. If the nongendered assignment of all believers is to "spur one another on toward love and good deeds,"[29] why wouldn't a woman be able to encourage a man toward the heart of Jesus?

I'm not the only one who would tell you that I have benefited greatly from Crystal having an equal spiritual voice in our marriage. She has been the audible and tangible representation of the Holy Spirit in my life more times than I can count. She's rightly pointed out when my words, actions, and not-so-hidden motives don't align with the Scripture I say I believe. I find that ironic, seeing as right before I got married my dad warned me about Crystal being a moral hazard. His exact words? After telling me he was begrudgingly giving his blessing to marry her, he declared, "She's going to bring you down spiritually." The opposite has been true from the beginning, and I'm only more grateful for that as I record more years with Jesus.

Not surprisingly, the further I've gotten away from the IFB oppression of my youth, the more my response to Crystal's exhortation has grown

---

29 Hebrews 10:24 NIV

opposite to my dad's reaction to any confrontation. When Crystal discreetly and respectfully recommended an addiction recovery ministry to my dad, the man who taught me that a husband and wife are one flesh angrily retorted that Crystal wasn't a legitimate member of our family. Thus, now, neither am I.

As I listen to the stories of refugees from IFB abuse—especially those who experienced sexual trauma—my dad's dismissal and dehumanization prove themselves the rule rather than the exception. Cover-ups are standard. Victim shaming is the norm. Demanding a victim to "forgive and forget" gets repeated as standard operating procedure. It's typical to tell a woman worthy of carrying the earth-shattering news of Christ's resurrection to his inner circle that her spiritual discoveries are beneath men. Some say it as succinctly as John MacArthur, a right-wing pastor whose church has been credibly reported to have covered for his parishioner's sexual abuse, did to Beth Moore behind her back: "Go home."

Can't you just hear Christ's disciples saying that to Mary?

If half of the people on the planet in a relationship with Jesus are forbidden from expressing what they're learning to the other half of that population, then the silencing of women isn't just a matter of religious or sexual abuse. It's a discipleship issue, if not a Gospel issue.

Were I one of the men who believe they'll stand before God for the women of the world, I'd hate to have that on my rap sheet.

14 MISALIGNED ALLEGIANCE

Unsafe churches made me assume we could worship both God and country, but Jesus has reminded me to pledge my allegiance only to his all-inclusive kingdom.

A few weeks ago, I drove by the football stadium on the campus of a Christian university. I found myself struck by the three flags held taut by the evening breeze. From the tallest pole waved the red, white, and blue of the United States. Below that swayed the red, white, and blue of the Commonwealth of Virginia and the red, white, and blue of the Christian flag.

If you're not familiar with the Christian flag, know that it's a staple of Christian school classrooms and even many IFB church sanctuaries. It's one of the few ecumenical symbols allowed in IFB ecosystems. IFB churches consider almost every other item dubbed ecumenical to be dangerous or evil. Every IFB church I attended considered other denominations as gatherings of the lost, the unsaved, the ignorant, or the deceived. But the Christian flag escaped that stigma. Even for a fundamentalist, it was hard to argue with the contents of the pledge to this cross-denominational flag: "I pledge allegiance to the Christian flag and to the Savior for whose kingdom it stands—one Savior, crucified, risen, and coming again with life and liberty for all who believe."

Not a single adult in my life batted an eye at the idea that we would start each day of IFB grade-school classes with a Pledge of Allegiance to the American flag, let alone that we also pledged allegiance to the Christian flag—and always second. In the context of pledging our allegiance to a country and its government, not once in my years inside the IFB movement did anyone bring up Jesus' words that no one can serve two masters or his call to seek first the kingdom of God.

IFB schools taught me that Virginians have at least twice historically needed to choose between loyalty to their commonwealth and their country. But my pastors, school administrators, and teachers seemed never to have considered that the two masters of the American empire and the kingdom of God might likewise disagree.

During any mention of a Christian's citizenship in heaven, it was always assumed there was some sort of dual citizenship deal. For all the times they told us we were spiritual pilgrims—strangers and foreigners in our current life—they always applied it to secular systems. I never heard a "man of God" ever apply that outsider reality to a Christian's status in the United States. Instead of embracing the potential of being a minority in our culture, the call was always to "pray for America" and to fight to restore America to its design as a "Christian nation."

That might sound benign or even optimistic as a call for everyone in our country to experience Jesus' healing power and salvation from their brokenness. But it's more sinister than that. I came to notice after leaving the IFB movement that followers of Jesus are actually called to desire salvation for the entire world, as Jesus did both when talking to Nicodemus and when saying goodbye to his first disciples at his ascension. Simon Peter said God wants nobody to perish and everyone to repent.

Fundamentalists support their partisan mission with a selective reading of Matthew 25:31–46, in which Jesus talks about sheep and goat nations. I say selective, because the passage's criteria of what makes a damned nation or blessed nation isn't beliefs, policies, or even cultural domination. When IFB preachers add Christian-nationalism undertones to the Great Commission with this passage, they fail to mention that the defining criteria of an honorable country is how a people group serves their hungry, thirsty, displaced, naked, sick, and imprisoned neighbors in Jesus' name.

In this prooftext, the King James Bible makes the gathering of the people groups and the separation of eternities about separating *nations*. (Other English translations interpret the Greek *ethnē* as *people* or *peoples*.) Due to some unfortunate pronoun references that follow *ethnē*, the KJV implication is that—despite every other Bible passage about eternal blessing and judgment being an *individual's* destiny—we'll be sorted for heaven and hell based on whether our *nation* is a sheep or a goat. While few IFB preachers would admit it, with that interpretation of Scripture, our nationality could produce a double jeopardy situation. According to this logic, true believers could lose their eternal security based on a binary evaluation of their country of residence.

Obviously, this is preposterous in the context of human history. Both the quantities and boundaries of nations have changed often—even in just in my lifetime. As I edit this chapter I am in northern Slovenia, which has belonged to more than a dozen different empires and countries in its history. No IFB preacher ever explained in front of me how this national sorting could take place across all of history's humanity when country borders change and cultural distinctions transition over time.

Despite this, the pastors of my youth used all of this sheep-and-goat-nations mindset to call congregants to "turn America back to God." They encouraged us to vote for Republicans. We had to do everything in our power to overturn Roe v Wade, get only Christian prayer back into official school use, censor explicit media, cement blue laws, and get behind anything that limited extramarital sex, alcohol consumption, and the teaching of evolution.

America's status as a representative theocracy depended on us making it predominantly Christian again. If we couldn't do that through attractive evangelism, our votes at the polls would be our next best bet.

These charges from the pulpit claimed Old Testament warnings and promises given to the monarchal nation of Israel over our democratic republic. In my history classes, I was taught that the founding fathers were mostly IFB-aligned believers who intended for the constitutional freedom of religion to *actually* be a protection for majority rule by conservative Protestants.

So, it shouldn't be a surprise that the manifest destiny taught to me came with the aura of the blessing of IFB's god. I was led to believe that a sovereign God had breathed European religion over a savage North America. Left unsaid but implied was the idea that the loss of life and autonomy for indigenous people and enslaved African people were necessary inconveniences along the path to our supernaturally predestinated greatness. The land and dignity we stole and the atrocities we committed were part of the Father's blessing for our religious fervor. While my teachers never claimed divine inspiration as the source of the Declaration of Independence or the Constitution, many IFB pastors have and still do. David Barton, a darling of IFB homeschoolers, toured the country with adjacent assertions. Unfortunately for the self-proclaimed archivist and historian, his claims were so thoroughly debunked that his publisher ceased the publication and distribution of one of his books that contained them.

Declarations like these used to be hidden in the backwater sanctuaries and revival tents of the fringe congregations in America. Now, the line between religious extremism and fascism is getting blurred beyond those assemblies across multiple denominations. Fundamentalists, evangelicals, and Catholics alike cheer for political cronies who tell them God blesses their partisanship. Michael Flynn, a man who served as the National Security Advisor for twenty-two whole days, later headlined a tour of churches that offered half-off tickets for pastors in attendance. At one of the tour stops, the man who needed to be pardoned for lying about matters of state declared, "If we are going to have one nation under God, which we must, we have to have one religion. One nation under God, and one religion under God."

This sentiment of a de facto state religion is not exclusive to fundamentalists, but its saturation levels are highest in the more extreme parts of the American church, including the IFB movement. Why would preachers who railed against the sexual scandals of Bill Clinton turn their churches into rallying places for an unabashedly sexually deviant Donald Trump? Why would extreme-right Christians storm the US Capitol with "JESUS" flags while wearing hats that said "GOD, GUNS, TRUMP"? Why would an alt-right pastor joke after the election of Joe Biden that he wouldn't stand in opposition "if assassination is part of God's plan"? Why would a professing Christian post a sign in their field that says, "Jesus, name above all names" and then unironically fly a TRUMP 2020 flag *above* it? Why would "LET'S GO BRANDON!" reverberate inside a San Antonio church?

The answers to those questions are many, and worthy of a full book of their own. I've included the works on these topics that I recommend in a list of books that helped my reconstruction in the "Helpful Resources" section at the end of this book.

But these expressions of nationalism in the church make sense especially in IFB churches. Preachers in this cult don't even try to appeal to a pluralistic culture with a winsome Jesus. These demagogues leverage fear to consolidate power and to make congregants conform to their extremely narrow view of the world. It appears as though they intentionally ignore that Jesus changed the world without a cultural majority, without political control, and without anyone in the highest seats of earthly power.

The IFB version of the Great Commission I experienced was never intended to help any other country, nation, or ethnic group thrive. Foreigners could accept our legalistic gospel, but they couldn't take our jobs. Democrats could accept Jesus as their Savior, but they needed to vote differently to prove their faith had thoroughly changed them.

My star-spangled god needed voters' help to keep his second-favorite nation in our—I mean, his—image. My weak savior needed those of us in the Moral Majority to secure dominance in the world for the sake of his kingdom. From what I can tell, this hasn't changed. Fundamentalism's partisan faith is not in a God of all nations but in a specific political ideology. Their highest aim is power and control, which requires a dominant America dominated by conservative Christianity, instead of unstoppable good news powered by the Holy Spirit. (As we've all seen over the past few years in America, widespread conversions and sacrificial service aren't what happen when an IFB-approved candidate gets into the White House.)

That all used to be true of me. I speak from experience (and chagrin), as one groomed by talk radio and the institutions of my youth toward jingoism. Between you and me, two decades ago as I was first leaving the IFB movement, I cranked the volume on my radio and cheered when Toby Keith sang:

> 'Cause we'll put a boot in your ass,
> It's the American way.
> Hey, Uncle Sam put your name at the top of his list;
> And the Statue of Liberty started shakin' her fist;
> And the eagle will fly and it's gonna be hell
> When you hear Mother Freedom start ringin' her bell
> And it feels like the whole wide world is raining down on you—
> Brought to you courtesy of the red, white, and blue.

The red, white, and blue of my American flag were the same red, white, and blue of my Christian flag, and I was happy to wrap state violence in both. I got a big kick out of US soldiers writing jokes about Allah on the bombs they mounted to the bottom of our war planes. I was the "some" in Psalm 20:7 (KJV) that says, "Some trust in chariots, and some in horses: but we will remember the name of the LORD our God." I was like my buddy who also grew up in IFB churches and who told me last year that he prefers his president with "bigger balls." Despite preachers in my life referencing Matthew 28 and Acts 1 dozens, if not scores, of times over the preceding decades, I failed to remember that Jesus loved the people on the other end of those explosions. Jesus desired reconciliation with the souls snuffed out on those night-vision video clips of detonations.

For sure, there's nuance around the discussion of national defense, a standing military, and the protection of innocents by the brave who willingly enter the theater of war. But there's no hint in the New Testament that nationalism, jingoism, or xenophobia are appropriate spiritual values. Jesus told us to love our enemies. He told his audience of oppressed Jews to serve their captors by walking conscripted loads twice as far as their captors required. He didn't promise it would be easy, but he also didn't present any excuses or caveats.

Jesus had compassion on his fellow Jews, but he wasn't preoccupied by political freedom. While burdened for his countrymen, he didn't seek to overthrow a government, a political party, or an ethnic group. Even all the kingdoms of the world that Satan offered him in the desert were too small a prize compared to "the joy set before him."[30] Neither his first-century disciples nor the guy pictured on my Indiana driver's license understood what Jesus was teaching through his example. So, Christ had to come right out and say it in John 18:36 (NLT): "My Kingdom is not an earthly kingdom. If it were, my followers would fight to keep me from being handed over to the Jewish leaders. But my Kingdom is not of this world."

Even having read those verses, it didn't occur to me until years later that Jesus wasn't a patriot or that patriotism wasn't a spiritual virtue. I eventually noticed that Jesus didn't storm Jerusalem as an insurrectionist. He rode in on a humble donkey and didn't resist arrest when fundamentalist leaders showed up with a band of armed guards to take him into custody. After the political zealot of his posse rebuked him for talking about his impending death by the religious leaders, Jesus volleyed back with a verbal bomb:

---

30 Hebrews 12:2 NASB

"Get behind me, Satan." And when Peter resorted to physical violence, Jesus responded by healing the man Peter attacked.

For Jesus, kingdom trumped country. The Gospel superseded nation. Eternal redemption took precedence over cultural shifts. He wanted to change hearts—not affiliations. He declared, "I came that they may have life"—not the American Dream®. He promised that those he set free would be "truly free."[31] But he wasn't selling a freedom from the Romans or the Hebrew tax collectors that worked for them. He didn't pitch a nationalist agenda. Quite the opposite, actually. Jesus knew what many American Christians don't: political freedom is too small a freedom for which to pine.

God uses the freedoms of our democratic republic to broadcast his truth, but he also watches the big-C Church grow like wildfire under totalitarian regimes. Even fundamentalists will admit that the Gospel's massive initial distribution came because of the persecution of a secular government.

If we Christians value our positions in our culture, our government, our socioeconomic status, or our geopolitical dominance more than we do our relationship with Jesus and his mission, we all but ask a jealous God to embarrass our idols. There's precedence for this. Each of the ten plagues that preceded the Israelites' escape from Egypt embarrassed one of the Egyptian gods. On Mount Carmel, God humiliated Baal and his prophets, while Elijah cracked jokes about their silent deity. In the second of the ten commandments—before we're told not to murder, lie, or steal—God commands all of his people not to have other gods before him.

Our idols aren't safe. God hates divorce, but I've seen men meet Jesus when the idol of their marriage got smashed in a circuit court. I've heard the stories of gifted athletes who surrendered to Jesus after career-ending injury. We know from the story of Job that Sovereignty allows the removal of even good and beautiful things to reveal our character. So, idols are definitely on the table of things he's willing to prune out of our lives.

I've found that out the hard way multiple times. Over the span of a few years, I lost around seventy thousand dollars and garnered unexpected bills for tens of thousands more after taking pride in my ability to generate wealth, to read the real estate market, and to design my own home. Self-sufficiency and independence stood atop pedestals as idols in my life. In my

---

31 John 8:36 NLT

1,300± square foot home office, the Dave from my earlier Panera story asked me, "It all comes back to money for you, doesn't it?"

It did. Often, sadly, it still does. But having watched my idols crack and splinter, I've become a more generous person.

Jesus isn't vindictive; he's just not opposed to object lessons that connect fully with our hearts. In my case, I needed to learn that "your heart follows your money." I had to practice putting my money into the kingdom so that my heart would head that way too. Eventually, that intentional generosity led to saying yes to caring for a daughter born into someone else's family. And being her dad has healed parts of my heart I didn't know were broken.

Speaking of the next generation, the kids who grew up in far-right churches are leaving organized religion—especially the fundamentalist side of it—in droves and for multiple reasons. Pollsters have asked them why. Often topping the various lists of reasons for jettisoned religion is the partisan corruption of church leadership. Pastors have wrapped political rhetoric and partisan values around theology. They'd rather have a Trump-supporting church or an elephant-led congregation than more souls in the seats. Pastor Andy Stanley encapsulated this hijacking of the church when he wrote, "When a local church becomes preoccupied with saving America at the expense of saving Americans, it has forsaken its mission."

Instead of asking themselves what they're doing to push parishioners away, patriot pastors disparage "defectors" as cowards, brainwashed by liberal elites. What's actually happening is what pastor and author Skye Jethani calls the "unbundling" of religion. Fundamentalists like to require a package deal of extra-biblical tenets that one must hold to remain in good standing with the "man of God," if not God himself. For some, when the bundle breaks, eternal truths and spiritual community become flotsam and jetsam. Because the package deal is untenable, they throw out the whole package.

This kingdom-over-partisanship deal applies to the left side of the aisle too. Many practices labeled "progressive" dehumanize bearers of the image of God. Donkeys aren't wiser than elephants. Pachyderms aren't holier than pack mules. Both Republicans and Democrats are willing to mistreat or even kill some categories of people for the profit, advantage, or convenience of others. Neither of the parties are completely pro-life. So neither align with the Holy One who came to give abundant life. But secular governments can't ever be expected to fulfill the justice only Jesus can sustain. No political movement can do what the Gospel can. And no partisan dogma or political movement can make us feel as secure as a safe church can.

Pastors who leverage the pulpit for any secular ideology or partisan power stand in danger of cheapening the Gospel by association. Jesus broke down cultural and national divides throughout his ministry to demonstrate his borderless love. He came for the oppressor and the oppressed, the liberal and the conservative. There are no foreigners in his kingdom because it has no borders. It holds no elections and contains no dictators. It welcomes people of every ethnicity and all cultures. He doesn't categorize his followers by flag, by party, or by how its leaders come to power. He sees a smooth blue marble whose only boundaries are between the land and the sea.

American exceptionalism and Christian nationalism look silly from the Creator's vantage point. Even mere human astronauts return to Earth with a new perspective on borders and patriotism. Back in 1987, space journalist Frank White coined the term "overview effect" to describe how astronauts who view our planet from their weightless distance see our shared humanity in a new context. Observing our planet in its entirety as a suspended globe makes both xenophobia and jingoism laughable. A few years ago, anthropologist Deana Weibel introduced another term, "ultraview effect," to describe the deep, incredible awe many astronauts experience when taking in their surroundings—moments and feelings these scientists categorize as religious experiences. They return home more open to faith and less connected to nationalism after getting a peek at Earth from God's vantage point.

While many pastors and their IFB flocks see the world as a grade-school globe with its thick black outlines and contrasting blocks of pastels, Jesus sees it as one big ball covered by people he loves. The more we let our hearts break for what breaks his, the easier it will be for us to pledge allegiance to his kingdom instead of our country. The more we see governments and borders as the human constructs they are, the more we'll try to influence culture with grace rather than attempt to vote it into submission. Maybe when we stop singing national anthems in sanctuaries, the Great Commission will echo more clearly from them.

15 AN ARTIFICIALLY WHITE GOD

Unsafe churches whispered that people of color were cursed, but Jesus has showcased the sovereign diversity of his eternal kingdom.

I was sitting on the couch with my daughter, who had just returned home on her first Christmas break from college. She started a new conversation with, "You know that thing on Facebook right now, where people are asking what decade they'd want to go back and live in? Yeah, I don't have a lot of options." We both knew what she meant. My daughter is Black, and the 2020s are the safest time in American history for her.

And that's not saying much.

We live about a half hour's drive from where Lee surrendered to Grant, but a lot of the locals still haven't conceded the Civil War. Even some of my good friends contend that the war was about state autonomy, even though most of the confederate state governments published declarations claiming otherwise in their temporary constitutions. I see a confederate flag in traffic at least once a week, because "it's about heritage." People with that "heritage" have regularly asked my daughter if they could be served by a white employee instead of her because they didn't want to hand their twenty-dollar bill to a Black girl.

"It happens all the time." D shrugs. She brought it up only as a baseline after detailing a traumatic encounter with someone whose heritage was offended by her employment at the corner market. This man walked past the white employees over to her register and started berating her over the Black Lives Matter movement. "You people are just like the [gay slur]!" he barked over her cash register. She wasn't wearing a BLM mask or sweatshirt.

The only thing that connected her in any way to the organization is that she's living a Black life. She hadn't said anything to this man before his tirade began other than the typical pleasantries of a convenience store cashier.

After writing the first half of this chapter, I returned home from the writing session to learn that my daughter had texted Crystal while I was in the library. Apparently, at her college, students with a heritage to preserve called her and her friends a disgusting, dehumanizing slur I can't even bring myself to quote here. This isn't a story from 1862 or 1962. That confederate flag heritage was spit at my daughter on March 17, 2022.

Jesus was kind to me by not letting me be there for these moments. I don't think I would've represented him well.

While I've always found it odd that some Southerners still get viscerally angry about a war somebody else lost 160 years ago, I do share some of their white supremacist heritage. I was born north of the Mason-Dixon line but raised in a culture that assumed the white way to do anything was the right way to do it. Hair. Music. Clothes. Traditions. The naming of children. All of that was reinforced by a whitewashed narrative of my country's past.

My American history curriculum celebrated a divine wind that swirled around the problematic realities of our empire's past. I was told the state of Maryland where we lived had originally been a Roman Catholic sanctuary but not that Maryland *churches* had been tasked with the brokerage of Black slaves and white or mixed-race indentured servants. Maryland *churches* determined the penalty for the perceived crime of interracial marriage. I learned about the various revivals of our past but not that our denomination had divided over the issue of slavery. I wasn't told that slaves were reminded at their baptisms that their freedom in Christ didn't offer any freedom from their human masters. I had to read about every battle of the Civil War, but no teacher or textbook mentioned the Tulsa Massacre, in which an angry white mob destroyed more than twelve hundred homes, churches, and businesses across thirty-five city blocks. We were reminded of the sadness of the six hundred thousand soldiers who lost their lives in the "War Between the States" but not the tragedy inherent in the genocide of the twelve *million* indigenous people whom the American colonizers exterminated.

Historians must make difficult choices about what to include in textbooks, but my history teachers spent time lionizing the fundamentalist preacher Billy Sunday rather than the Tuskegee Airmen. The lore of circuit-riding preachers was reinforced rather than spending a few minutes teaching us about the plight of early Chinese immigrants, conquered Hawaiians, or interned Japanese Americans. My IFB school curriculum didn't discuss Jim Crow laws or that Black patriots in World War II weren't granted the GI bill that white veterans received when they returned home. My IFB textbooks failed to note that people of color were redlined by the banking and real estate industries—forced to live only on the other side of the tracks.

It wasn't just history class. Racism crept into Bible classes and chapel services, particularly in the story of Ham seeing his dad, Noah, drunk and naked. Something unsaid between the lines of our English version of the Bible seems to indicate that Ham committed some sort of cultural impropriety or even sinful behavior. Noah's other two sons covered up their father while walking backward and without looking at him. When Noah sobered up, he burned in anger at Ham and cursed Ham's son, Canaan. I was taught that after this incident, Ham's descendants moved to Africa. The implication: since Africa is associated with Black ethnicities, the plight of Black people may be attributable to Noah's curse. (Parenthetically, God didn't curse Ham or Canaan. A hungover Noah did.) You can imagine the unhealthy assumptions that spiral out from the idea that Black people originated from a curse.

This all makes sense in the cultural context of the IFB day schools of my youth. The Christian school movement exploded during the fifteen years before I attended an IFB kindergarten—which just so happened to be the fifteen years that followed the Civil Rights Act. In the American South, those schools were also known as "segregation academies." In other words, "Christian school" was practically a euphemism for "white school." In his succinct book *Bad Faith*, Randall Balmer points out that after these segregation academies sprang to life, the population of white students in Holmes County, Mississippi, public schools dropped from 771 to *zero* within two school years. The direction of that white flight was almost exclusively toward "Christian" schools.

After conservative leaders initially struggled to build a religious voting bloc around reinstituting school prayer, fighting pornography, and even making abortion illegal again, they found their galvanizing issue in their fight to allow Christian schools to stay segregated. When the IRS threatened to remove the tax-exempt status of BJU, the college begrudgingly allowed married Black students on campus but not anyone who might have the potential to date white students. Their sole Black student left after only one month into his part-time studies. When BJU refused to change their racist policies, the IRS withdrew the university's tax-exempt status. This wasn't during the era of black-and-white television. This was 1976—the year before I was born. This case brought white evangelicals together into what is now the Religious Right.

The founders of my college and the creators of the curriculum used in my elementary, middle school, high school, and undergraduate classes graduated from that same BJU. Their alma mater fought the United States government in the Supreme Court, contending that the right to enact segregation was protected under freedom of religion. If you're scoring at home, yes: their contention was that the God of our IFB faith condoned institutional racism. BJU lost that case in 1983—just eight months before I started kindergarten. This case for faith-based segregation wasn't exclusive to one college or one day school. Jerry Falwell, before he distanced himself from the fundamentalist movement, publicly groused at forced desegregation too. In my eight academic years across three different IFB day schools in three different states on both sides of the Mason-Dixon line, I had only two classmates of color.

I don't recall my parents ever saying anything disparaging about people of color while I was growing up. In fact, they intentionally welcomed our Black neighbor over to the house—including on the Christmas morning where my big gift was a bean bag chair. I do remember a white widower from our church my parents invited over for dinner. The retiree contended that the n-word is a neutral term because "there are white [n-word] and Black [n-word]." Back then, the whole "respect your elders" thing was probably in play when they didn't push back on his racism. There was no follow-up conversation after he left to correct that declaration. While I didn't say that word aloud, I did take that old man's perspective with me to college.

Thankfully, when I got there, God sovereignly roomed me with a soccer fullback from Zambia. The computer science major was dating a white criminal justice major. I remember him asking me if I would ever consider dating a Black girl. I told him the cultural differences would probably be too big a hurdle for me. My ensuing conversations with Timeo started my journey exploring other cultures, reading biographies of people with different worldviews, taking Black friends up on their offers for awkward conversations, and asking myself tough questions. That journey eventuated not only to Black teenagers laughing in my house until all hours of the night but also to helping Black Americans feel seen in a predominantly white church—especially on my serving team.

I say all of that to let you know that racism is a choice, and even those nurtured by white supremacy can heal the cracks in their Gospel over time. I still have so much to learn, but my posture includes open hands. The more I let Jesus knead my heart, the more I realize how my childhood religion resisted being brokenhearted for the plight of people of color. What I've learned about that Dixie heritage is that it's selective. I've also realized that both its inherent racism and the excuses for it are sins. And sins require repentance.

On May 8, 2020, I cried throughout the first two miles of a memorial walk to reflect on the murder of Ahmaud Arbery. Those tears surrounded a prayer of repentance. I asked Jesus to forgive me for being complicit through my ambivalence, avoidance, and lack of empathy. The milieu of my upbringing programmed me to be a racist, and it's been work not to follow that trajectory. But even as the father of a Black woman, I knew there was more cancer to eradicate from my worldview.

Fundamentalists will admit that racism exists—just not that it's an ongoing systemic issue anymore. That makes sense in light of a faith system that emphasizes individual effort and responsibility. But it's ironic when these same fundamentalists protest against systemic sins such as abortion, pornography, and human trafficking. (According to my Facebook feed, my IFB peers would add liberalism to that list.) Social scientists have documented that Christians—particularly conservative ones—are more susceptible to conspiracy theories like QAnon than the population at large. In other words, fundamentalists, more than any other category of American, see systems where they aren't. So, it's ironic that they refuse to see the systems that do exist, systems that operate out in the open.

Fundamentalists believe in systemic issues when they themselves are in the cultural minority—or they perceive themselves to be the minority—but struggle to see the issues where they are in the cultural majority.

I've seen reports that demonstrate how people of color with the same financial ratings as white people still pay higher interest rates —if they are granted loans at all. Black-owned businesses are turned down for loans at twice the rate of white applicants. In scientific studies, similarly qualified candidates with ethnic names like Jamal or José on résumés get interviews at significantly lower rates than those with European names like James or Joe. Data scientists have shown that criminals of color are given longer sentences than their white counterparts for the same crimes with the same number of previous infractions—even when judges make decisions based on standardized algorithms. Predominantly Black public schools receive less funding per student and have more students per classroom than schools in predominantly white districts. That's in large part due to the far-reaching ramifications of redlining after World War II. An even greater expense? Black American women are more than twice as likely to die in childbirth than Caucasian women are.

Those aren't bugs in a cultural infrastructure; they are features woven into our country's fabric. The prejudice that fostered these and other malignant realities was in place long before the Civil Rights Act of 1964, and it didn't suddenly disappear when President Johnson signed it into law. Conservative attorney David French noted on his Advisory Opinions podcast that part of what makes this all so complicated is that you have people without malignant intent or racist motives operating within and overseeing systems that were designed by racists.

So, as culturally progressive as our nation might appear in many areas, this sickness remains. I like how Dr. Derwin Gray addresses this disease in his book *How to Heal Our Racial Divide*. He presents a doctor discussing lung cancer with a patient who'd spent years of their life smoking. When the physician asked the patient about their history with cigarettes, the patient interrupted and pointed out that smoking was part of his past, not his present. So, it didn't need to be discussed. This story hit home for me because the last time I saw my grandfather, he was in a casket in my grandma's parlor after losing both of his lungs from smoking two packs a day.

Everyone reading this paragraph knows the importance of a smoker discussing their past with their pulmonary oncologist for the best hope of healing. Well, the American church smoked two packs a day for more than three *centuries* and protested its right to smoke until the early years of my life. In particular, the sect of the American church that reared me burned through more Marlboros than probably any other denomination.

Baptist missionaries who wanted to be able to minister while owning slaves split their denomination and created what is now the Southern Baptist Convention. IFB pastors started segregation academies. IFB administrators sued the government to have segregated colleges. And an IFB pastor sat on my living room couch in 2016 contending that slavery was a net positive for "the Blacks" because it got them off their native continent. If I remember correctly, that was the last time my dad was in my house.

Probably not a single person who is reading this book, and especially this chapter, was an accomplice or even a bystander to any of this horrible history. And none of us can single-handedly overturn the cultural forces and entrenched systems that continue to treat people of color differently than it does those of European descent. So, what do we all do with this information—and more importantly, this reality?

I've asked myself the same question. My inquiry has led to conversations about racism with my Black friends and neighbors. I've been reading books authored by people of color and listening to podcasts that feature Black voices. It's an ongoing learning process for me, but somewhere along the way I found a good example in Nehemiah, who rebuilt the walls of Jerusalem around 440 BCE. When Nehemiah learned of the damage incurred by past generations and by other countrymen, he wept.

If you haven't mourned over the tragedies and residual disparities of people of color, my guess is you haven't been truly curious about their plight. I don't say that as someone with a long history of racial empathy. I didn't engage much with this cultural chasm until the 2010s. I've learned that I need to include more people of color in the content I absorb and spend more time with people who look and believe differently than I do. That education has accelerated as I intentionally refrain from any "Yeah, but what about . . ." retorts.

More sympathy and empathy have come when I've sat with minor discomforts. I remember reading Austin Channing Brown's book *I'm Still Here*. She capitalized *Black* but not *white* throughout the manuscript. That subtlety lit a light bulb above my head about how details of preference feel to someone on the other side of them. I remember a literary agent turning me down as a client because she was looking for authors of color, particularly women of color. After centuries of Black authors facing closed doors, I reminded myself that it was time for their voices to be heard and that any closed door for me was a small price to pay for nonwhite voices to be deservedly platformed. To take it a step further, I bought stacks of books published by Black, Asian, Latinx, and indigenous authors. I learned that if my money doesn't flow toward people different from me, my heart won't either. And if I don't absorb other narratives of my past and present, I can't get a complete picture of what actually happened.

After his realization and time of mourning, Nehemiah talked to God about the problem. More than that, he asked his Father to forgive him, his family, and his country for their sins. He didn't minimize or rationalize the malignant behavior. Over the next few years of his life, Nehemiah proved himself to be a major part of the solution for his broken homeland, but he started by owning his past. This wasn't self-flagellation. He wasn't wallowing in shame. It was a beautiful fusion of empathy and repentance.

In *What If Jesus Was Serious About Prayer?* Skye Jethani wrote, "Scripture teaches us this uncomfortable truth: we cannot claim the blessings of our community but deny the burden of its sins." He added, "Most Americans are eager to accept the benefits of this land even though we are probably not personally responsible for them, but we are reluctant to own the sins of America because we did not directly participate in them."

If we're going to ask Jesus to root prejudice out of our hearts and racism out of our institutions, it's healthy for each of us to confess influences that got us respectively where we are. That confession makes it easier for us to notice and be soft in moments of future revelation.

After praying, Nehemiah let his sorrow move him to action. He asked for help and resources. He committed a season of his life to restoring a broken aspect of his homeland. For us, that means more than just voting, signing petitions, or even walking in peaceful protests. We need to cede some of our opportunities in predominantly white spaces to our deserving friends of color or at the very least welcome diverse voices into our circles of faith. And that means we need to pursue friendships with people whose lives are filled with different music, wardrobes, values, hair, religious practices, and heritages. We need to celebrate our differences, not minimize or assimilate them. As Derwin Gray says, "We need to be color-blessed not color-blind." Our diversity showcases the vibrant creativity of our Maker.

We need to listen far more than we talk—and always *before* we talk. The humility and meekness of active listening will lead us to authentic empathy.

One of my favorite stories of this kind of empathy comes from the life of Mahatma Gandhi. A mother brought her son to Gandhi and asked him to tell the boy to stop eating sugar. Gandhi declined but asked the woman to return a couple of weeks later. When she did, Gandhi told the boy to stop eating sugar. Puzzled, the woman asked Gandhi why he didn't just say that the first time she came to him. He replied something along the lines of, "Two weeks ago, I was still eating sugar." He felt the need to give up sugar himself before he could tell someone else that they should.

Before we sell our version of history, our perspective on racial topics, or our nuanced solutions to cultural problems, it's wise to absorb those of others—even our opponents. What we intentionally hear and read might change our worldview. It might not. Either way, we'll be better for it. Empathy is not agreement, but empathy helps people feel seen and heard. Accepted people don't have to agree to feel valued.

And that's the underlying root of it all: for everyone to feel valued and valuable. Jesus called us to love our neighbor in the same way that we love and care for ourselves. The converted fundamentalist, Saul of Tarsus, took that a step further in his letter to believers in the Greek city of Philippi. He charged believers in this multicultural metropolis to humbly consider others as *better* than themselves. We reflect Jesus when we offer more dignity to people of other ethnicities, when we encourage others of diverse cultures.

It took decades for me to realize that the primary place in our world that should see ethnic diversity is the church. The church should be the first place people find warm welcome from those who look different from them. If there's any organization that should be equally concerned about the white refugees of Ukraine and the brown refugees at our southern border, it should be the church. If there were any list of institutions willing to acknowledge mistakes and problematic history, the church should be at the top of that list. If anyone goes to other cultures in other countries with humility and curiosity instead of with a savior mentality, it should be Christians. If anyone lobbies for justice, it should be those who follow the Creator of Equality.

I've discovered that the more I get curious, the more I care. The more I care, the more I learn. And the more I learn, the more God breaks my heart for what breaks his. In that process in the upside-down kingdom, my heart has found healing.

16 HEAVEN HATH NO FURY

Unsafe churches glorified the wrath of God, but Jesus has asked me to let him take care of justice and vengeance.

I can't tell you if it was causation or just correlation, but my journey out of the IFB movement began the year after the September 11 attacks. Crystal and I bought an eleven-inch television on that watershed day and signed up for cable. Neither of us wanted to huddle in the break room at my work to get televised news anymore. (We had watched the long Bush-Gore election results reporting up there.)

Over the next few years, we took in a lot of content to make up for the lost time of our TV-less years of college and marriage. Amidst that deluge of content were my first encounters with cable news, and most of that news (outside of ESPN) was about terrorism and the response to it. I remember only vignettes from those years with Fox News. Looking back, I should've paid attention to one of the labels that reporters and pundits kept applying to the terrorists.

Fundamentalist.

For most people outside of the fundamentalist wing of any religion, *fundamentalist* carries a pejorative connotation. It implies that someone has gone beyond the zealot stage to a stage of extremism. For years, though, I was one of the fundamentalists who viewed their fervent legalism as evidence that they were on the narrow path toward the narrow gate.

The fundamentalists of my youth had proudly used that branding to describe their ultraconservative approach to Christianity. They found it unfair that Muslim extremists would be considered similar to them. Their badge of honor now scrolled atop footage of smoking carnage around the clock.

The connection was fair, though. Both versions of fundamentalism silence their women, cover them in bolts of fabric, and treat them as second-class citizens. Both are led by sectarian shamans who aren't accountable to elders. Both put strict limits on the kind of music played in their midst. Both treat gay people as a specific caste of evildoers. Both hold to a specific archaic English translation of their holy book, despite most practitioners of their faith preferring more modern translations. (At the time of writing, Wikipedia shows sixty-two different English translations of the Qur'an.) Both rail against secular culture while withdrawing from it rather than engaging with it. Both use virgins as incentives for young men to observe their faith properly. Both believe their governments should be run by their religious values rather than those agreed upon by a representative democracy. Both leverage shame for compliance.

Both are sustained by angst and communicated through anger.

I don't have enough fingers and toes to count how many times I've endured anger-fueled sermons. The IFB movement showcases the kind of orators who spit vitriol like World War II fascists. Its leaders glorify pacing screamers and stationary insulters alike. When a preacher calls a category of people a pejorative name, you'll hear shouts of "Amen," "Preach it," and "Come on" from men in the audience. If an IFB preacher doesn't hear an immediate response to his invective, you'll often see him lean toward the audience and cup his hand to his ear—or just verbally demand an amen from the pews.

On Easter Sunday this year, I watched a "man of God" scream at his Georgia congregation about how he liked it back "when a preacher just ate a bag of 16-penny nails, chased it with diesel fuel, shut his hand in the car door about five times, and stubbed his toe on the way to the pulpit, and preached the devil out of us." (He went on to say we need more pastors to preach against women who wear "britches" and men who wear shorts.) It made me think about the accounts I've read of elite athletes getting themselves pumped for maximum performance by reading disparaging tweets or news clippings. We've all seen the moment in a movie when a hero loses a friend to the enemy and then goes berserk , charging toward his buddy's killers. There's some sort of connection between rage and adrenaline that makes fury a performance enhancer. So, I could see why—in a culture that celebrates a sweaty, spitting, red-faced delivery—these IFB preachers work themselves into a public temper tantrum.

The problem is that Jesus asked those who believed in him to—well—follow him. That's a big news flash, I know. For the two thousand years since Christ's ascension, that assignment has required us to follow his transcribed example. Church leaders, especially, should be those most closely following his precedents. Fundamentalists diverge from these ancient landmarks every time they re-platform a belligerent preacher because Jesus' default setting was meekness. Christ's standard was compassion. He typically used stories or questions—not insults—to challenge someone's worldview. He claimed that the primary marker of our discipleship would be our love. Not our rage, not our volume, not our insults.

Our love.

The exceptions to Christ's pattern of grace were never the Romans, the secular world, or even parishioners. Jesus reserved his holy anger and labels like "brood of vipers" and "whitewashed sepulchers" for the fundamentalists of his day—not the people who couldn't live up to their standards.

Trying to justify their rage, angry pastors like to point to the story of Jesus flipping tables and flailing his homemade whip in the temple as justification for holy anger, specifically their "righteous indignation."

Only after leaving the IFB movement was I able to recognize problems with that rationale. First, the Romans Road that fundamentalists taught me starts with "There is none righteous, no, not one."[32] The only one righteous enough to sustain righteous anger is God, and he never deputized any of us to carry the weight of retribution. In fact, both the Jewish Torah and the New Testament relay that the Lord commanded his people to let him take care of vengeance. The apostle Paul warned his friends not to let anger from one day spill into another. So, the bitterness inherent in incessant ranting isn't holy. It's not healthy for the human who holds it, either, especially in the quantities demonstrated by IFB preachers. Of course, it could be performative anger—living in caricature—but that hypocrisy wouldn't be healthy nor would it be blessed by the Source of All Truth.

The second problem is that this was the exception for our Messiah, not his modus operandi. People flocked to him for multiple reasons: to experience his healing, to witness his miracles, to hear his unorthodox teaching, to watch him confound their religious leaders, or just to be

32 Romans 3:10 KJV

accepted by a religious leader when other rabbis didn't. People left Christ's presence feeling less shame, not more. Jesus instructed both a man and a woman specifically not to sin, but he didn't shout it at them. He didn't need to yell. His moral authority came not from his volume, not from a pulpit, and not from a platform. He confronted sin within arm's reach as someone who wanted better for someone he loved. He knew that a life with less sin is a life with fewer regrets by the sinner and less damage to those around them.

Also, Christ's disciples didn't flip any tables. They didn't weave his cat o' nine tails for him or make their own copies. He didn't roll up to the money changers with a posse. The Sermon on the Mount doesn't say, "Blessed are the indignant." We don't read anywhere else in the New Testament that an apostle or other disciple was given a special dispensation of righteous anger. Even during immense persecution, Christ's disciples didn't act as though the Gospel was so fragile that it needed protection by acts of rage.

What made Jesus angry was injustice. In particular, his indignation was aimed at those who made it more difficult for seekers to access him. He wanted women and children and the common man to know they could be equal heirs to his kingdom. Jesus communicated that they didn't need to adhere to the onerous burdens of the hypocritical, self-righteous elites. The men who stood in these seekers' way weren't liberals, pagans, addicts, outcasts, entertainers, people with same-sex attraction, women who wore yoga pants, or straight men who wore pink. Apparently, though, that's who a lot of IFB preachers assume need to feel the anger of the "man of God." (Seriously, I watched an IFB evangelist smugly brag from the pulpit about making two preschoolers cry because their mom dressed them in plaid shirts that included pink stripes after he had railed from the pulpit earlier against the effeminate act of a man wearing pink.)

Jesus longed for a world of justice, of a return to shalom. He asked us to pray for life on earth to reflect that of heaven. I don't know if you've ever thought about this, but there will be no anger in heaven. We will all be 100 percent holy, and nobody will be yelling at us to keep in line. Jesus knew—and knows—what modern social scientists have confirmed: shame is a short-lived motivator. A jockey can go to the whip only so much. A coach who defaults to rage alienates elite athletes, and his hyperbolic ranting eventually falls on deaf ears. The most skilled drill instructors don't need to torture their recruits constantly. As someone who was beaten for years with both shaming words and strong hands, I can tell you that bruised fruit is neither attractive nor sweet.

People who study human behavior tell us that anger is a secondary emotion. We feel rage *after* we feel hurt, scared, rejected, humiliated, or frustrated. Outrage follows loss, pain, fear, loneliness, embarrassment, or a loss of autonomy. Cable news networks and social media algorithms are programmed to exploit this reality. To keep ratings and app usage up, they need to exacerbate outrage and stoke the flames of argument. They show us stories and panel arguments about the topics that appeal to the negative emotions that eventuate in anger.

IFB preachers have been using these tactics since long before Facebook and Fox News. Instead of discipling their congregations toward kingdom focus, personal integrity, and ways to love our neighbor as ourselves, they crack their whips. They use the propaganda techniques of populist demagogues. They make you scared of those with different values and skeptical of their equal humanity. They offer you a path to feeling morally superior to the majority of the world by inciting disgust. It shouldn't surprise us that neuroscientists have found that the part of the brain that lights up in FMRI machines when humans are disgusted flashes brightest in study subjects who self-report as religious conservatives.

We all know hurt people hurt people. So, it's with grace that I contend that IFB preachers who regularly capitalize on petulance and anger need help. I'm not a professional psychologist, but I have to believe they are just transferring the abuse or shame—or both—leveraged on them.

It makes me wonder what happened to New Jersey IFB pastor, Eric Dammann, who bragged from the pulpit in a sermon posted online how he got the attention of a teen in his youth group. "Bright kid, which didn't help things, right? Made him more dangerous . . . I punched him in the chest as hard as—I crumpled the kid. I just crumpled him . . . I led that man to the Lord right there. There's times that might be needed."

At some point, whether we're a "man of God" or not, we have to deal with the root causes that lead to anger. I drop the worst words when someone discounts my expertise. My fists clench when I hear of what men—especially "men of God"—have done to women and children. When I learn about something hurtful that has been said about my wife or to my daughter, I instinctively envision acts of violence. I've been confronted by both Crystal and my therapist for getting irrationally angry at perceived injustices committed by other drivers, despite all of the inappropriate moves I've made in traffic.

Violent anger runs in my family. Supposedly—though I've never seen a copy—one of my ancestors was the title subject of a book written about the "meanest man in America." My great-grandfather beat my Grampa George—with chains. Multiple members of my extended family have told me stories about acts of despicable abuse and unjustifiable violence.

When my dad didn't use his muscles against me, he used his words and his religion. He and my mom both went to the shame whip, and that hurt me far more than the wide brown leather belt I can't purge from my memory. When I protested what my parents wanted me to do, they reminded me how selfish I was—that I had always been selfish, that my first word was "mine."

There's a picture of kindergarten-age me with a purple face. In it, I'm being choked from behind by my preschooler sister. Instead of pulling her off my back, one of my parents ran and got their camera to capture the "justice" of the moment. My parents laughed and told me it served me right for kicking her years earlier when they had brought my newborn sister home from the hospital. Fast forward thirty-seven years from that choking incident, and you'd have heard my mom repeatedly tell my sister that I deserved my dad's physical abuse. My mom never tried to stop him—at least not in front of me. I flinched and braced for impact the one time she cocked her hand to slap me across the face. She pulled back her hand, smirked, and then hit me instead with the threat of "just wait until your father gets home." As you can guess, I would've preferred her slap.

So, I have some sympathy for how these IFB dragons develop their fiery breath. I don't yet have a lot of empathy, though, because I've learned that an angry lifestyle is a choice. There is a way out. It's not easy. It requires curiosity and humility. For some folks, it probably also requires an accountability that can get uncomfortable. But those who want out can get out—especially if they follow the example of Jesus.

Having seen how unattractive the Gospel looks when slathered in outrage, I've worked to de-escalate my heart when it goes code red. I'm learning how to process those triggers and how to regulate those emotions of helplessness, embarrassment, and frustration. In my journey of healing, I use long hot showers and daily journaling, walks in the woods and prompt confession, sunset drives, and therapy sessions. I remind myself of God's goodness and sovereignty—that he wants what's best for me, that he didn't miss what just happened, and that his love isn't based on my performance.

Despite decades of intentionality, it's still work to lift my foot off the gas pedal rather than take my red-lining heart to passive aggression or straight-up aggression. It's still a weekly struggle, but the other day I bought breakfast for the rude driver behind me who honked his displeasure at me in a drive-through line.

I've never raised my voice at my daughter. On one of my mom's last visits to my house, she watched my teenager and I crack jokes on each other and laugh through our differences of opinion. My mom asked, "Is that how you talk to your daughter?" I smiled as I proudly answered, "Yes!" I'm glad my daughter can trust me with her hot takes and her real thoughts. D regularly confronts my lack of consistency, and I'm better for it.

It's a sovereign gift that my kid likes me and isn't afraid of me. I'm working now to repair the damage from the acid of my insecurities that spilled all over Crystal earlier in our marriage. Our disagreements no longer become the kinds of fights I'm ashamed to have escalated in years past. In professional and other relationships, the mental filter of the Gospel has caused me to backspace hundreds, if not thousands, of lines from emails and text messages.

I guess what I'm saying is that *actually* following Jesus makes me less angry, not more. The more I've learned of his heart, the softer mine has become. The more I've realized what has been forgiven in my past and present, the more grace I feel compelled to extend to others. Anger is a warning light on the dashboard of my life, a reminder to ask myself what's the core irritant behind my emotion. That curiosity leads me to prayer, contemplation, Scripture, nonfiction books, confession, and professional counseling. In an indirect way, anger leads me to healing—or at least points me in the direction of it.

Of any man who ever walked this planet, Jesus had the most reasons to be angry. Nobody was as profoundly mistreated as he was. He could've lived in a constant state of outrage for the future torture and murder he knew fundamentalists were orchestrating for him. He could've called down fire on his religious enemies and brimstone on the Roman soldiers who mocked him. He could've preached with more deserved angst than any of the IFB preachers you can watch on YouTube, Instagram, and probably TikTok. If anything, the fact that he only turned over a few tables and yelled at some religious grifters shows us that the most impressive shepherds are meek.

The Messiah knew the indignities he suffered said more about his opposition than about him.

The Father knew that his pending justice was both appropriate and secure.

Christ knew inescapable truth was stronger than violence.

Jesus knew he only needed to crack his whip once.

Our Savior knew our gratitude for the red he was about to shed would lead us to a more abundant life than decades of red-faced sermons ever could.

17 SELECTIVE TIME TRAVEL

Unsafe churches convinced me that God's voice is hidden behind arbitrary walls, but the Holy Spirit whispers to all of us in our heart languages.

My best friend in high school returned from a youth conference in the Chicago suburbs with a beautiful, long-distance girlfriend and a story—neither of which I've ever forgotten. He told me how the famous preacher who hosted the event went berserk in the pulpit. The old man in thick black glasses grabbed a copy of an NIV Bible, tore batches of pages out of it, and threw those handfuls of crumpled paper out over the students in the crowd. Then Jack Hyles shouted, "This! Is not! The Word! Of God!"

A few years later, Hyles (whose own daughter called him "a cult leader") spent his last sermon of his forty-two years in the pulpit on the topic of the King James Version of the Bible (KJV). He contended that anyone who surrendered their life to Jesus after hearing Scripture from any other version of the Bible wasn't truly saved. They couldn't be a true Christian, because what germinated in them was "a corruptible seed."

The math problem of that assertion is jaw-dropping. In a world with more than seven thousand languages, this pastor and other fundamentalists contend that the only people who can follow Jesus and go to heaven are those who were presented the Gospel in one specific version of one specific translation into one specific language. I say "one specific version" because there were four major and hundreds of minor versions of the King James Bible between 1611 and 1769. (This conference host and every fundamentalist pastor I've ever sat under read out of the 1769, despite the rampant claims of the infallibility of "the 1611.")

Anyway, lest you think this ridiculous assertion is a fringe occurrence, this "man of God" at one time presided over the largest fundamentalist church in the country that claimed twenty thousand parishioners in regular Sunday attendance and one hundred thousand on the church membership roll. Hyles touted both the largest Sunday school and the largest bus ministry in America. His Bible college trained one of my dad's best friends, a future church planter. The megachurch pastor's bus ministry spawned a lot of copycats, including the one that occupied my dad on Sunday afternoons while we lived in Tennessee.

Less than a year before this demagogue's final KJV sermon, my fiancée and I sat with the rest of our college senior class in our last gathering before graduation. Previous senior classes held picnics or some other communal events that included slideshow retrospectives of their undergrad years. This was four years before the birth of Facebook and six years before the world got Twitter, and I assumed this gathering would be one of the last hoorahs with people I'd likely never see again. I had been looking forward to a party, but we were directed into a ballroom with big screens. Those big white rectangles filled with the latest installment in a series of videos against BJU's liberal view that the KJV wasn't the only English translation that could be used for evangelism and discipleship. When the video started, a collective moan emanated from the crowd of seven-hundred-and-some of us kids in our early twenties. Later in the video, laughter erupted at the preposterousness of the claim coming from the overhead speakers.

I looked around at the deans standing along the outskirts of the room. These men—of course only men—had just started a seminary with the KJV as its cornerstone doctrinal differentiation. Their eyes widened. They scanned the crowd with what looked like shock or maybe disbelief on their faces. They must have expected applause or nodding heads. My guess is that they were surprised that after four years of inculcation, many of us had rejected their idol of belief enough to feel comfortable laughing about it in front of classmates who were heading into that seminary the following semester.

What they didn't realize is how thoroughly they had illustrated the ridiculousness of their untenable positions. Our college library showcased "the Bible room," a curated collection of English Bibles from centuries gone by. A pair of massive volumes of the 1611 King James Bible sat under glass in the center of this miniature museum. Anyone who looked at them could tell they weren't what we were required to read and memorize for class. What was read and quoted on our stages wasn't what was on those pages.

Greek translation classes were a requirement for all ministerial majors, and anyone whose translation homework read like the KJV was given a score of zero on their work for cheating. The very professors who led students toward the seminary knew no modern person would translate the truth of Scripture in Shakespearean prose.

That makes sense for anyone reading this book, but it didn't for Jack Hyles or tens of thousands of IFB preachers. The most extreme King James-only zealots disparage any Bible teacher or preacher who reads the KJV and then says, "in other words" or "as we would say today." Some have even warned against those who would tell their audiences about the original Greek or Hebrew words along with other ways those words could be translated into English. Even though some Greek, Hebrew, and Aramaic words were translated two or more different ways into the same King James Bible, most in the IFB cult don't have a category for the nuance of translation between languages. Many are so ride-or-die for the idea that the KJV had received a second divine inspiration from God that even the original language texts are considered inferior. One guest preacher at my alma mater compared the NIV translation of the Bible to HIV/AIDS because of the scourge it was on the world.

I swam in the water of this misunderstanding for two decades. I memorized so many verses from the 1769 version of the KJV that when I'm trying to remember a verse for a blog post or book chapter, I often Google the colonial-era language I remember. As a former card-carrying fundamentalist, I know how and why these extreme views take hold.

Almost none of these pontificators speak a second language. Few understand that languages don't always match up words one-to-one—let alone that other languages have words for ideas that we English speakers don't. These pastors and evangelists won't show you vacation pictures from other continents, and I'd bet a paycheck that the vast majority of these men don't have friends from other American subcultures—let alone from contrasting international cultures. Myopia always breeds false confidence. When you close down your world to those just like you, it's easier to make sweeping generalizations about your exclusive status or exceptional knowledge.

The differences between the translations are categorically minute. IFB leaders admit this about all of the differences in their beloved King James translation, which underwent significant edits in 1629, 1638, 1760, and finally 1769—along with hundreds of minor adjustments made in editions between those dates. One of those updates replaced "unicorn" with "wild ox," preventing probably dozens of popular children's books that might have filled shelves at Lifeway and Mardel stores centuries later. While some of the changes in articles ("a" vs. "the") or names do alter an aspect of some passages, they don't detract from the congruency of Scripture. And they definitely don't change the Gospel.

One of the few dissenting voices I ever experienced in IFB churches came from a Sunday school teacher at the IFB church I attended in Indiana. Nathan had earned his degree in ancient cultures and had studied multiple archaic languages. In fact, for his senior capstone project at the University of Michigan, he translated the entire book of Acts. I'll never forget when he chuckled after telling our class, "If [modern Bible translators] were trying to remove Christ and his deity from the Bible, they did a *really* poor job."

I can confirm this from my weekly group interactions with holy texts. At my Wednesday night Bible study, we read a Scripture passage aloud around the circle in two or three translations and often add a paraphrase to get a better picture of what that section of the Bible means. Contrary to what fundamentalists would tell you, the differences don't bring confusion but instead clarity. As we sit around a fire or a picnic table, the immutable truth of what we're reading becomes clearer and more certain. Not less. The variations are intriguing but not life changing. We don't need tiny details to be able to redraw the big picture. The more translations we consult, the less that is lost in translation. How we live out the truth we know is more important than what we believe about that truth, anyway. For instance, I couldn't quote you the exact words Crystal promised in her custom vows at our beach wedding. But she's lived them in such a way that there's no doubt about her love or her commitment. I know what's true about her commitment because of what she's proven. If we truly believe that Jesus and his Gospel are the hope of the world, figuring out the most livable and practical truths inherent in the Bible should occupy our time more than defending a document from 1769.

Hubris keeps King James-only zealots from asking, "What if these tiny differences indicate more of an error in *my* favorite translation instead of in everyone else's?" Not once during my years inside the fist-grip of fundamentalism did I hear a pastor address the potential influence of King James' Anglican values on his sponsorship of the translation. It wasn't until after I left the cult that I learned about that influence. For instance, King James' religion practiced baptism by sprinkling rather than by immersion. When the translators got to the Greek word for baptize, which means "to dip," they knew their sponsor wouldn't be a fan of that precedent making it into the English version. So, they just transliterated it as "baptize" to keep those passages flexible and ambiguous. One of my mentors joked, "If the translators of the King James Bible had held to the strength of their convictions, we'd know John the Baptist as John the Dipper." That makes me laugh at how my life could've been different. I could've been reared as an independent dipper, could've been trained as a fundamentalist immerser, or attended a dunkers college. In high school, I could've been even more confused when my coworker called me a "dipshit."

Most of these men have an insecure view of the inerrancy of Scripture. They can't handle the nuance of a perfect Gospel communicated through imperfect people translating it through inadequate languages. If the Holy Spirit must translate our prayers "with groanings that cannot be expressed in words,"[33] why would Scripture not surpass our human ability to communicate?

Many of these IFB preachers take the claim from Jesus in Matthew 5:18 out of context. This quote in Christ's biography states that no small detail will disappear from the Law until it is fulfilled. KJV fanboys apply this to a New Testament that hadn't even been written yet and wouldn't be canonized for another three hundred years after it was transcribed. Plus, the context of that verse was Jesus saying he wasn't coming to abolish the writings of Moses and Old Testament prophets but to fulfill them. Without a DeLorean modified with a flux capacitor, you can't fulfill a prophecy before it's prophesied. So, Christ wasn't even referencing the Bible as we know it.

For some reason, holding an enduring faith in the inerrancy of the God of their Bible requires a myth of perfection around how the Bible came to

---

33 Romans 8:26 NLT

their language and culture. Trying to squeeze a limitless God through the limits of language, they must create a narrative to dismiss the tensions of reality. In search of certainty, they have built a religious proxy for faith.

The former fundamentalist Paul explained why even the Bible isn't everything there is to know about God. In his first letter to members of a dysfunctional church, he wrote, "Now we see things imperfectly, like puzzling reflections in a mirror, but then we will see everything with perfect clarity. All that I know now is partial and incomplete, but then I will know everything completely, just as God knows me completely."[34]

Instead of looking for the guiding principles of the biblical canon, these English speakers parse and litigate specific words—some of whose meanings have changed over hundreds of years through various cultures. That's the way of the Pharisee: to find the loopholes. I know because I'm a recovering Pharisee. My whole life, I've been highly skilled at finding gaps in fences. In fact, I put a new application to a rule in my alma mater's handbook because as Dean Hurst told me, "We don't make the rules here. Students do." What Dean Hurst meant was that new rules came from students defying the spirit of the law by finding ways to flout it through new technicalities.

The reverse is also true. Adhering to the letter of the law gives us justification for disobeying the spirit of the law. That's why Jesus reduced the 613 rules of the Talmud to just two: (1) love your Creator King with everything you have and (2) love your neighbor as yourself. One of the fundamentalists who heard Jesus declare these two guiding principles wanted a legalistic way around that difficult simplicity and asked, "So, who's my neighbor?" This fundamentalist's first response was an attempt to carve out exceptions. None of us can throw stones at him, though. We're all bent toward that comfort and self-justification. Professor and author Karen Swallow Prior succinctly explained this default setting well when she wrote, "Adhering to rules is much easier than exercising wisdom."

These inane arguments about translation originate from privilege. You know who isn't arguing about the minutia of their Bible translations? People who follow Jesus under totalitarian governments, within authoritarian religious regimes, and without pervasive copies of Scripture in their native tongue. It's like any other thing humans consume: the richer and

---

34 1 Corinthians 13:12 NLT

freer a culture is, the more they can explore random details and debate tertiary topics. Refugees in resettlement camps don't complain about the short ripeness span of avocados or the superiority of mayonnaise over Miracle Whip. Potato farmers in the Andes don't spend time comparing pink Himalayan salt to sea salt. Many don't even have the luxury of a food pyramid.

By creating a subculture around something as ancillary as a single version of a single translation for a single language, these KJV extremists inadvertently reveal how far they are from the needy we're called to serve. These KJV apologists' books, pamphlets, sermons, and lectures all illustrate how much of their spiritual energy they've devoted to insignificant goals and less-than-great commissions.

Here's why that's a big deal. That privilege becomes dangerous when it creates barriers between truth and freedom. There's an insidious desire to make the Bible exclusive rather than inclusive. Pharisees have been trying to make it harder to attain their status for millennia. The church has often fought against the Bible's truth getting into the hands of those it controlled. In fact, William Tyndale may have been martyred for trying to bring the Bible to English (a language that didn't even exist when Jesus gave the Great Commission). Five hundred years after Tyndale's death, fundamentalists are still trying to keep the Bible in an ancient, less-accessible form. As part of their caste system, a less relatable (and in some cases, less accurate) holy book helps them feel smarter, holier, and more distinctly separated from the hordes of heathens outside their church's walls. They demand that parishioners embrace the discomfort of the 1787 version of the King James Bible with a straight face. That has long puzzled me. If they're just picking arbitrary reading discomfort, why don't they pick the actual 1611 version that they claim to cherish? I mean, if you're going to do something, go all the way.

Most fundamentalists refuse to accept that language changes—and that none of us can alter that inevitability. Every year we read about the new words added to the dictionary. (My favorite addition from last year is *deplatform,* for reasons you can probably guess.) Each generation adopts new words and verbal shortcuts their parents find odd. My daughter rolls her eyes when I use the word *hip* instead of *cool*. She told me not even to try to use *yeet* in a sentence.

If we want to get the Gospel and Scripture's other inerrant truths absorbed by a changing culture, it makes sense that we'd want to make the Bible as easy to understand as possible. If our goal is to feel like we own some exclusive caste position, it makes sense that the password to our speakeasy is a phrase from a language that predates the first Webster's dictionary. If I have to choose a side of history—if I must decide between making Scripture easier or harder to understand—I'd rather stand for accessibility.

18 MISREPRESENTING ORTHODOXY

Unsafe churches defended their hypocrisy at all costs, but Jesus has called those who share his heart to follow his authentic example.

My dad put Dr. Martin Luther King, Jr., into a category similar to opportunists like Al Sharpton. As American cities named boulevards and schools after the murdered Baptist pastor, my dad disagreed with the elevated status the civil rights crusader posthumously achieved. At some point, my dad finally vocalized his problem with the federal holiday and other notoriety surrounding Dr. King's martyrdom. He told me that Dr. King was a philanderer, and that his adulterous affairs negated his work for social justice and his message of equality.

I've also listened to survivors of unsafe churches describe their inability to listen to anything proclaimed by their former pastors, denominations, and affiliated organizations. While they might eat the meat and spit out the bones in other contexts, specific voices lost all value. I get it. After watching *The Secrets of Hillsong* documentary, I deleted all Hillsong music from my playlists. After the deeds of Ravi Zacharias were exposed, I didn't finish his audiobook that I had downloaded to my phone. And after I learned about his predations, I no longer consult my dad about home and auto repairs.

So, while I extend grace to anyone whose trauma or values discount hypocritical voices in culture, I found my dad's objections to Dr. King incredibly ironic in light of how my dad fought to be allowed to return to the pulpit. He'd been caught not only cheating on his wife but also directing his sexual energy to minors in his church. Dr. King's dalliances were sinful but at least they were between consenting adults.

While that irony plays out on the micro level of my family, I can't escape the more macro irony in my dad's disregard for Dr. King. In the unsafe churches of my youth, beliefs were an idol, and hypocrisy was defended as a way to protect the Gospel. Dogmatism took precedence over following the example of Jesus. Doctrine was more important than authenticity, curiosity, or compassion. "Speak the truth in love" just meant "tough love," and you spoke that truth only to those of lower castes.

The fundamentalists of the seventies proved a Christian could justify racist segregation as long as their kids went to Christian school. The eighties proved fundamentalists could be uncompassionate about the gay victims of the HIV crisis as long as the believers went to four church services a week. Starting in the nineties, ultraconservative Christians murdered abortion practitioners while proclaiming their belief that unborn lives already showcase the image of God. The first decade of the new century proved fundamentalists could hate their country's enemies as long as they also preached against contemporary Christian music. The decade after that proved that Baptists could unironically share a portrait of Daniel in the lions' den that replaced that man of integrity with a thrice-divorced, unrepentant sexual assaulter who'd cheated on his pregnant wife with a porn star. This inappropriateness was excused because fundamentalists believe Democrats might be the greatest of all threats to Christianity.

After parenting and grandparenting through these decades, IFB pastors now denigrate the ensuing generations who have left their churches en masse over their inherent hypocrisies. I've watched multiple pastors rail about those of us who've abandoned "the old paths." These condescending preachers accuse Gen Xers and millennials of compromise—of chasing after the world—when many of us have actually been searching for an authentic faith.

We refugees of IFB churches have noted that the black suits circle the wagons around their deviants and monsters, especially their "men of God," but then damn any number of categorical outsiders to hell. We've learned that the same men who preach against dancing at a wedding also steal the innocence of children. We've heard the same preachers who remind us that "God so loved the world" talk about the people they hate—from their pulpits. Those who've contended that truth was determined once and for all in 1611 have also massaged truth by gaslighting men, women, and children about their abuse. Men who've taught "there is no condemnation for those who belong to Christ Jesus"[35] have leveraged shame as a weapon. Obese men at the "sacred desk" have commanded women to keep themselves in the same trim shape they were in when they got married. I'm still waiting for one of these out-of-breath, southern-fried pastors who've weaponized a misinterpretation of Proverbs 31 against women to unpack an earlier proverb that recommends gluttons put a knife to their throats to avoid overindulging with food.

These moral disconnects arise not from paradox but from hypocrisy. These ironies stem from a selective self-righteousness. You could row the entire *Argo* through the holes in the IFB gospel.

While rebuilding my faith system, I needed to wrestle with these inconsistencies in my own heart. Had I fixated on the hypocrisy of the voices of my youth or the influencers in the news, I might never have moved past deconstruction. Instead, I focused on pursuing a life consistent with the words and example of Jesus—to be the change I wanted to see in the religious world.

What IFB preachers fail to understand is that it doesn't matter what you believe about Jesus, the Bible, or "sound doctrine," if you aren't living like Jesus. The apostle James wrote that our *behavior* verifies our faith—that even demons believe the right things about God and tremble as a result of that belief. I like how Christian counselors Jeff and Terra Mattson simplified James' statement about this congruency issue in their book *Shrinking the Integrity Gap*. They wrote, "Faith is what faith does."

Jesus' brother also wrote that true religion is taking care of widows and orphans. Not following a creed, not reading from a specific translation of Scripture, not avoiding music with a syncopated beat, not wearing specific clothes, and not gathering at a specific place at a specific time. None of the drums of culture war that IFB preachers beat are among the Old Testament criteria that the prophet Micah documented, either: "And what does Yahweh ask from you but to do justice, and to love kindness, and to walk humbly with your God?"[36] If that list is too ambiguous for modern-day Pharisees to game, imagine their frustration at Christ's two priorities: love our Creator with everything we have and love our neighbors as we love ourselves.

---

35 Romans 8:1 NLT

36 Micah 6:8 LEB

For the IFB movement, believing the "right" stuff has supplanted growth, surrender, and authenticity. In contrast, I've resonated with the trajectory of Bob Goff, my favorite humanitarian. Bob noted that the way he practices his faith has changed a lot over the past five decades because he's learned that "the best theology is loving people like Jesus loved people."

But loving people is hard. Caring for the sick, naked, hungry, displaced, orphaned, widowed, imprisoned, and disenfranchised like Jesus did would take everything we have. So, IFB preachers have drafted a newer and different priority list to tend. They've elevated belief above actions and creed above authenticity. Their doctrine has allowed them to rail against a changing culture and churches that adapt to it. Their dogma has permitted them to use dehumanizing terms to describe people who are not like them. Those like my dad use the beliefs they have deemed correct to offset or excuse their own disgusting acts committed against the vulnerable. Their unwillingness to change has carved an idol out of arbitrary rules they pretend are old.

Speaking of old things that IFB preachers carve into idols, no book about this movement would be complete without discussing their utter devotion to a narrow slice of hymnbooks. Second only to the King James Version of the Bible, an IFB preacher's favorite old thing to venerate is their IFB hymnal. Despite Paul's encouragement to minister to each other in "psalms, hymns, and spiritual songs" IFB preachers disparage anything other than hymns. I've even heard brimstone hurled at just the words "praise and worship." In particular, IFB churches avoid most hymns created after the Korean War. They mask their prejudice for familiarity by saying their hymnals are full of sound doctrine, and the new stuff is emotional drivel at best and Satanic deception or sexualized liturgy at worst.

Personally, I've been more convicted of unhealthy perspectives and sinful behavior by songs written in my lifetime than anything you'll find in a hymnal. I've publicly sobbed on the floor of my church's auditorium and cried with arms raised while walking mountain trails because of the eternal truth in modern worship songs. At the same time, I'm still moved by updated arrangements of traditional hymns and by psalms set to music. Sometimes it's a loud celebration; sometimes it's an acoustic contemplation complete with a cello.

There's beauty in all of it, but for the sake of this book, I wanted to check the claims of superior hymnal doctrine. So, I jumped on Amazon and bought a copy of a hymnal I recognized from my college years. If you remove the offertories and spoken-word benedictions, it holds 590 songs. I went through with a highlighter and marked the ones I recalled singing in IFB churches. For some, I couldn't remember the melody until I listened to them on YouTube, but that cursory tour led to a list of 303 hymns I had sung. I've long forgotten all of the four-part assignments from my time as a tenor in an IFB quartet competition and my year as a bass in my college's student choir. I wish I could forget all of the hours I spent singing those lyrics in front of men in jackets robotically waving their right hands.

As I perused the lyrics within the hardback book, I found the same things I've found in some modern worship songs: incorrect theology, a focus on our benefit and feelings, and obscure biblical references that'd make an outsider scratch their head. Some hymns made claims we'd now attribute to the prosperity gospel. Some really sat down in shame. One equated the crosses we individually bear to the one Jesus carried. A surprising number of the hymns I recognized focused on the rapture—getting out of Dodge instead of influencing our world. For some reason, the United States' national anthem was in there, since worshipping the American flag is—you know—sound doctrine. I guess they didn't sell that hymnal in Canada.

I also found statements of expensive surrender, respectful reverence, and gratitude for Christ's rescue. So, if you're scoring at home, both hymns and modern church music can move us toward Jesus. Both catalogs hold problematic lyrics. Both appeal to a specific subculture. Both have their place in humanity's expression of faith.

Hymns are obviously more conservative in demeanor, and they're undeniably older. Those two attributes make the hymnal a sacred cow for fundamentalists. The preachers of my youth associated a deeper theology with more restraint. They categorically held that older expressions of truth somehow make truth truer. I guess it's like how British accents make people sound more erudite, and so we assume what they have to say is more profound.

But Jesus didn't call us to profundity. He didn't start any seminaries. He debated the fundamentalists of his day to illustrate the emptiness of their well-parsed legalism. People flocked away from the Pharisees' old path to his new one because he offered healing, freedom from shame, and a simpler framework for connecting with God. People felt seen and known and liberated. Women felt valued. So did kids. Tax-collecting grifters felt forgiveness equal to their regret. Outcasts felt welcomed. A thief on a cross felt worthy to speak to God Incarnate.

Jesus didn't ask his disciples to believe the right things about him. He asked them to follow him. He taught along the way, but he modeled at least as much as he taught. In a letter to his friends, Paul explained that Jesus is "the visible image of the invisible God."[37] So, if we want to know the heart of God—and not just well-parsed theology—we need to look first to Christ's example. And the measure of what we believe is how well we're following his example—not how well we can diagram a letter written to a first-century church we can't attend in a town whose culture we cannot fully know.

Loving our neighbors sacrificially isn't a soft Gospel. Living from a wellspring of authenticity, meekness, and compassion isn't shallow doctrine. Adhering to Jesus' incredibly short list of priorities isn't a new path. It's the oldest one—inherent in two of the first words he told his first disciples: "Follow me."

Bestselling author and teaching pastor Shauna Niequist explained Christ's countercultural value of new paths. She said, "Jesus did not preserve boundaries and traditions at the expense of humans. He valued humans at the expense of previously held boundaries and traditions." The Messiah's example spoke as loudly as his sermons, and his example always defaulted to the question: What would Eternal Love do here?

Jesus blessed the humble not the brash, the meek not the petulant, the repentant not the self-righteous. He didn't chide seekers who proved earnest but errant. Instead, he called out fundamentalist teachers. He exposed the vanity of the doctrine police, the first-century version of our twenty-first century "Theobros." Here are five English translations of Matthew 15:9, when he put those legalists on blast:

> "In vain do they worship me, teaching as doctrines the commandments of men." ESV

37 Colossians 1:15 NLT

> "It is no use for them to worship me, because they teach human rules as though they were my laws!" GNT

> "Their worship of me is worthless. The things they teach are nothing but human rules they have memorized." ICB

> "They act like they're worshiping me, but they don't mean it. They just use me as a cover for teaching whatever suits their fancy." MSG

> "Their worship is a farce, for they teach man-made ideas as commands from God." NLT

As I mentioned earlier, my Bible study buddies and I like reading multiple English translations of whatever passage we're excavating because the juxtaposition makes the big ideas clearer. Absorption becomes less about dissecting and more about asking ourselves, "What's the overarching message here?" That process for Matthew 15:9 clearly contrasts the real and the artificial, the divine and the human. Jesus tells us not to waste our time with worship—hymns or otherwise—if we're majoring on minors, if we're elevating arbitrary standards over his immutable commands. It clearly doesn't matter how many human "fundamentals" we get right if we aren't following what Jesus said are his critical assignments.

Our worship is meaningless if our doctrines are nullified by our hypocrisy.

For the past century, IFB preachers have used *doctrine* to mean "a core, existential belief." But when you see *doctrine* used in the New Testament, it refers to what someone taught. Jesus and the apostles had doctrine, but so did the Pharisees. What did the Pharisees teach? They taught that good Jews had to adhere to strict legalism to make it into heaven or at least to have religious status on earth. What did Jesus teach? Well, he didn't teach about women keeping silent, specific translations of holy texts, or what kind of music he didn't like. He didn't bark about political rivals. He didn't yell about secular influences on children or people with chemical dependencies.

Jesus gave difficult, counterinstinctual commands, and he didn't cosign on the version of fundamentalist doctrines of his day. We know from the Old Testament prophet Isaiah that the God who knows our thoughts sees our attempts at self-righteousness as filthy rags.[38] Extraneous doctrines emit the opposite of the sweet fragrance that should waft from a Jesus-centric life.

As the New Testament church was coming together, Luke reported that new believers followed in the apostles' teaching.[39] Whatever they were teaching led to sacrificial living, daily accountability, and eventually martyrdom. So, I'm guessing it wasn't light stuff. It also wasn't old stuff, because Jesus had just left a few months earlier. He didn't leave them a written New Testament, a bulleted list of doctrines for their website, or even a well-parsed creed. Nope. Just his example and his words.

In my life, I've found that if I want more than Jesus' words and example, it's probably because I want to shift attention away from my inability to follow them. Because of this, my antennae bristle when I see someone stack unnecessary weights on people trying to follow Jesus. When they give the impression that "thus saith the Lord," I remind myself of who drew Jesus' rebuke. And when they perpetuate a dehumanizing movement out of their invalid doctrine, I take heart in the assertion of Dr. King: "The arc of the moral universe is long, but it bends toward justice."

---

38 Isaiah 64:6 NLT

39 Acts 2:42 NLT

19 SAYING THE MAGIC WORDS

Unsafe churches attempted to make a relationship with God a magic formula, but Jesus has never called us to go through the motions.

During the twenty-one years since I started my business, I don't need all of the fingers on one hand to count the number of cold sales calls I've made. Actually, I might not need any fingers to count them. I passed my mandatory sales class in college only because I was randomly assigned the biggest of all past advertisers to hit up for ads in our campus activities guide. Every year, they purchased the entire back cover of the publication—enough advertising dollars to earn me an A on the assignment.

So, you can imagine the internal anxiety when, as a teenager, I was assigned to canvass a neighborhood to sell the IFB gospel door-to-door—as the lead speaker. It had been excruciating enough just to stand there next to my dad all the times that I had been his "soul-winning" partner. It was especially awkward the time a woman behind the door told my mom that she wouldn't attend "that church" because the pastor of the church we represented was having an affair. When my mom protested that she was the pastor's wife and that she could vouch for that not being true, the stranger scoffed. "Well, you don't know your husband." At the time, I thought the lady was mistaken. Now I don't know.

Almost every Thursday night, my dad, a former Catholic altar boy, led pairs of Baptist parishioners to strangers' doors to ask about their faith and their attachment, or lack thereof, to a local church. As residents of Maryland, the colonial refuge for Catholics, most people who did come to the door claimed Saint Christopher's as their church home. Or at least, they answered, "I'm Catholic." Kent Island had two towns, and both of those zip codes show a Saint Mary's Road on their maps. I lived on one of those Saint Mary's Roads for six months. At that time, our island held roughly thirty thousand residents, and Saint Christopher's couldn't have housed even 20 percent of the people who claimed to attend there. Still, I was sent out to convince complete strangers that their generationally entrenched belief system was wrong.

On top of that, we lived in an affluent area—a state that competes annually for the highest per capita income in the nation. The island served as a bedroom community for the capital district around Annapolis, Maryland, and Washington, DC. I was told at the time that the county south of us held more millionaires per thousand residents than any county in America. I didn't question that, not with all the multimillion-dollar estates down Carmichael Road, some owned by presidents of multinational corporations. No joke: I once ran a count of the Lamborghinis and Ferraris that drove past our rural driveway. It should come as no surprise, then, that people who'd done well in life felt they had done it on their own, that they didn't need the perceived crutch of religion. The perfect person to convince them otherwise had to be a gangly high school student who made a little bit more than minimum wage reshelving books at the county free library.

On one of my first nights as the primary spokesman, an elderly woman invited us in. She consented to everything in my spiel. No questions. No reservations. But also, no emotion or eagerness. I vaguely remember that she even regurgitated a version of the sinner's prayer. That was a first for me.

But it was too easy.

I wondered if she had figured utter compliance was the fastest way to get us out of her house. To me, it felt like when a football coach lets the other team walk into the end zone so his team can get the ball back with plenty of clock left for the winning field goal. She had us out of there in time to see Alex Trebek announce the Final Jeopardy! category. As we left, I remember thinking, "Now what?" Having made the sale, we killed time before our rendezvous with the others. As we walked, I wrestled with so many questions I didn't dare ask out loud.

She said the magic prayer. Did that count?

Was there any advice we should've given her for what to do next?

What was her name again?

• • •

One of the tenets of fundamentalism I still believe is that what you do with Jesus is the most important decision of your life. I was rightfully taught that my relationship with my Eternal Groom was even more important than the one with my earthly spouse. Despite feeling that deeply, it felt weird to walk from house to house, asking strangers if they wanted to marry my friend. "No? Okay. Well, do you want to check out his house?"

Note to self: Don't tell them that there'll be a dude there with a high-pressure sales pitch. And he'll probably tell them about the Mack truck . . .

If you didn't grow up in IFB spaces, you may not know about the Mack truck. I don't know why it was always a Mack truck. Peterbilt and Kenworth trucks are just as big and formidable. Anyway, IFB preachers used to tell us we had to accept Jesus as our personal Savior before we walked out the door. We could be hit by a Mack truck and have to stand before Jesus that very day. And then it would be too late to make the right decision.

Even people who pitch timeshares or Amway don't resort to that level of pressure.

Jesus did talk about eternal consequences to our decisions. There's a lot about hell we don't know from the Bible; but we know that multiple times Jesus referenced a place of torment in the afterlife. IFB preachers will tell you that Jesus spent more recorded discourse on hell than he did on heaven; but in a 2015 piece for Patheos, Dan Wilkinson proved the reverse is true. Wilkinson documented that 3 percent (60 verses) of Jesus' red-letter paragraphs referenced hell or eternal judgment, while 10 percent (192 verses) discussed heaven or his coming kingdom.

Reading through Christ's biographies, you'd be hard pressed to find him putting on a hard press. Even with no more than a few hours to live, he didn't ask anyone to say a specific prayer. He didn't need to. He knew the fundamentalists who put him on the cross weren't going to change their minds. One of the Roman soldiers representing the government on the scene recognized his deity, but we're not told if he became a follower after Christ's resurrection. We are told that one of the other criminals on an adjacent cross received the promise of an afterlife in paradise. Jesus assured him of this without asking him to pray a prayer, let alone the standard magic one.

IFB preachers place more emphasis on *the* prayer than Jesus did, because Jesus sees our hearts and reads our thoughts.

I'm not trying to be flippant about the sinner's prayer. The ex-fundamentalist Paul said any unbeliever who confesses aloud Christ's lordship and acknowledges his divine resurrection shall be saved. Earlier in that same letter, though, Paul said Abraham's accredited righteousness came from his faith. No prayer was mentioned—no specific moment in time, actually. (Was it when he started the journey with Isaac? When he answered Isaac's question? When he put Isaac on the altar? When he raised his knife?)

The biographies of Jesus prove that a verbal prayer or even a silent prayer is not the only way to salvation. Jesus told a woman the fundamentalists of his day had labeled "immoral" that her faith had saved her—after she wept on his feet and wiped those fallen tears with her hair. Philip baptized the Ethiopian eunuch after explaining Isaiah's prophecies were about Jesus—not after a prayer or even a transcribed conversion process.

Despite this, IFB preachers place a ton of emphasis on getting people to *the* prayer or even just to a church service where the prayer will be quoted in a closing invitation. If we bring visitors, the preacher all but promises to ask for bowed heads, closed eyes, and a "repeat after me" prayer. Fundamentalists put a lot of weight on getting the uninitiated to that altar call and the silently parroted prayer. Few will respond, but the more people endure the awkward pressure the more of a chance that someone will raise a hand, fill out a card, or say a prayer. It's what basketball fans call "volume shooting."

The first church of this persuasion my parents attended held a contest to see who could bring the most visitors to church. The prize—I kid you not—was a shotgun. Not money. Not a fancy Bible. Not Christian music on vinyl or 8-track tape. Not even a hunting rifle. (Oh, and—surprise—not anything most of the women in the church had on their wish lists.)

If you get past the idea of a violent weapon as the prize, the next problem is that there was a prize in the first place. Think about what that says to each person you invited. "So, if I go to one church service with you, you might win a gun?" In other words, "What you experienced in your faith community wasn't attractive and life-giving enough on its own for you to invite your friends to experience it? But a giveaway is?" What does that tell the people you invited about the value you place on your faith and its practice?

Also, this broader approach treats people as belt notches. In multilevel marketing terms, those who are invited are potential "downlines." That strategy is not exclusive to fundamentalists, but it's baked into their intrinsic theology. Nobody sells "fire insurance" like an IFB preacher. And no pastor tenders get-out-of-hell-free cards as frequently, either. I can't tell you how many church services I've sat through with fewer than thirty people—all of whom had prayed *the* prayer or at least had been asked to pray it on multiple occasions—in which we still had to endure a thorough "if you should die tonight" spiel and an "every head bowed, every eye closed" invitation. We would go months—sometimes many months—between a new person walking through the front door (other than maybe a visiting family member), and yet almost every Sunday morning, the sermon would aim for conversions at least as much as it worked at equipping the saints. Based on the opening scene of this book, maybe those invitations were all aimed at me.

To their credit, though, IFB preachers get a lot of people to sign up using these tactics. Itinerate evangelists and summer camp speakers put a new shine on well-worn talking points and persuade the most people to walk the aisle.

Unfortunately, there's a wide gulf between assent and conversion. There's a difference between people who don't want to go to hell and those who want to follow Jesus. It can be quite a few steps between parroting a prayer—even *the* prayer—and becoming a disciple. Following an invitation to come forward doesn't always eventuate in following Jesus as his pupil and apprentice.

Please hear this: I'm not trying to cast doubt on what may be your faith origin story. There will be fundamentalists on my street in heaven. We'll walk past Anglican and Methodist and Episcopal neighbors' places. If we have jobs there, I'll probably work with Roman Catholics, Pentecostals, and people of Aboriginal faiths. I don't think my nondenominational church or anyone else's local assembly will have neighborhoods to themselves. I'm sure someone will be surprised to bump into me in the next life, especially since I was baptized into three different religious traditions all before my thirtieth birthday.

No matter your faith system, you can't negotiate someone into affection. Outside of some weird psychological manipulation, you can't scare someone into love. Arranged marriages often do find a version of romance, if not true love. The same goes for mail-order bride situations. So, technically, it's possible that someone *could* step into the best thing that ever happened to them on the other side of a screen door from a religious salesperson. Jesus himself sent pairs of people to visit Jewish villages, stay in strangers' homes, and tell them the good news that their promised Messiah had finally arrived.

With those two caveats registered, I'd like to add a big *BUT*: I wrote this chapter because I've seen those magic prayers hinder kingdom work.

I've encountered wandering souls who haven't done anything with their faith in years or who haven't engaged authentically with Jesus in decades who will spurn a thoroughly life-changing experience because of an aisle they walked, a hand they raised, a prayer they parroted, or a baptismal tank they entered at a younger age. I've seen people have to wrestle with what they'd been told about following Jesus, while choosing death in different areas of their life.

"Nah. I'm good. I got that covered. Thanks, though."

Conversely, some of my friends and family members have weighed potential blowback from stakeholders in their life before admitting that what they had in the past wasn't real. I have too. I didn't tell my parents I'd been baptized outside of their religion until well after the fact. Even though my dad shouted at me that he prayed I would find salvation, I knew he wouldn't approve of how that prayer was answered a decade later. When my sister surrendered fully to Jesus a few years after graduating from college, my disgraced-pastor dad argued on the phone with me for two hours that her baptism was unbiblical. (For the record, there is not a single verse in the New Testament that says you can't get baptized more than once.)

"It's in there."

People will go through the motions of conversion for various reasons, including good intentions. It can be a challenge to build safeguards around the process to keep that number of motives to a minimum. One way to do that is to move away from treating converts as pelts. People who chase after Jesus can walk patiently with people before, during, and well after the moment they cross the line of eternal surrender. We can teach them prayers such as "Lord, I believe. Help my unbelief," and the prayers of repentance David wrote in Psalm 51. We can invite people into our homes and our lives—not just our churches. We can serve them instead of using them for organizational or internal contests. We can live a life so drenched in love that they'll crave to be married to someone like our groom.

In other words, our compassion, not our incantations, will draw people to luxuriate in the Eternal Love that guides our safe church. If it was Christ's kindness that led us to repentance, why would we leverage anything devaluing or impersonal to woo people to the promise of eternal life?

20 PROTECTING THE FIEFDOM

Unsafe churches prided themselves on their independent, unaccountable despots, but God has existed in plurality and has called his churches to do the same.

I love introducing friends and even strangers to beautiful places and enriching experiences. I can easily discern when someone is new to my church, my rock climbing gym, or one of my favorite disc golf courses, and it makes my heart happy to show them the ropes. So, I was a natural fit as a table leader at my church's new attendee orientations. I'm an adrenaline junkie and untamable extrovert. (Sorry; that means I'm the guy who talks to you on a plane.) As such, I approached those tables like a game of conversational roulette. Often, the discussions led to laughter, serendipity, and connection. I usually returned home with an energized heart and a smile on my face.

Usually. But not always.

I remember one gruff couple. I never saw them at our church after orientation night, but that wasn't a surprise. They announced two stipulations for sticking around—ways our church of over three thousand people could adapt to their preferences to woo them into staying. First, we needed to open a chapter of American Heritage Girls, a "Christian alternative to the Girl Scouts of the USA" whose highest rank is—you guessed it—patriot. That was strike one.

Second, they needed to know "Where does the buck stop here?" I explained that we had a senior management team for organizational decisions and a group of elders for spiritual direction. "What happens when they can't agree?" they asked. I explained that decisions were either unanimous after prayer and discussion, or our leaders would fall back to a plan of action they could all support. My church doesn't do majority rule. There's no voting—even for new elders. When a new elder position becomes available, staff and volunteer team leaders are asked to submit names of people who are following Jesus authentically and without reproach. Weeks of fasting and prayer over the accumulated list of names follow. When the current elders have agreed upon a candidate, they spend a Sunday teaching what the Bible says about elders and the standards to which elders are held. Then the church body is given an email address to which they can submit any objections they have to being led by that candidate. If after a few weeks there aren't any objections, the new elder is welcomed into the fellowship of those already serving.

This model frustrated the two-stipulations couple at my orientation table. I assume they wanted to figure out how to court the man who made the final calls on stuff. They insisted that someone had to rule over everyone else in leadership. "We don't have one of those," I rebutted. Seeing their incredulity, I invited our founding pastor over to the table to chat. I can't remember if they asked him about where the buck stopped—if they assumed I was just kept out of the know. I do remember chuckling about the exchange later during our table leader debriefing session.

For the past seventeen years, a "man of God," pyramid-style church has thankfully been relegated to rare flashbacks. I remember explaining my current church's model to my dad, who bristled at the idea of leadership plurality and accountability. His objections at the time make more sense now that I know he was hiding the sexual abuse of his congregants. You'd think anyone who had studied the Trinity or who had read Paul's letters to his mentees wouldn't be able to make a case against shared and equal church leadership from Scripture. I assumed that, but my dad proved me wrong.

My dad said elders can't be trusted, that the practice wasn't wise. To defend this claim, he pointed to the twelve spies Moses dispatched into Canaan. My dad asserted that Israel spent forty years wandering in the desert because they trusted the majority of those informants. This ridiculous analogy breaks down because (1) the spies were military operatives, not national elders; (2) Israel didn't operate under egalitarian leadership; (3) Moses—not the spies—made the call not to invade Canaan; and (4) the nation of Israel wasn't a New Testament church.

The mental gymnastics it takes to get around plurality of leadership would be sufficient training for one of those laser fields a thief navigates in a heist movie. The contortions needed to make accountability seem unwise and even ungodly would get you to at least the second round on *America's Got Talent*—and maybe into a gig at a traveling circus. But connivers have been wrapping their self-serving arguments around healthy ideas since the Garden of Eden, and humans have been shaping their worldview around their myopia for almost as long. It's easier to create ideology, theology, and cultures in our own image when we don't expose them to critique.

Narcissists crave the control of an org chart with a single seat at the top. The pride that drives that ambition can't hide. Thankfully, it's usually obvious when someone wants to build a miniature kingdom in their likeness.

One antidote for that selfishness is accountability, because plurality frustrates despots. Since all who follow Jesus are commissioned to seek first *his* kingdom and do *his* will, it makes sense that Sovereignty would sprinkle roughly fifty "one another" commands throughout the New Testament. For a God who exists in equal plurality, it makes sense that his church would follow his example.

It's not just the power hungry who contend for control to be centralized in one man. It's also the charlatans and the predators. A more covert maneuvering of the "man of God" model stems from a desire to avoid accountability. These men want to portray an aura of holiness that contradicts their hidden sins, habits, and even lifestyles. They live in an ever-widening integrity gap. This happens in churches with elders, too, and we've all read those headlines. But the IFB movement incentivizes hypocrisy with its hyperfocus on image management.

My dad copped to this. In between lies about one of the teenagers he sexually assaulted, he admitted to me that he couldn't reveal his struggles to anyone in his tiny church. He claimed that if he had disclosed his sin, he would've lost spiritual authority. To him, as a sinner, he couldn't say "Thus saith the Lord." So, every Sunday morning, Sunday night, and Wednesday night, he had to get behind "the sacred desk" with a growing internal dissonance. He had to pretend he had his spiritual house in order so he could tell others to get right with God.

I've found multiple problems with this line of thinking.

As has played out in news headlines over and over again, the pressure this secrecy creates eventually explodes catastrophically for the pastor and his victims. Preventive measures could've made it more difficult for my dad's gross temptations to become grievous sins and then despicable habits. It's a long shot, but maybe he could've learned different responses to his dangerous impulses and built new neural pathways within protective guardrails. Infusions of thorough rebuke might've redirected my dad's trajectory. Maybe that would've meant leaving his pastoral position years earlier than he did. Either way, it could've saved his victims from grievous harm.

Every pastor is a sinner. Every pastor struggles to follow Jesus fully. Every spiritual leader falls short of the glory of God. No church leader gets everything right in every area of his or her life. Even the apostle Paul opined in his letter to Roman believers about how he struggled to do what was right and to avoid what he knew was wrong. He went hyperbolic and claimed to be the chief of sinners.[40] Paul could do that because his authority wasn't birthed from aestheticism or perfection but from surrender. When the Lycaonians praised Paul and Barnabas as gods, the missionaries ran into the crowd, tore their clothes in dismay, and rebuked the audience. They shouted, "We are men just like you!" They wanted even the people they were trying to proselytize to see their humanity.

As a sheep feeder, part of a pastor's ministry of reconciliation is modeling the processes of confession, repentance, and reformation. Instead of "You should do this," the messaging becomes "This is how I've learned to do this" or "This is what I've learned about God when obeying him this way." If anything, authentically sharing about a struggle encourages congregants that they aren't alone. That doesn't mean that a pastor has to share from his pulpit everything that he would share with his wife, close friends, therapist, or spiritual director. But a pastor who portrays a spiritual superiority is less relatable and less believable than a vulnerable teacher.

Our pain, regret, and failures make a great backdrop for God's grace, perfection, and sovereignty. Paul wrote that our weaknesses showcase Christ's strength. One of the things I love most about my current church is that its teaching team builds on this reality often. They will look at the topic scheduled for a particular week and then often ask the team member who has wrestled most with that particular surrender or principle to be the one who takes the stage on that Sunday. That chosen teacher can speak

40 1 Timothy 1:15

about the challenges of obedience more authentically. After those talks, these teachers don't need to hold an altar call, let alone a heavy-handed one. After people have heard their own stories reflected in the story told from the platform, they approach that stage, unsolicited, for advice, prayer, and encouragement.

I've been one of those people multiple times. I remember the Sunday five years ago when our senior pastor talked about fighting the desire for personal significance over kingdom building. He called us to put our pursuit of legacy on the altar of our hearts. As someone who has chased affirmation literally across all seven continents and into both polar circles, I wanted to compare notes with a shepherd who'd traveled with me and battled the same longings. He assigned me to (1) go on an adventure, (2) not take any photos or videos, and (3) not share about it online. He wanted me to feel the withdrawal of that outside recognition, to wrestle with the surrender of not leveraging a cool experience for hits of online dopamine. It was hard, because my next adventure was really cool and a bit of a status symbol for the adventurers at my church. But I did my assignment, and the adventure was beautiful. Two years later, I started a therapy journey that has often reinforced that pastoral assignment by addressing the ache that drives my pursuit of an enviable legacy.

I write all of that to say that I'm healthier as a sheep, as a congregant, and as a human because that message was given by a vulnerable fellow wrestler.

For all of the IFB "men of God" who weaponize Paul's invitation to "follow me as I follow Christ,"[41] I've not heard them spend much of their time revealing their own thorn in the flesh, their unanswered prayers, their unmet longings, or their Romans 7 struggles. Parishioners and the unchurched alike don't want to hear "Have faith!" They crave a story where someone says, "I struggled to believe God was good in this one aspect of my life, but this is how he revealed his heart in that struggle." People both inside and outside the church walls don't want clichés about God's nearness in their pain. They want to commiserate with those whose hearts were comforted by the Holy Spirit during similar stress or suffering.

The challenge of this authenticity is that it requires us to wrestle with our demons. It's only safe for us to reveal an issue if we actually want to

---

41 1 Corinthians 11:1

resolve it. Accountability is hard because it affronts our will and exposes our weaknesses. That's probably part of why so many IFB pastors preach so loudly from their pulpits against professional therapy and counseling. Giving others permission to speak truth to our assumptions and proclivities means we'll probably have to surrender our favorite guilty pleasures and swap out our preferred coping mechanisms.

The stakes grow higher for those in leadership, particularly in spiritual environments. Pastors and teachers typically dispense more scriptural truth on a weekly basis than do most parishioners. That means there's more content to compare against their character. Managing the integrity gap gets harder the more truth we tell to others. Personally, I think that's part of why the pulpit-and-rows model can become unhealthy in ways circles of sheep don't. I'm not convinced that the first-century church modeled a clergy-and-laity setup. It presented itself as a one-another body—an everyone-is-gifted organism in which all believers were equal heirs, all ministers of the Gospel, and all commissioned ambassadors.

In my life journey, I've found that a diversity of accountability accentuates its effects. I bare my heart on different topics and in different ways to my wife, my friends, my pastors, my counselor, and my online connections. If I actually want to be more like Jesus, I've discovered that it's good to give permission to people to confront me when I'm off course. Those who've been given that access have often used it to address malignant tumors on my soul. On the verge of tears, one of my mentors—after hearing me describe a line of unhealthy thinking—even called me stupid for a lie I was telling myself. He was right.

At multiple inflection points of my adult life, I've received the gift of comfort, counsel, or confrontation. Sovereignty has used all three to push me to surrender or to draw me into a refining challenge. (Usually, the assignment is a sacrifice of my time, autonomy, or disposable income.) Relinquishing my grip has given my soul rope burn a few times, but I'm now grateful that I let go. Doing the hard assignment has given me spiritual and relational capital when I've later challenged another believer to lean into a stout faithfulness. Denying my ego and disclosing my insecurities has diverted the trajectory of my life further and further away from the course my dad and other IFB voices of my youth have traveled.

I wouldn't have gotten there on my own. Wounds would've festered longer and pushed me into hiding. Disease would've hardened my heart. Self-righteousness would've infected me with more arrogance and higher doses of disdain. Entropy would've guided the devolution of beautiful things in my life. Cognitive dissonance would've led me to create a gerrymandered theology. Like my dad and many of his peers, the rivets on my stressed boiler would've eventually burst and sent shrapnel into the lives of people I care about.

We can minister and even lead people to Jesus—for a while—as fakes. We can serve Jesus without surrendering to him. We can preach and counsel in a widening chasm between our stated beliefs and our daily practice. Our façades don't challenge the promise that God's Word will not return empty. Pastor Rich Villodas pointed out this tempting dichotomy through the life of the reluctant prophet Jonah when he tweeted, "Preaching through the book of Jonah . . . Among many things, the end of the book is a warning to preachers like me. It's possible to lead others to repentance but be unrepentant ourselves."[42] Unfortunately, the preachers in my life and the pastors in the news weren't the first and won't be the last to live a double life. But I hope this book helps people get out from under the ticking time bombs of their respective "men of God."

It takes humility to admit we are "broken"—not just in general but as part of a fallen world. We must summon heaping helpings of courage to pull back the curtain on the show we broadcast on social media, at church, and everywhere else we're tempted to hide. That especially includes a church platform. But the size of our integrity gap is a choice. Accountability is a discipline, a muscle that needs frequent exercise to avoid atrophy. Honoring the challenging questions of our peers requires courage.

That challenge only grows for those who care for other souls. Sharing leadership between equals costs us freedom but fosters creativity and better solutions. Egalitarian environments wound our egos but illustrate our triune God. Diversity of perspective—from Bible studies to elder gatherings—leads to colorful beauty we couldn't have painted on our own.

I've experienced multiple churches built in a pastor's image as well as congregations birthed from prayerful collaboration. Neither type is free from the influence of human depravity, but only one of those systems is

---

42 https://x.com/richvillodas/status/1496130344151568395?s=20

modeled after examples in the New Testament. From decades of observation, I can understand why Jesus called his church to be collections of differently-gifted-but-equal people rather than a bunch of authoritarian fiefdoms. Diversity shines light from different angles into an organization's shadows.

I've witnessed firsthand and heard reports of the church splits, factions, and even physical fighting that occurs in churches where a "man of God" is large and in charge. As a fifth grader, I watched red-faced yelling in a church business meeting when public comments were the only accountability that my dad had in his church. In so many of these "my way or the highway" assemblies, parishioners take the arrogant preacher up on his offer. They leave—even when that leaving comes with shaming or shunning. Half of my dad's congregation did just that after one of those public arguments on a Wednesday night.

If Jesus came to give us abundant life, we shouldn't assume he blesses the systems that lead to splintering, wounding, and catastrophic moral failure. Since he's rooting for vibrant life, it makes sense that he's a proponent of the accountability required to corral our selfishness. If the Creator of the Universe is willing to exist in egalitarian plurality, why aren't the men who claim to represent him?

Maybe it's because they don't.

21 AFRAID OF OUR OWN HUMANITY

Unsafe churches admitted that they're scared of what music could do; but Jesus has regularly invited me into diverse, intimate ways to worship him.

My IFB college deputized all of their students to turn each other in for any infraction of their draconian rule book. In addition, the school paid students handpicked by the deans to do this as their work-study job and quoted Jesus' little brother in their semester kickoff meetings: "Therefore to him that knoweth to do good, and doeth it not, to him it is sin."[43] These deans twisted the earnestness of these young men and women with an ultimatum: to "lay your head on your pillow at night with a clean conscience," they had to turn their fellow students in for everything from unmade beds to walking with a member of the opposite sex on certain sidewalks at certain times.

After the opening revival services each September, though, we knew what they were doing the most sniffing for in the guys' dorms: music violations. You'd think it would be porn, but they limited Internet access only to public spaces like the library to prevent that. (Although after my roommate's workmate—the son of a large IFB church's pastor—got busted with printed porn, the deans' henchmen broke my dorm room's ceiling tiles looking for hidden *Playboys* that neither I nor my roommate ever had.)

Anyway, here's the music we could listen to:

43 James 4:17 KJV

- Anything by the college's traveling singing groups
- Any album sold in the campus bookstore
- Other Christian music without guitars or drums (submitted to authorities first for approval)
- Classical music
- Movie soundtracks that were at least seven years old

To make sure illegal music use could be caught, (1) headphones were not allowed on campus except in the academic media labs; and (2) no dorm room included a lock on the door. My floor leaders almost always knocked, but I'm not sure they were required to. The guys who stole my camera and hundreds of dollars from under my bed didn't knock first, or at all. The college had to make borrowing anything—including clothes—illegal because so many people got caught with someone else's belongings and excused themselves with, "Oh, I was just borrowing."

As a rebel, I hid my contraband. Not well and not for long. I got busted with—I kid you not—the music from Disney's Main Street Electrical Parade. My cassette tape was confiscated and returned to me at the end of the semester. It wasn't a great loss, since my roommate had Tupac going in our room. (I remember the day Tupac died only because my roommate, who had lived on three continents, got condolence calls from around the world.) But the stakes for me and Timeo were small. Neither he nor I were prayer leaders or even assistant prayer leaders.

All of our residence halls were segmented into groups of three or four dorm rooms. All students were required to meet in their assigned group at 10:30 four nights a week for spiritual direction, and then all the rooms on our floor met together in the atrium on Saturday nights. One room in each group held the prayer leader. The other rooms were headed by assistant prayer leaders. The assistant prayer leader for Young Tower 4319—my room the year after living with Timeo—was Dan, a youth ministries major and shooting guard from Holland, Michigan. When Dan got busted with illegal music, he was removed not just from his assistant prayer leader duties but from our room and from his good friend, Dave. They had requested to be roommates, and the deans had approved that request. (The college's brass didn't want bad influences rooming together.

In fact, they did away with assigned seating at meals only a year before I arrived on campus—because "birds of a feather flock together.")

Dan's infraction? He had a CD of songs inspired by Oswald Chambers' convicting masterpiece, *My Utmost for His Highest*. The 1995 album held songs titled "You Are Holy," "God of All of Me," and "Where He Leads Me." You know—dangerous ideas.

To be fair, while "men of God" malign the lyrics of spiritual songs written after 1970, they often concede that it's the musical instruments and the melodies of more modern worship songs that are a threat to someone's standing with Jesus. IFB thought leaders have written extensively on the dangers of syncopated rhythm in music. They attribute this style of music to "savage" African tribes and usually tie it into how that leads to sensual, demonically inspired dancing. In short: music with a beat leads to dancing, and dancing leads to sex. Thus, any music with drums or a syncopated rhythm is immoral, and church music with a beat brings sexuality into the worship experience. With the IFB spin on evangelicalism's purity culture, it's no wonder why "men of God" are afraid of anything remotely connected to physicality.

Interestingly enough, they could use Israel's King David dancing in what was either vulgar attire or a vulgar lack of attire to emphasize their point. They probably don't bring this case-solidifying anecdote up from the pulpit because David rebutted his disgusted wife's snarky review of his worship exuberance with, "I am willing to look even more foolish than this, even to be humiliated in my own eyes!"[44] The prolific psalmist considered both royal decorum and Hebrew tradition as expendable in order to fully immerse himself in the exaltation experience and lead his people in worship. The king dubbed "the man after God's heart" knew to be true what pastor Francis Chan posits: Worship isn't about our comfort. In his book *Letters to the Church*, Chan tells the story of a congregant who complained to him about not liking the music part of the service. Chan answered him—and I'm paraphrasing here—"That's okay. We weren't worshipping you."

Whether we're more comfortable with an Anglican songbook, a Baptist hymnal, or more modern song lyrics on screens, our preferences are only that: personal preferences. While we are asked to share "psalms, hymns, and spiritual songs" with each other, the call to do that ends

---

44 2 Samuel 6:22a NLT

with an imperative to offer them to the Lord. While we can certainly feel connected to each other and to the divine in this offering, the primary recipient of that praise isn't us. It's God.

So, what kind of worship did God say he didn't like? What parameters did he place around the music of the church?

I thought the best place to research that would be the Psalms, since the red letters of Jesus' biographies don't include much about music. I offered Facebook friends each $150 to read through Psalms in the course of a month with a spreadsheet I gave them. Each grabbed a different English translation since nobody who responded to my offer could read Hebrew. I had them each record in the spreadsheet each time the psalmist referenced any of the following:

- Contemplation or silence
- Physical position during worship
- Specific mentions of instruments
- Particular volume of voices or instruments
- Physical activity during worship
- Calls to declare or say something
- Singing

The first thing I learned was that I needed a more scientific way to do this research, but the most important thing I discovered was that Psalms is a study of worship contrasts. We're asked to be still and quiet—*and also* to make a loud noise or even shout our praise. We're told to speak declarations of truth about God *and* to sing praise. We're admonished to bow in reverence *and* to lift our hands, clap them, and even dance. These contrasts don't speak to a conflict of commands but instead of a diversity of ways to approach the Source of Creativity and the Maker of Humanity.

If you've ever seen a baby dance when a song comes on in a restaurant or at a wedding or in a movie, you know dance isn't always sensual. It's just part of the human experience. If you've ever gotten a big interview, a huge business deal, or a client you've been chasing, you've probably pumped your fists with excitement. If you're like me, you've even jumped around a bit—and maybe even said some undignified things. When your kid scores in their sport of choice, you jump up and down in the stands and shout praise. When you see a beautiful moment in a play, a musical, or a dance recital, clapping or crying is just a reflection of the beauty inherent in that moment. The father-daughter dance that fundamentalists avoid at their weddings usually puts a lump in everyone's throats or a gregarious laugh in the air. These human moments aren't about sex. Our emotional responses arise instinctively from the part of us that was made in the image of God—the part where a triune deity said, "Let *us* make mankind in *our* image."[45]

IFB preachers, especially on Super Bowl Sunday, will rail against a culture that draws more people to stadiums than churches. They opine about people shouting and celebrating in stands but not in "the house of the Lord."

My response to these pontificators has for decades been a question: "What if they were allowed?" What if people felt as free to celebrate in church the way they do at sporting events? What if the places we could feel *most* human and *most* connected to the human experience were gatherings of believers? What if—seven days a week—congregants were encouraged to search out and experience the beauty and diversity of the volumes, postures, emotions, and expressions built into how God designed us?

We should have songs of lament in our liturgy, but we should also have exhilarating anthems. We should have lyric-less times of reflection and also bold proclamations of truth. We should feel comfortable to bow down, kneel, and even lay prostrate on the ground. When God created us in his image, he gave us bodies. Why wouldn't he want us to experience him with our senses and postures and movements? Anything less is at least a partial picture of what worship should be and at most disobedience to the calls of the canonized Psalms.

The rigid limitations on physical and emotional connection during IFB church services lock congregants in their intellects and directs them away from a holistic encounter with our Creator. Disembodied minds don't reveal the full image of God.

I've read about victims of abuse crying the first time they tried a stretching exercise like yoga or Pilates. Feeling their own physical strength and their own body's autonomy opened new doors to their emotional healing. That illustrates what the Old Testament prophet Ezekiel described in terms of what restoration would look like between Yahweh and his

---

45 Genesis 1:26 NASB

beloved Israel. Part of that reclamation included replacing their hard hearts with softer ones. In most translations, the passage says the old hearts of stone would be replaced by new and better hearts of *flesh*.[46] In other words, as Jesus makes all things new, we become more human—not less. And why not? We were human before Adam and Eve brought death on us all, and God called that humanness good. When Jesus wanted to prove his eternal love and mercy, he did so through humanness.

Embracing the diversity of our humanity—both the differences between our own emotions and the differences between our instincts and those of others—allows us to absorb more fully the complexity of the God we serve. Before Paul told the Colossians to speak "psalms, hymns, and spiritual songs" over each other, he told us to let the truths of Jesus' words dwell in us richly. That makes me think of marinating—of letting sweet, sour, spicy, or salty juices permeate something we want to savor later. If cooking competition shows and Michelin-rated restaurant reviews are to be believed, the best dishes are the ones that juxtapose contrasting textures and flavors. The most creative chefs are the ones who successfully pull off uncommon taste combinations.

Likewise, an enriching church experience is built on a diversity of human talents and expression rather than a monolith of conformity. If you've ever attended a church service in a different culture or even just a different language, you get a hint of this enrichment. From my church experiences on five continents, I can confirm that you don't have to know the songs or understand the preacher to feel connected to something bigger than yourself. One of my South Korean brothers prayed over me and my buddies one night in his native tongue. His prayer was unlike anything I'd ever experienced—the rhythm, the pacing, the sound of his syllables. The guys at Dude Group had no idea what he said, but when he got to his version of "amen," we felt ready to run toward hell with water buckets. I picture the Holy Spirit smiling as he watched. I don't know what prayers smell like, but I imagine that moment wafted as a sweet fragrance toward his nostrils.

It wasn't about us Americans. It wasn't about Hwang. That moment drew our focus to the One Thing we had in common. The posture of our hearts connected us with the heart of Jesus. Whether we were weeping

---

46 Ezekiel 36:26 CSB

or leaping in God's name, God would've inhabited our praise and prayers. Whether we were reflecting in silence or shouting about attributes of his character, he would've heard his name as a term of endearment.

It's ridiculous to dogmatically discount worship music newer than what IFB gatekeepers consider acceptable because every song sung in any church today is new compared to the "psalms, hymns, and spiritual songs" that Paul and his Colossian friends sang with each other. Even when we sing the Psalms, we are only proclaiming what songwriters Dante Bowe, Brandon Lake, and Chandler Moore call "just an old hallelujah with a new melody."

My journey away from fundamentalism's arbitrary parameters around music and its interference with worship has become a pursuit of authentic encounters with the Holy Spirit. Wherever my heart is before I enter into worship experiences, I've moved more and more toward abandon during those moments of worship. In whatever circumstances that swirl outside of my holy encounters, I've learned to bring a sacrifice of praise. While I selfishly still hope for an emotional connection or soul-level prompting, I'm learning to bring my humanness as an offering.

Sometimes, I can't get words out. Sometimes, I jump up and down shouting them. I've cried hot, cathartic tears listening to worship music in church services and on woodland trails. I've lain prostrate on an auditorium's floor and in a corn field. I've yelled attributes of God into gale-force winds blowing off a remote Patagonia glacier and quietly locked arms with men on a patch of suburban asphalt as we thanked God for his presence.

It was all worship because worship isn't limited to music—let alone a confined segment of music. When I start forgetting that or start evaluating worship by what I get out of the deal, I retreat to these lyrics of "Clear the Stage" from Jimmy Needham:

> Take a break from all the plans that you have made,
> And sit at home alone and wait for God to whisper.
> Beg Him please to open up His mouth and speak,
> And pray for real upon your knees until they blister.
> Shine the light on every corner of your life
> Until the pride and lust and lies are in the open.
> Then read the Word and put to test the things you've heard
> Until your heart and soul are stirred and rocked and broken.

> ...
> We must not worship something that's not even worth it.
> Clear the stage, make some space for the One who deserves it.
> ...
> 'Cause I can sing all I want to;
> Yes, I can sing all I want to;
> And we can sing all we want to
> And we can sing all we want to
> We can sing all we want to
> And still get it wrong.
> Worship is more than a song.

Another practice that I learned to remove my ego from the equation and engage as authentically as possible started as an experiment. I participate in the prayer and music portions of a service with my eyes closed. If I feel compelled to sit or stand, raise my arms or pump my fists, kneel or lie on the floor, I just follow internal prompts. I have no idea whether others are doing the same. It doesn't matter. I'm not worshipping them. I'm uniting with the One who invented music and sound, rhythm and energy, emotion and connection. Somehow, in being present in my humanity, I get a better glimpse of the ethereal realities of my soul.

Those transcendent moments have grown more and more frequent the fewer parameters I put around my spiritual encounters. The more I bring worship into my daily experience, the less I'm dependent on Sundays to feel connected to my Creator. The further I've gotten from the limitations that legalists put on worship, the more of it I've experienced . . . and the more I've felt alive.

PART 3

LIFE IN GREENER PASTURES

“The grass is always greener over the septic tank.”

— ERMA BOMBECK,
author and humorist

22 CHOOSING GROWTH OVER COMFORT

Unsafe churches indoctrinated me to avoid change at all costs, but Jesus has welcomed me into a lifestyle of constant renewal.

In his book *But What If We're Wrong*, Chuck Klosterman asks a couple of questions that have stuck with me for years. The first is whether we think that ten years from now we'll agree with all of our current beliefs and decisions. Since most self-aware and intellectually honest people answer "no," Klosterman then asks us why we're so sure of all of our opinions right now. Basically: If we know life experience and intentional learning will shape us over time, why are we so opinionated, so sure others are wrong? How is it that we're so confident in our perspective that we feel safe to combat family, friends, and strangers online? (Or from an IFB pulpit?)

These questions would've caused my internal hard drive to smolder when I was younger. When fundamentalism was all I knew, I couldn't imagine a world where any of my beliefs were wrong. As a proud conservator of a specific subset of Christianity, I couldn't imagine that truth had escaped me. So, I resisted change, adaptation, and progress.

Back then, growth meant gaining more ways to defend my beliefs and finding more discipline to abide by the legalist parameters of my religion. I didn't realize that some of those extra-biblical standards were younger than the incandescent light bulb and, in some cases, younger than my grandparents—far from centuries-old orthodoxy. All I knew was I was part of the purest religion, the rightest faith, and the holiest church; and I wanted to hold up my end of the deal.

Ironically, during those teen years with this definition of growth, my life verse was Luke 2:52 (NIV): "And Jesus increased in wisdom and stature, and in favor with God and with people." As a backward teenager, I longed for the favor of my peers—especially those of the opposite gender. I knew I was socially awkward, and this short piece of Scripture gave me hope.

Parenthetically, almost every true IFB adherent can tell you their life verse. It's a big deal. It reveals the focus of their piety and, in some cases, their familiarity with obscure Bible passages. After revival services or other guest-preacher events during my decades on the inside of the IFB movement, congregants would queue next to the stage for the "man of God" to sign their Bibles. Even kids did this—like grade-schoolers along the railing at a Major League Baseball game during batting practice. I got in the queue a couple times with my maroon Scofield Reference Bible. Can you imagine what the apostles would say to Bible-signing lines? When Cornelius bowed in front of Peter, the early church father blurted, "Stand up! I am a human just like you!" Anyway, preachers typically wrote the reference to their life verse under their signature; and we'd always look those up. My buddies and I joked that we should make ours a snippet from Song of Solomon. (That joke was affirmed in an episode of *The Waltons* where the boys did something similar when asked by a nun for their favorite verse.)

My life verse didn't mention breasts that look like baby deer or the taste of my wife's garden. It also didn't hold a command to grow. It was just a word picture of what I longed for—the Scripture version of the Michael Jordan "Wings" poster on my dorm room wall. I wanted to grow up in all of the ways Jesus did. I hoped to hit six foot three by the end of my freshman year and be popular with my peers. I figured college would take care of the wisdom part. I didn't know what growing in favor with God would look like, but that would be just a cherry on top anyway.

I didn't gain any height or much wisdom in college. I left grateful for answered prayers about my career, but somewhat disillusioned by the faith system I was given to approach God. While knowing I was supposed to "grow in Christ," I wasn't sure I had—despite almost fifteen hundred church services, chapel sessions, Bible classes, mandatory devotionals, and revival sermons during my time on that campus. Or the five hundred required prayer group gatherings.

My life verse had let me down. The list I had hoped to be prescriptive for me proved to be only descriptive of Jesus. I underwent more spiritual movement during my seven weeks as a camp counselor the summer before my junior year than in all 130 weeks as a college student. I left college with better career skills than when I'd arrived, but I was probably no closer to Jesus.

The difference between my academic and spiritual growth was humility. I came to college as an knowledge-absorbing sponge. I understood that I didn't know enough about writing, design, and advertising, and I was paying out of my own savings accounts to close those knowledge gaps. Most of what I was hearing was new. I couldn't say that on the religious side of the college experience. I learned interesting tidbits about the Bible in my eight required Bible courses and a handful of the sermons I endured, but little of that reinforcing content helped me see Jesus more clearly. Fundamentalism only has so many talking points, and as an IFB preacher's son, I already knew them well coming into my freshman year. The pastors the college paraded on stage only proved that.

The hurdle I didn't jump is the same hurdle that keeps fundamentalists from growing. That obstacle is a simple but difficult reality: growth requires change. Change requires recognizing a need for change, and the first step of that recognition is humility. We have to admit our situation isn't ideal, let alone perfect.

We have to be willing to say, "I don't know."

But "I don't know" is anathema to a fundamentalist. The IFB movement requires certainty about whatever it is you're trying to conserve. How else do you know what you're conserving?

In fact—I kid you not—IFB preachers from multiple states gather at an annual doctrine convention called "Certainty Conference." At this event, guest speakers rail against people who believe differently than them. Pastor Brett Bartlett used his talk there to proudly claim his view of the King James Bible is the same he has of God. You know, because those are equivalents. (He went on to call someone who reads from multiple English versions of the Bible a liar for saying they believe the Bible is true.)

Anyway, growth fights against the very premise of dogmatism. Our bodies conserve resources for survival when facing malnutrition, so physical growth happens only when our bodies move past simple conservation. This is the spiritual version of what my friends Judson and Megan experienced when they adopted boys from the Democratic Republic of the Congo. When they met their new sons at the airport, they were shocked by how much smaller the boys were than American kids of the same age—due to conditions in their orphanage. Their stunted growth reversed once they were introduced to better nutrition. This same scenario proved true in my own life when I left the IFB movement for a more nutritious faith experience.

I never left an IFB service filled up. Somehow, I was still hungry, even though I was force-fed from a short list of topics. Back then I didn't leave feeling "better is one day in your courts than a thousand elsewhere."[47] But I can't tell you how many times I've left a church service or Bible study or service project in the last two decades with my soul brimming. Hope and joy have spilled onto my face more times than I can count. Awe and wonder have overflowed onto my soul. Even when I've driven home from a gentle rebuke or awkward conversation, there's been a sense that a faithful hand guides my path. I felt like I was in the right place at the right time. It's not every Sunday. I don't feel that way after every Dude Group gathering. Sometimes checking my phone is an incredible temptation, but now my expectations have a higher ceiling.

Part of that newfound fullness started with the desire to change. The reward for change has become habit-forming. I now fully expect to change, because I don't want to be the same me a year from now—let alone in ten. I've found that renovation sometimes requires demolition of my pride, my habits, and my assumptions. During physical growth as kids, our hearts and heads predictably get further away from the ground. They literally move away from where they used to be. In my spiritual journey, I've found the same to be true. I've physically grown fifty-four inches since my first day on the planet, and I'd guess that my faith has stretched at least that much.

In contrast, just today (as part of my work to verify that my memories match what others are still experiencing) I watched a video of a California pastor bragging to his audience, "I'm not gonna change after preaching here forty-six years." I've heard others warn about the dangers of change, of bringing anything new into their "old-time religion." A few days ago, I watched another of the IFB fraternity yell, "The old path leads to the

---

47 Psalm 84:10 NIV

throne of God. The old path is the way of holiness. It is the way of peace. It's where God walks." In fundamentalism, old is good, and new is literally from the devil.

But old is not categorically better than young. Some old houses draw the rightful attention of *Southern Living*, while others deserve the laminated orange notices that warn people not to live in them. Some old cars belong in the Petersen Museum and some in a salvage yard. The Constitution is older than its amendments, but you won't find many IFB pastors who'll contend that the First Amendment is a heretical departure from the heart of the original revelation.

Some old people are classics that bear the beautiful artifacts of their formative years mixed with their evolution over subsequent decades. Others have hardened into cantankerous vessels of infinite bitterness. We all know elderly souls filled with kindness and wisdom as well as seniors stuck in the prejudice and myopia of an era when doctors recommended specific brands of cigarettes.

Spend enough time in any IFB establishment, and you'll hear a man on stage quote King Solomon's proverb that warns against moving ancient landmarks.[48] The problem comes in the implication that the "separated" standards of IFB churches are ancient. Not one professor or pastor in my twenty years on the inside ever admitted that we were part of a movement instead of an orthodoxy—let alone that the movement was founded in the same decade when entrepreneurs started Hallmark Cards, Black+Decker, and Whirlpool. People were flying in airplanes before the IFB sect came into being. It blew me away when I learned that Christian Science is an older cult than the one I repped into my early twenties. While I was writing the first draft of this chapter, Kane Tanaka of Fukuoka, Japan, was almost a decade older than the IFB movement. She passed away at the age of 119 before my final draft left for press. She was old for a person, but she'd have been young for a religion.

The IFB movement's founders may have started their schism with good intentions and a holy discontent. I can't speak to that. But the havoc wreaked over the past eleven decades by this worldview has pushed hundreds of thousands of people away from faith in Jesus.

48 Proverbs 23:10

In fairness, nostalgia can be a beautiful thing. It can remind us of our formative values, our former dreams, and a simpler existence. But it can also push us away from change. It's good for our hearts when we revisit a favorite restaurant, but we miss out on so much yummy goodness when we visit only that restaurant every time we go out for dinner. Eventually, we can even grow tired of what used to be a treat. The law of diminishing returns eventuates in a dissatisfaction with even good things.

In other words, a monotonous experience can grow into a sedentary boredom. A lack of change can lead to a loss of contentment. I've seen that in IFB circles too. It's not surprising that many who loop the same track grow more bitter, more rigid, and more judgmental. I've watched people burrow deeper into their conformity rather than grow into their full potential.

At the same time, we shouldn't chase change for the sake of change. Growth and change can become idols as much as tradition and certainty can. The tension between change and static faith arrives in pragmatism. If we hold onto what we know with humility, we can let go of opinions or practices that don't serve our current expression of the Great Commission. If we are "walking in step with the Spirit,"[49] we'll know which handles to hold tightly and which to release. Simon Peter, one of the founders of the New Testament church, had to change a foundational approach to ministry—two decades into his leadership. Why would we, who have no canonized speeches or letters to our credit, be any less needful of correction or adaptation?

We don't have to chase change, because change finds us easily enough. We're all growing in one way or another. Over time we grow more or less sedentary, more or less vulnerable, more or less humble, more or less curious, more or less dogmatic, more or less empathetic. All of that spiritual growth—just as with our physical bodies—holds the potential for growing pains. On so many nights, I've wished for a spiritual ibuprofen. During times of stretching, I've wished heaven sold some emotional version of Aleve. But those aches have let me know Luke 2:52 was happening in my life. In fact, if I haven't experienced the pangs of stretching spiritual bones and tendons in a while, an internal alert buzzes like a fitness tracker to warn that I haven't moved in a while.

---

49 Galatians 5:16

The surrender inherent in growth can be quite expensive. At least it has for me. I've had to relinquish pride and security, time and money, surety and familiarity. Oh, and lots of comfort. I remember looking at my watch in the waiting room before my first session with my therapist. My beats per minute jumped from fifty-five to eighty-three. It felt like when I've walked to the edge of a bridge to bungee jump or stood at an open door on an airplane thirteen thousand feet off the ground. I was scared to talk about what was swirling in my heart and mind. It took multiple sessions before I started to reveal the causes instead of just the symptoms of my brokenness. I learned what I needed to change in myself along with how hard and expensive that growth would be. I had to choose change in order to find healing. While relinquishing my self-preservation, I've found a life I didn't know I could live. The more vulnerable and pragmatic I've become, the more life has permeated my days.

You don't have to take my word for it. Bible teacher Jada Edwards explained this reality well: "We can't expect deep moves of God if we offer shallow surrender. We need consistent, specific, and reflective confession to stay humble and be used greatly by God." Author and TED Talk presenter Susan David, PhD, also summed this idea well: "Discomfort is the price of admission to a meaningful life."[50] And the apostle James promised that "God opposes the proud but gives grace to the humble."[51]

Part of that grace is growth. Part of grace's inherent reward is progress. When we're humble enough to say, "I don't know," we make space for new understanding. I like bestselling author Shauna Niequist's catchphrase: "I guess I haven't learned that yet." This regular response assumes she's on a path of continual learning. Like her, I hope I never get off the grand expedition that's been my faith journey. I use *journey* intentionally, because I anticipate new scenery and a path that continuously looks different from where I started. I want to see a wiser, deeper—better—version of me in the mirror on my birthday every year. I hope you do too.

Learning displaces both ignorance and incorrect knowledge. So much of our training as apprentices to Jesus requires replacing lies with truth, swapping out the malignant with the benevolent, and supplanting

---

50 https://twitter.com/SusanDavid_PhD/status/1349747542209286144

51 James 4:6 LEB

assumptions with exposure to reality. If what we're being taught isn't changing what we know and experience of God, we aren't growing. If our teachers aren't growing, we can't expect that we will either.

Personally, the pastors and mentors who've influenced me most are the ones who've been the least dogmatic and the most pragmatic. It's true of my peers too. I've found my most healthy and intriguing friends to be those who absorb diverse voices, including those with opposite perspectives. Truth is truth wherever it resides; and it often lives behind a different flag, a different culture, or a different tradition. That doesn't mean we give equal weight to everyone's opinions, but growth gets a lot harder when we hide from opposing points of view—like within the confines of a Certainty Conference.

Last week on Instagram I watched an influential fundamentalist pray in front of his congregation for "preachers not to change, not to buy into becoming relevant. Help them to stay with the old-fashioned way." I wonder if that blind guide realized he was praying not to grow.

My editors have asked me why, twenty years removed from attending an IFB church, I watch videos of problematic preachers. This spot is probably the best place to explain that.

Multiple times while writing this book, I've wondered if I'm describing ghosts—artifacts of the past that no longer exist. *Why raise a red flag if fundamentalism might be on its way out?* That question pushed me to social media accounts that document recent sermons recorded and posted by IFB institutions. These social media clips confirm the stories and quotes I heard last night from my niece, whose parents required her to watch the livestreams of services from their IFB church while she vacationed here in the Blue Ridge Mountains. Until her visit, those clips of preacher rants were what reminded me of the stakes of this book.

Last night, as I listened to the pain and frustration of her religious experience, I recognized the makings of a future refugee from this malignant movement. There are hundreds of thousands of men and women who've gone before her and might follow after her. This cult is real and current and proudly practiced. What hasn't changed since my departure is how IFB preachers demand conformity and claim certainty. In so doing, they've supplanted an invitation to growth.

When we put blinders on our faith and our worldview, we miss the nuance and color and diversity designed into our planet. That's not a big sacrifice if you only want to walk old paths or loop the same track, but it is a problem if you want to experience everything that the Holy Spirit can bring into your life. It's also a problem because both Old Testament and New Testament writers declared "The just shall live by faith."[52] You don't need much faith if your spiritual practice is just a repetition of the familiar.

We're all drawn to comfort. That goes for people who enjoy the predictability of high church liturgy and those who prefer the less-scripted rituals of low church gatherings. For sure, it also applies to those of us in the nondenominational movement. We like the coffee bars, the high production value, and the TED Talk vibe of our Sunday mornings. None of these religious lanes have the corner on truth. All people of faith prefer to interact with organized religion on our favorite set of terms, and we all fight the temptation to feel like exclusive knowers of what church should look like. I've learned that I need to hold onto rituals and preferences with a loose grip. My hands need to be easily emptied so I can hold onto a sovereign hand as he guides me over new and unknown terrain.

We all feel the pull toward stasis. The challenge is to put that status quo on the altar of things we're willing to sacrifice for the sake of the Gospel. The goal isn't discomfort. It's obedience. The Great Commission has proven itself adaptable to cultures and subcultures but only through pragmatic believers who themselves are willing to adapt. There's a lot of space in between what we do know for sure from the Bible's human authors, but that space makes Scripture more adaptable in different contexts.

52 Habakkuk 2:4 and Romans 1:17 KJV

23 REAL ADVENTURE INSTEAD OF COSPLAY

Unsafe churches tried to enlist me into culture wars, but Jesus has invited me onto a grand faith expedition where we're all loved equally.

In 2019, I went on more trips and experienced more extreme activities than in any other year of my life. I took my first class in wing walking (hanging out on the wing of a biplane while it's doing aerobatic maneuvers). I surfed in the Arctic Circle, climbed a frozen Colorado waterfall eleven thousand feet above sea level, snorkeled between tectonic plates in Iceland, standup paddle-boarded on an alpine glacier in British Columbia, learned how to fly fish in Montana, and attended rally racing school near Seattle, Washington.

All of this didn't happen because I put Tim McGraw's "Live Like You Were Dying" on repeat. I didn't get a fatal diagnosis from a frowning oncologist. I didn't collect a big windfall or win a gameshow prize. Nope. 2019 held the day I finally sought help from a professional counselor. During the summer of 2019 I joined Ruthie in telling our families about my dad's abuse and then confronting my dad again. I wrestled all that year with the manuscript of my previous book and with a freelance gig I was transitioning to a different business emphasis. Oh, and I also chose to accept the challenge of becoming a father to someone else's biological child.

It was a lot—even without knowing COVID was about to rock everyone's world.

I fasted and prayed. Crystal and I spent hours almost every week in good-but-heavy conversations. I consulted other wise voices in my life. I read the Bible cover to cover that year. And I ran from my emotions. Some people run from their pain to a controlled substance, an addictive habit, or an inappropriate relationship. I ran, per my usual, toward adventure.

When my heart feels overwhelmed, I gravitate toward physical escape. When stressed, I Google places to fly. When sad, I Google adrenaline rushes to try. When overwhelmed by work, relationships, or loss, I feel an almost equal pressure to get the heck out of wherever I am. When the bells and whistles are ringing in my heart, I review my saved posts from travel influencers on Instagram and check how many American Express points I have left in my account.

In his beautiful sovereignty, God redeemed those "hard year" adventures. More accurately, he waited for me to show up with my unhealthy motives and then revealed a part of his character to me when I arrived. I'll spare you the details on that process here. I've written literally a whole book about that.

I tell you all of that as backstory to my last counseling session. I was telling my therapist about how much I worked in high school, how much of my paychecks I saved for college, how much I planned for the future—how badly I wanted to leave home and be as self-sufficient as possible as early as possible. Lindsey asked me a haunting question: "What were you trying to escape?"

I left home for a college with even more rules. So, my motives weren't just freedom from parenting. I transitioned from an IFB church to an IFB college. So, it wasn't a protest against my required religion. I loved my brother fiercely and enjoyed my time with my sisters. So, I wasn't trying to escape family.

I wanted more options.

I pined for a girlfriend. I craved more friends my age. Since I hadn't been allowed to play sports as a kid and I didn't even try out for sports in high school, I wanted to see if I was coordinated enough to play intramural sports. I hated that I had to argue for autonomy and that I was shamed for my interests and questions. I wanted a chance not to be haunted by past bullies and current workmates (who, after they learned I was a virgin, circled around me and chanted "MAST-UR-BAY-TOR" in unison).

I wanted freedom and a better life.

College scratched some of those itches, but I was limited by more than just the constraints of IFB rules. Freedom really didn't arrive until after college. My early career success gave me a second shot, especially a few years after I started my company. Disposable income arrived for me right about the time we all got social media, and that concoction was as dangerous for me as a Molotov cocktail.

I started the GoPro life back when GoPro sold only wrist-mounted 35mm film cameras. While others drank alcohol for "liquid courage," I turned on my action cameras for "digital courage." I threw myself into a big jump, a fast lap, or a scary paddle—right after I heard the beep that told me a red light was blinking and an MP4 file was being created. I wanted to be interesting because I thought that was the only way to make people interested in me. That's also why I was an early adopter of podcasts and why I've listened to hundreds of nonfiction books. I tried to build an on-ramp to almost any conversation that could happen around me.

I wanted to be wanted.

That desire led me to some incredible experiences and into relationships with some really cool people. Over the years, I've found healing for a lot of what ailed me. I still struggle with a compulsion to capture my adventures for online distribution, but I'm more careful about it now. I try to share from exuberance rather than insecurity. I amplify the beautifully human moments of my life at least as much as the impressive ones. I tell stories of my friends instead of just myself. I season the mix with vulnerable stories of what I'm learning.

In my forties, I'm finally practicing self-regulation. I've learned to run to local creeks and forests several times a week because nature acts as a release valve for the tension in my chest. My wife, friends, and therapist regularly inquire about my motives, and they aren't afraid of rebuking me when I'm off-kilter. I've grown accustomed to discussing uncomfortable realities, and I work at developing proper responses to emotional triggers.

For good or bad, though, my global travels have created a monster—or maybe just an addict. I now crave adventure. I get antsy when there isn't an activity that requires a safety harness on my calendar. So, I understand that I might want more excitement in my faith experience than others do. I assume not everyone longs for adventure in their life, let alone in their spiritual journey. That said, I would bet a lot of religious folks do want more energy, more life, and maybe even more challenge in their souls.

In my current faith tradition, I'm surrounded by people who fully embrace adventure. Even before Crystal and I adopted our daughter, we rubbed shoulders with multiple foster and adoptive parents every Sunday and on many days in between. I need two hands to count the friends from my church who've upped and left to work in a developing country for ministry reasons. I know servants who have given up impressive corporate salaries, comfortable positions, or an established career track to move into nonprofit work. My ministry teammates have leaned into reconciliation with unfaithful partners. One of my buddies and his wife moved their family into a neighborhood where others in their socioeconomic situation typically don't, to be closer to the needs of our inner city. Fellow congregants have leveraged their own trauma to counsel others with similar stories. One of my friends has had to operate his international ministry under an alias because of his dangerous work, and a group of my friends serve as a security team for an annual conference of pastors of underground churches. My pastors and mentors have augmented their spiritual adventures with pastimes like racing motorcycles, whitewater paddling, flying experimental aircraft, and summiting snowcapped mountains. One of my unchurched buddies told me if he went to a church, he'd want to go to "your adventure church."

I reflected on all of this adventure after seeing a video on Instagram this morning of a fundamentalist pastor yelling from his pulpit in front of an empty choir loft.[53] The North Carolina minister compared the apostle Paul to Stalin—specifically in how Stalin ordered his soldiers to shoot other Russians when they retreated. This proud preacher seemed to praise Paul for angrily dismissing John Mark and splitting with Barnabas. He declared that we "need more pastors like General Patton." He railed against those who would leave his church, calling them deserters. He punctuated his critique by telling the kind of man who would leave to go get his "wife's girly boots." I watched a well-traveled IFB evangelist refer to non-fundamentalist pastors as "Pee-wee Herman wannabes." I recently watched an IFB evangelist attack the intelligence of IFB refugees: "These little pinheads that have left our churches, they've never been in a fight. They're so smart they're stupid. They don't have the camaraderie like we do."

I recently watched a Nebraska pastor opine on his podcast, "They are *such* losers—I mean *the* biggest . . . Every time I think of recovering

---

53 @badsermons

fundies and all of these people—they are just the biggest losers. They are the biggest losers because they used to be [in] our kinds of churches but flunked out—flunked out."

These name-callers aren't outliers. You'll find this sentiment throughout the IFB movement. It goes beyond toxic masculinity and even narcissism with those that throw grenades from behind pulpits. The "man of God" is the general; his church is his division of soldiers; and anyone who can't hack it under their command wasn't cut out to be a soldier. They'll use the "you're either with me or against me" ultimatum and then disparage you for choosing the healthier option. And in cases I've heard from people I know, shunning soon follows. Abusive pastors bend the Matthew 18 parameters of church discipline to apply to those who seek a more biblical church experience in another assembly.

It hit me after watching the Stalin and Patton video that this war motif is a disguised cry for adventure. Many of these sedentary pastors don't have any mountains to climb in their respective lives. No grand expeditions loom on their horizons. Their legalism insulates them from nuanced tensions. Their arbitrary fences keep them safe from the stout challenges inherent in loving someone into the kingdom. Most of these pastors aren't confronting their physical fears, visiting multiple continents, or even trying a variety of ethnic food. So, they must manufacture meaning and adventure through fiction. Like the trope of grown men living in their parents' basement, they are drawn into proxy wars. Instead of video games, though, these "men of God" participate in culture wars.

This war motif convinces cult members that they're under constant attack. Their legalism thus proves their vigilance. Manufactured missions bind the congregants together as foxhole comrades. It offers them an intoxicating sense of exclusive virtue—"us against the world." IFB preachers, much like politicians, have more to gain by an ongoing battle than a conquered foe. Culture wars make for a constant supply of sermon fodder and energetic amens.

Some of these battles are just hilarious. Take the war on Christmas. Christmas is under the assault of greed but not from atheists, liberals, or Muslims. Nobody pickets Christmas Eve services. Nobody protests Christmas card retailers or manufacturers for including options with Bible verses on them. You won't hear about a petition to take faith-based

Christmas carols out of mall speakers or radio rotations. "Happy holidays" is just easier to say in a pluralistic society than "Happy Hannukah, Advent, Christmas, Kwanzaa, Boxing Day, and New Year's!" Take it from someone who works in advertising, you don't want to try to design all of that into a store sign. Besides, as KB and nobigdyl declare in "King Jesus," their rap collaboration: "People don't care if you keep Christ in Christmas if they cannot see that there's Christ in the Christian."

Then there's the war on Christianity itself. Polling companies have found that a significant percentage of conservative evangelicals believe they're an oppressed population. The fundamentalists in my social media feeds only reinforce this, and IFB leaders stoke this fire. I would dare these Chicken Littles to express these feelings in front of the apostle Paul or current believers in China. Earlier this month, I heard the testimony of an Afghan believer who assumes she will die for her faith—because people in her church already have. When asked what Americans can pray for her, she asked that when she is martyred that her death would happen quickly.

American Christians are not even on a slippery slope to that type of persecution. There is a chaplain for every MLB, NBA, and NFL team, and many MLS and NHL teams. NASCAR events include a prayer before "Start your engines!" Sessions of Congress open with prayer. The president of our country typically attends the National Prayer Breakfast. At each presidential inauguration, the incoming commander in chief is sworn into office with his hand—not on the Constitution—but on a copy of the Bible. Our national currency has "In God We Trust," printed on it or carved into it. Our federal holidays include Christian holidays but not a single Jewish, Islamic, or Satanist one. There are more than fifteen hundred Christian radio stations in the United States—that's at least three for every casino in our country. Christian movies show in secular theaters from coast to coast. Churches are tax-exempt in every state, and donations to them are tax-deductible. You could make the argument that tax law has created a government subsidy *for* Christians.

If there's a war in America on Christians, the Christians are definitely winning. It's not even close. For more than a decade, the Supreme Court has upheld Christian liberties in almost every case they have considered.

Fundamentalism has also created a fictitious war against its liturgical style. I shake my head at the IFB depictions of night club music and androgynous men. One of my current worship leaders wears the same jeans on stage that he does in a skid loader or while splitting wood by hand. He walks on stage in the steel-toed boots he was issued for his work in a factory. The man who most reframed worship for me posts his inspirational YouTube videos from his woodworking shop and earned his living on a commercial fishing boat before he led on our stage. And the hipster guys who serve on rotation at my church are no less anointed (and no less masculine) for wearing their Carhartt beanies, skinny jeans, or V-neck shirts.

• • •

People leave IFB churches for the same reason they leave funeral homes. After catching up with friends and family, they want to go back to the land of the living. We're leavers, not quitters. We just want to escape the pallor of a dying religion. We don't want to be gaslit about our substantial problems with artificial orthodoxy and then forced to endure the ensuing defibrillator of revival services. We're alive, and we want a faith community that is too.

Instead of soldiers of fortune, we want to be co-conspirators on a grand caper. We want to be on the crew manifest of a grand expedition with fellow explorers. Instead of focusing on all the things some shaman tells us we can't do, we want to be constantly reminded of our incredible and universal calling—visions of what could be. We want to hear stories of lives changing, not sporadic announcements of "professions of faith."

Not every refugee from abusive theology craves adventure like I do, but we are all drawn to life, light, and energy. We all prefer reminders of what Jesus is for instead of regular displays of what propagandists are against. The younger we are, the more we gravitate to leaders on a mission as opposed to dinosaurs roaring about their insecurities. And most of us have met enough bitter, old fundamentalists to know we don't want to do whatever got them to their judgmental angst or unattractive boredom.

One of my pastors has a seminary PhD *and* a video of himself jumping out of an airplane with me. He didn't realize what a contrast he was setting the first time he told me, "Whenever Jesus showed up in the Bible—whatever it was—it wasn't boring."

People who followed the God of Abraham, Isaac, and Jacob constantly had to be told, "Fear not." They wouldn't have needed that assurance were they not in situations that reasonably caused fear. In contrast, during my decades inside fundamentalism and my years observing it from the outside, I've noticed its pastors have the opposite message. These pulpit pounders are fearmongers. They create war and oppression where it isn't, cheapening very real spiritual warfare and persecution in our shared world. They prove the words of G. K. Chesterton to be true: "Idolatry is committed, not merely by setting up false gods, but also setting up false devils."

Compassion for the world is swapped out by fear of it. The messaging is geared toward exclusivity instead of inclusivity, defensiveness instead of openness, close-minded protection instead of full-hearted vulnerability. It makes sense, then, that IFB preachers gravitate to the analogy of soldiers rather than to the Bible's other analogies of betrothed lovers, unified families, productive farmers, patient runners, and healthy bodies.

While the library of Scripture reinforces the consistent aspects of God's character and patterns of his behavior, the grand narrative of the Bible includes wild stories of rescue and adventure. He asked Noah to build a floating zoo; he asked priests to hike in circles then into a whitewater river. He leveraged Ehud's left-handedness as an assassin and Rahab's cover as a prostitute. He directed a talking donkey to run Balaam into a wall and showcased Ruth initiating a romantic relationship by pushing cultural boundaries. The Creator of the Stars held the sun still for Joshua and told Gideon to break pottery in the dark. He never gave a proper name for the food he placed each night around Hebrew tents. That's probably why they called it *manna*, which in English means "What is this?"

While we know with great certainty the attributes of God, we can't predict how he'll work. It's better that way. We'd probably try to game the system, if we could know his plans. And I'd much rather spend my life as an explorer of God's goodness than as a cosplayer in make-believe wars.

24 EMBRACING UNCERTAINTY

Unsafe churches keep their god in a tiny, manageable box, but Jesus invited us into an awe that comes only from unpredictable energy.

I absolutely love where I live. The Blue Ridge Mountains have unlocked something in my heart I didn't know was there. I'm not a fan of our mercilessly muggy summers, but watching lightning storms might be my favorite activity when the thermometer surpasses spring temperatures. As bolts explode behind our local peaks, the silhouettes of our mountains appear and then disappear. The ridge lines look like spines of giant, huddled creatures guarding those of us in the valley from electrocution.

In our bedroom, Crystal and I have large windows that face south, and I watch a lot of lightning from our bed. But when a storm comes, I have a standing hall pass from Crystal to scurry out to my car and drive to some of my favorite lightning-watching spots. For some storms, I head to the parking lot below our airport's control tower for sweeping vistas facing east. For most storms, though, I have a couple of parking spots on a nearby hill that give me unobstructed views north toward Apple Orchard Mountain. I use an app that alerts me when lightning strikes within twenty-five miles of my location and maps where strikes hit the ground. It lets me know which of my favorite spots to drive to.

A couple of nights after a recent Independence Day, I raced to one of those overlooks and found the sky to be mostly clear overhead. So, I parked my MINI Cooper and hiked to the top of the hill. There, in a small meadow, I stood for about an hour, watching heat lighting billow in the clouds and then strike bolts along the horizon to the north. I couldn't hear much of the thunder or of the hustle and bustle of the civilization at the bottom of the hill. Just the gossipy whisper of the tall, wild grasses. Up there, it was just me and the warm breath of summer. Folks in the valley shot off their last batches of fireworks from the holiday weekend. Even though I couldn't hear their explosions, I watched the fireworks from above their colorful crowns.

I love fireworks. My heart gets giddy immediately after that *fuh-woomp* sound the tall fireworks make when they launch. I revel in the colors and the crackles. I can't get enough of the resounding booms. I even like the metallic smell of the smoke that trails in the air. For a half hour each Independence Day, I feel like a kid again—especially when I sit under the explosions with my nieces and nephews.

Up on top of the mountain that night after the Fourth of July, the fireworks below didn't take me back to childhood memories or the kid in my soul. They took me back to the days that followed the 2016 election.

After the caustic transition of presidential power, pundits everywhere told us that our divided country was the result of echo chambers and isolation. They pontificated. They opined. They said we all needed to invite voices of dissent into our lives—to entertain contrary ideas, to converse with folks who held opposing viewpoints.

So, I did.

Over the next five years, I read more than two hundred nonfiction books. Many, if not most, of those works were authored by writers who didn't share my faith, my gender, my heritage, or my political ideology. Some opposed my views of morality, sexuality, and even my definition of monogamy. In one of my favorite books from this journey, its German author mocked anyone who believed what I do about the origin of human existence (even while he marveled at the incredible design of his scientific subject matter). Podcasts and blog posts joined the mix too. I listened to atheists, agnostics, and even people who entertained the merits of anarchy.

During this expedition, I noticed how many of my friends and evangelical celebrities had walked away from faith in Jesus. So, I started reading books by deconstructionists and those who saw Jesus, God, and the Bible very differently than I do. As a writer, I enjoyed how eloquently they penned their assertions. As someone who enjoys my daily interactions with pragmatic analytics, I absorbed logical cases for their conclusions.

These men and women moved some furniture in the sanctuary of my soul. By that I mean that some of my peripheral beliefs grew less dogmatic, or they actually changed. I gained sympathy, maybe even empathy for people whose life experiences led them to different spiritual places than mine had. At the same time, because of the transcendence I've experienced after different choices, I felt a profound sadness. Many of those authors, podcasters, and social media influencers hadn't just moved furniture. They had gone all Chip Gaines on the load-bearing walls of their souls. I wouldn't be surprised if a bulldozer or an excavator was involved. At times, the deconstruction about which I read felt more like demolition.

Many of those who followed this demolition with some sort of reconstruction process seemed to rebuild their *Argo* squarely within the limitations of their own reasoning. Most of them had crafted their respective gods in their own image and built their spirituality around their own sensibilities. Dissatisfied with a God of lightning, they seemed to prefer the relatively manageable explosions of fireworks. They wanted to pick the size, the color, the height, and the noise level of their interactions with their inspiration. They chose to interact with explosive power at designated times and in specific places. They still wanted wonder and excitement but within comfortable boundaries.

That's what I thought about in the meadow on top of that hill. As I watched the massive bolts of lightning sporadically strike mountains, the fireworks in the foreground felt puny—almost comical. Both created bright light in the darkness, but each generated massively different power. As an electrical storm pummeled along a storm front many miles wide, the fireworks spritzed up within relatively tiny boxes of high school football fields. While attributes of the fireworks varied from one to another, they didn't create the unique shapes of heat lightning clouds or the jagged ground strikes that followed later.

That evening's juxtaposition of man-made power and high-altitude acts of God led me to a moment of worship. I thanked God for being lightning in my life. I thanked God for being unable to be stopped or harnessed or otherwise controlled.

The God to whom I regularly surrender doesn't always act in predictable ways. Omniscience doesn't always whisper the same prompts to me, and I'm sure I get different Holy Spirit shoulder taps than my wife and friends feel.

Both in the stories of the Bible and in my real life experience, God's constant, unconditional love appears overlapped with a fierce holiness. When even just his angelic messengers showed up in the library of Scripture, they often had to start the encounter with, "Don't be afraid."

God is scary. Jesus is dangerous. The Holy Spirit is unable to be captured or contained. The omnipotence of the King of Kings, when filtered through our finiteness, can feel inexplicable and even capricious. The flashes of Eternity's presence tear into the soil of our façades and shine white, hot light into the darkest parts of our hearts.

Something deep inside me craves a lightning storm instead of a fireworks show. Thunder scares me, but I'll take those rumbles over the silence of a deity I could carve for myself. The fear inherent in God's unknown is worth what I've watched that explosive power do in my life and the lives around me. As an adrenaline junkie with a short attention span, I enjoy the supernatural surprises of my spiritual journey—even if I don't always welcome the impromptu assignments that punctuate those divine encounters.

I used to think I was weird for wanting a God I can't understand, until my life filled up with others who share that desire. I'm wired to need a Sovereignty that has hidden wonders at both the cellular and galactic levels. I crave a deity that regularly blows my mind and explodes new things in my heart. I love that my Creator reveals something new about himself as often as his mercies are renewed—or at least that he can. As I've leaned into that more mysterious and enigmatic faith, I'm growing more comfortable with the inadequacy I bring to it. While I can describe the hope that lies within me and walk someone down a Romans Road, I can't draw immutable lines around God. I'm learning that anything I write about Jesus needs to be transcribed in pencil and not pen. I don't know how he time-releases his revelation in each of our respective hearts—in the specific order we each need those realizations—but I don't need to. He's the one sitting in the director's chair.

Embracing the mysteries of the library of Scripture and its God has revealed how small my imagination is. My spiritual journey has regularly illustrated the infinitesimal size of my understanding in contrast to what there is to be understood. Saying "I don't know" to good questions about the absurd stuff in the Bible has led me to a humbler faith. My inadequacy has rooted out many of my dogmatic tendencies.

That reality doesn't just place me across the street from those who refuse to give faith a second chance. It also puts me at odds with the fundamentalists of my youth.

I grew up in a weird version of deism. God was mostly defined by the past instead of the present. I was given very strict rules and even tighter parameters for how to appease a judgmental police officer who promised life—but a highly limited life. Jesus' red-letter promise of abundant life felt like hyperbole in light of how close the guard rails were to my fenders. I was inundated with the phrase "power in the blood," but that power didn't look like lightning. Frankly, it rarely even looked like fireworks. Sparklers, maybe. My IFB faith avoided unpredictability. I didn't need as much faith that way, and my imagination didn't have to stretch. As constrained as my faith experience was, it promised a type of safety.

Lightning is arbitrary and sometimes destructive. It sets forests ablaze. It kills people. Lightning doesn't follow logical patterns or predictable paths. It makes the hair on the back of my neck stand up. When thunder is close, it shakes more than just my rib cage. My heart feels it. Lightning is fierce. There's something primal about our encounters with the electricity, the torn air, and the crackling booms. It's both the scary and impressive connotations of the word *terrific*.

I would never have described my first two decades of religious experience as terrific. To be fair, I don't know that I'd label the permanently deconstructed life that way, either. Neither are joyless—don't get me wrong. But what they gain in control and containability comes at the expense of at least some measure of wonder. That's a trade too expensive for me because most of the transcendent moments of my life have arisen from wonder. I can't speak for those who've completely walked away from faith, but I can draw from decades in abusive theology. And I can tell you that moments of wonder were few and far between in my old religious system.

Both fundamentalists and those who've rebuilt their spirituality a la cart are creating fireworks as proxies for a life with lightning. To be fair—to some degree—all humans create our gods or lack thereof in our own image. All religions reflect the values of their originating cultures, and few faiths have more splintered variations than the Christian faith. Two millennia in, and it still adds factions and new spins on old heresies. Right now, in America alone, a sizable percentage of the population is rebuilding their theology around the politics of their favorite demagogues. Anne Lamott captured this shape-shifting idolatry well when she quoted her friend Tom Weston in *Bird by Bird*, "You can safely assume you've created God in your image when it turns out God hates all the same people you do."

Whether we build our beliefs around our fears or our wounds, our culture, or our traditions, we need to step back from our orthopraxy regularly and ask ourselves if we are forming our faith or if our faith is forming us. I regularly have to wrestle with whether I'm building my worldview on the space between what Jesus actually said or on the pattern he lived. By listening to the contentions of people on the other side of various lines, I'm ricocheted back to Scripture to see what it actually says—and especially what it describes of Jesus' life.

If my theology doesn't lead me to awkward conversations and uncomfortable moments, it isn't led by Jesus. If my spirituality feels warm and comfortable, it isn't powered by faith. If I'm becoming more and more sure about tertiary topics and more likely to spend my headspace there, I'm not obeying the simplicity of the Great Commission. At the same time, if my lifestyle leads me more and more away from assembling with other believers, I'm not on the right path, either. If God somehow always agrees with me, he's too flawed and finite to be worshipped.

Maybe it's just my personality style, but the fire alarms of my faith start chirping when the power in my life looks more like fireworks instead of lightning. I crave a spirituality that makes my heart rate jump on occasion. I'm not saying that we should strive for discomfort. Spiritual masochism can make our religious experience about our effort instead of God's grace, love, and mercy. At the same time, the biographic accounts from the New Testament show followers of The Way being stretched and changed, confronted and challenged. The writers of the Gospels, Epistles, and Acts showcase a Messiah and a church that manage a tension between afflicting the comfortable and comforting the afflicted.

That tension is not moral relativism. It's not "all paths lead to heaven." We're called to an expedition that's somewhere between "work out your own salvation" and "the just shall live by faith." There's clarity in who God is and what our Great Commission assignment is, but mystery is a feature—not a bug—of our finite following of the Infinite One. After Saul of Tarsus became Paul the Apostle, he wrote, "Now we see things imperfectly, like puzzling reflections in a mirror, but then we will see everything with perfect clarity. All that I know now is partial and incomplete, but then I will know everything completely, just as God now knows me completely."[54]

Whether we tend to the atheist or the fundamentalist ends of the faith spectrum, momentum leads us away from explosive surprises toward manageable predictability. The closer we get to the irreligious and dogmatic terminals of belief, the further we get from nuance, mystery, and humility. The further we move from the unknown and the "puzzling reflections," the more our beliefs resemble our own images instead of the One in whose image we were made. The more enamored we get by fireworks, the less we'll notice the lightning above the mountains.

---

54 1 Corinthians 13:12 NLT

25 A HEALTHIER KIND OF UNITY

Unsafe churches equated conformity with unity, but Jesus has a track record of rebuking those who obstructed diverse paths to his mercy.

Earlier on the day I'm writing this chapter, my church hosted one of what has been dubbed "Table Sundays." On a Table Sunday, all of the rows of padded chairs in our auditorium are replaced with round white tables and black folding chairs. After a shortened time of communal singing, the rest of the service happens around scores of circles. The pastor on the platform guides the interactive experience with setup and discussion prompts for Scripture discovery, group participation, and sometimes intercessory prayer. Then he walks offstage for eight or ten minutes at a time.

There are no church staff planted at the tables, no assigned seating, no volunteer leaders positioned at strategic spots. Nobody in leadership knows in advance who will sit with whom—whether there will even be a mature believer at every table. No pastors walk around to interject into the conversations they overhear. The organic circles flower with disparate exchanges, supervised only by the Holy Spirit. It's beautiful. It's engaging. It feels more like gatherings I've read about in the book of Acts than anything I ever experienced during my decades in the IFB movement.

As both an extrovert and someone who has sat through more than six thousand sermons, lectures, and required devotionals, I love Table Sundays. I bring this up not just to contrast my past with my present—though that comparison leads me to gratitude and worship. No, I told the other six people at my table this morning that I'd tell you something.

We were studying Luke 7:36–50. In those verses, the first-century doctor retells a story relayed to him about a night Jesus spent at a fundamentalist's house. As Jesus ate with a group of religious men, Mary Magdalene, a woman whose reputation was as "a sinner," knelt behind Jesus, cried onto his feet, wiped his feet with her hair, and kissed his feet repeatedly. Then she applied what we're told was expensive perfume. The fundamentalist leader in the room judged Jesus for letting Mary touch him. Jesus read Simon's mind and presented him with a riddle and then a very personal application that would've embarrassed me, if I were Simon. Jesus let the self-righteous leader sit in that chagrin while he told Mary that her sins were forgiven, that her faith had saved her, and that she could go in peace. For all future, worldwide readers of his biography, Jesus changed Mary's reputation as a sinner in her town to the woman who washed the Son of God's feet.

Everyone at my table this morning pulled different primary takeaways from this story. Mine was that I tend to label some people by their sin. I confessed that I often call my father a "serial sex offender" or a "child molester" instead of just "my dad." When our pastor asked us what we would do this week about what we shared with our tables, I knew I had to pray for my dad and for the leaders of the cult from which I had escaped. I had to want for them to find Jesus as much as I wanted it for anyone else. I needed to root for them to have a road-to-Damascus experience like the fundamentalist henchman Saul of Tarsus did. Instead of looking forward to their comeuppance, I had to wish for their forgiveness.

Then my pastor interjected into our discussion. He asked us to tell our tablemates the answer to the question, "Who are you going to tell about what just told your table?" I told Josiah, Bailey, Nate, Adam, Courtney, and Kira that I'd tell you—whoever's reading or listening to my book.

With that confession, I should add that this tension has been maybe the biggest struggle in writing this book. From my deepest core, I want to end the spiritual, relational, verbal, physical, and sexual abuse rampant in the IFB movement. At the same time, I have to remind myself that several generations of people with good intentions are just parroting what they've been deceived to believe.

I've worked harder in this book than I have in real life to wrap love around truth. But I've also not been 100 percent sure how much love I should afford a predator when warning fellow sheep about what victim advocate Tiffany Bluhm calls "a wolf in shepherd's clothing." What exactly do you pray for the pilots who drop bombs on your home, your church, and your playgrounds? Is this a matter of "Father, forgive them, for they don't know what they are doing"?[55]

I've found commiseration in the writings of Dr. Chuck DeGroat. The pastor, seminary professor, professional counselor, and church consultant says that the overwhelming majority of the narcissist pastors he's faced haven't responded well to coaching, counseling, or confrontation. Few have found healing. At the same time, he struggles not to label these wolves as narcissists but as people who struggle with the sin of narcissism.

I've talked to Jesus about my tendency toward categorization. I've prayed dozens of times for my own dysfunctions to be healed just as I've prayed for my mom and dad to find healing. For years, I've needed to ask God a modified version of what a distraught dad asked Jesus in Mark 9:24. My exclamation? "Lord, I hope. Help my lack of hope." As I wait for the answer to that prayer, I've held onto the kind of hope described in a proverb dubiously attributed to Saint Augustine of Hippo: "Hope has two beautiful daughters; their names are Anger and Courage. Anger at the way things are, and Courage to see that they do not remain as they are."

My indignation probably isn't righteous, but most days it smolders more from love than revenge. I would've endured far more abuse if it meant my dad and his IFB peers would have never stolen any girl's innocence. I can afford frequent therapy and have a robust accountability network that other victims don't yet have. Augustine's hope has been fanned ablaze in me during all waking hours, consuming my bones during long sessions at my laptop. That hope's courage has helped me weigh the relational consequences of this book and find them worth what my story might free in others.

Ironically, the shouting IFB preachers I see online call people like me "limp-wristed" and "effeminate." I've watched clips of these guys saying that refugees of their cult "have no fight in 'em"—that we're cowards. Those are the indictments of bullies. Those are the invectives a Goliath yells across a valley to Israelite soldiers. I'd guess these preachers don't spend much

---

55 Luke 23:34 NLT

time on 2 Timothy 2:24, where Paul tells his protégé, Timothy, that a man of God shouldn't quarrel but must be kind to everyone.

That pastoral qualification sounds counterintuitive to these IFB foot soldiers. I use *foot soldiers* because that's the term the vice president of my college used for us students, to remind us who we were before sending us home for Christmas break. Kindness doesn't make sense to people who sing "Battle Hymn of the Republic" on Sunday mornings. I know I'm turning into a broken record here, but Timothy's mentor told the house churches in Rome that it's God's *kindness* that leads us to repentance. Not his wrath. Not his rules. His kindness.

For sure, Jesus said his truth would divide families. It has mine. New Testament authors refer to God's Word as a sword in multiple places, and it has pierced my conscience more times than I can count. But that sharpness has been offset with the healing softness of acceptance, the welcome roundness of grace, and the dull ache that there's something more. More beautiful. More wholesome. More adventurous.

The Holy Spirit has used the voices of pastors, the words of authors, the lyrics of songwriters, and the transcribers of Scripture to spur me into prayers of repentance. At the same time, he's used exuberance-fueled moments of adrenaline, extremely personal moments in nature, and inescapably kind moments with loved ones to reveal his pursuit of my heart. And I've watched him do the same for others.

Fundamentalists won't tell you that in all of the times believers are likened to soldiers in the New Testament, the enemy isn't other Christians or even other people but instead the dark forces that swirl around humanity. In fact, the oft-referenced "armor of God" passage in Ephesians 6 ends with a reminder that we don't fight against flesh and blood but against evil in its ethereal forms.

It's not just IFB preachers that need to hear that truth. I do too. A sliver of my immature side would enjoy it if those who act as pulpit flamethrowers would see this book as a rebuttal, a rebuke, or a retaliation. Part of me wants a chance to tell those wolves that I didn't get out of the kitchen because it was too hot; I left because the putrid air made me vomit. I'm grateful to the editors who flagged places in my original drafts of this book where I delved into that, because a defense against abusive pastors is not ultimately the heart behind this book. This isn't a return volley in a tiny war. I just want to shepherd hearts away from danger. I've prayed for the "men of God" represented in this book—especially my dad.

Multiple times in the New Testament, we're told to pursue unity—even to be of the same mind. And Jesus told his disciples that their love for one another will prove to the world that they were his disciples.[56] As this book has come together, I've had to wrestle with how it fits into the call to unity and the love for which all believers should be known.

I spent a summer listening to Francis Chan's book *Until Unity*. I really like where he landed on the tension between unity and confrontation. This is a rough paraphrase from a nuanced book-length treatment of the topic, but what should unify us is the unadulterated Gospel. Paul exhorted the church of Ephesus to "make every effort to keep yourselves united in the Spirit, binding yourselves together with peace. For there is one body and one Spirit, just as you've been called to one glorious hope for the future."[57] Toward that goal, Jesus and New Testament authors (1) corrected those who mistakenly believed lies about different aspects of that Gospel and (2) confronted those who malignantly distorted Scripture for their own benefit.

The big-C Church needs to be unified around loving others as ourselves, gracious around tertiary interpretations, and resistant to anyone who soils the Gospel with artificial regulations and intentional distortions. Unity says that our kingdom-driven cause is paramount. In unity, we regularly remind each other that our mission is of utter importance in a fallen world.

The global community of believers can't have unity if different factions keep creating more doctrines, more extra-biblical requirements. The straightest and easiest path to a contagious unity is a focus on the words and example of Jesus. We must sacrifice our self-righteous nonessentials on the altar of the Great Commission.

Our fallen nature loves debate. That's why there's so much money in sports talk shows, cable news networks, and social media. (I admit this as someone who makes my living on digital platforms that monetize divisiveness.) At the same time, the closest the secular world at large gets to the vision for the church is when throngs unify during sporting events, rally together in massive protests, collectively raise money after natural disasters,

56 John 13:35 NLT

57 Ephesians 4:3–4 NLT

or join hands in serving the displaced. These movements create moments when strangers hug each other, when diverse people sing together, and when combatants temporarily lay down their prejudices over a shared cause. Both Catholics and Baptists across Boston hate the Yankees. Both Republicans and Democrats stand during the ovation after their children's school play. Both Black and white activists cheer for fellow citizens on the Olympic medals stand. Both gay and straight Americans put Ukrainian flags in their profile pictures after Russia invaded a country they'd never visited.

For followers of the Way, what unites us is more important than gender, ethnicity, denomination, political party, or sexual orientation. Our shared Gospel definitely trumps the style of music in a church service, what the minister is wearing, or which version of the English Bible is being read in the front of the room. That unity eventuates in unified and unifying fruit. We shouldn't be surprised when unity blossoms like that because Jesus (1) prayed that we'd be one like he was one with the Father and the Holy Spirit, and (2) said believers shall be known for their fruit. You don't need to spend as much time inside the IFB cult as I did to see that the fruit of its dogma is rarely love, joy, peace, patience, kindness, goodness, faithfulness, gentleness, or self-control.

People outside the church recognize that contrast more than pew sitters who listen to red-faced preachers multiple days a week. At least part of the reason for that is because unsafe congregations are indoctrinated into their myopia by men who gain from the sleight-of-hand show. Leaders within the cult get their ego stroked, their opinions validated, their status cemented, and sometimes even their deviant sexual desires met. Both the men on stage and the followers in the pews gain a self-righteousness by comparing themselves with other people who don't check the arbitrary boxes of what constitutes spiritual maturity.

None of those perks align with the Great Commission. None of those goals pour from the Gospel. None of that rotten produce grows out of what should unite us. We know from Jesus' parables that weeds get separated from thorns and fruitless branches get pruned from vines. Jesus directed his ire at the religious leaders who contorted faith in the ways unsafe pastors do today. So, every once in a while, unity has to confront the forces that fight against it. Part of creating harmony is removing the discordance from fingers that strike the wrong strings or keys. Often peace requires removing a distraction, if not confronting an invasion. Preserving solidarity sometimes requires addressing the uncooperative.

Protecting sheep will irritate some wolves, but safe shepherds and churches confront predators.

26 THE POWER OF TELLING OUR STORIES

Unsafe churches encouraged me to run and hide, but Jesus has often invited me into healing light.

From fourth grade until I left for college, I lived in the attic of a house next to a truck stop. Because of the way the stairs and my only window were juxtaposed, my bedroom didn't have a door. All the LEGO bricks in our home were stored in my room. So were the tiny soccer goals made out of PVC pipes. My room held the home's only CD player—the only stereo that wasn't my parents' vinyl turntable. Also, as the attic, it was away from all of our homeschool books and kitchen chores. So, my youngest siblings and their friends crashed my place on a regular basis. Most of the time I didn't mind, but I was a teenager.

In one of those high school moments, I kept telling Ruthie—yes, that Ruthie—to stay out of my room. The second grader wouldn't listen, wouldn't leave. I'm embarrassed to admit that I—as a high school senior—physically kicked her out of my room. She fell onto the vinyl tile floor and maybe down a few wooden steps before collecting herself. Crying, she slinked downstairs. I don't know if she reported my physical abuse to my sisters first. What I do know is that—as she should have—she told my dad what I'd done.

My dad stormed up the stairs. I don't remember his first words. I just remember him picking me up and chest passing me across my room. I went back later and measured. I had flown more than eight feet laterally. I cleared my bed in the air and broke through the drywall. Thankfully, my spine hit between two studs in the wall. The raging pastor asked me how I liked being on the other end of a bully. He acknowledged my terror and told me that's what Ruthie, as an elementary student, felt on the other end of my kick. "Don't ever touch Ruthie again!" he barked. The thunder and the lightning immediately exited my room with him. They left behind a rain of frenzied survival.

Unfortunately, my dad didn't obey the mandate he gave to me. Six years later, he sexually molested Ruthie and then told the middle school girl he thought she'd be okay with it. He then prayed a prayer of forgiveness in front of her, informed her that Jesus had forgiven him, and told her that she didn't need to tell anyone. Ruthie obeyed that command for nearly a decade.

That's where the story from chapter 2 picks up. During team training for a trip to work with refugees from the Nicaraguan sex trade, the recent college graduate Ruthie confessed her trauma for the first time to her trip leader. That's when my pastor showed up at my door. That's when Woody and Crystal's shepherd hearts helped mine beat slower. That's when, with Ruthie's approval, I learned that the man who beat me and told me not to bully her had also stolen her innocence.

I don't remember what Ruthie and I talked about during our five-hour drive alone to my parents' house. I do remember my nervous heart as I marveled at the incredible courage she summoned to invite my dad out to his parked vehicle at dawn. I slid into the middle row of the van and leaned forward into the gap between the front seats as she confronted him for his assaults and their toll on the past decade of her life. That was the first time I recorded a conversation with my dad. I didn't know then that I'd be recording lots of conversations with him over the ensuing decade. I didn't know then that he'd change his stories, his claims, and his defenses each time.

I held Ruthie's secret away from her family and mine until she said she was ready for those revelations, though I told it often to my friends at church. I needed prayer for my anger and confusion, and I've never been a fan of unspoken prayer requests.

During those years of waiting, Ruthie got into counseling. I assured her that her secret was safe with me until she was comfortable moving forward with the process of telling stakeholders in our respective families. My dad knew I knew. He knew Crystal knew. He knew Ruthie's family and the rest of mine didn't. Every December at my family's Christmas gathering, where up to nineteen people lived in my parents' house at the same time, the secret burned in my arteries. My dad pretended nothing had ever happened. I felt like a fake, a hypocrite, a foreign agent. It's not surprising that I ended up spending December nights in a zero-degree sleeping bag in my parents' back yard. Each year on the drive home, I felt like I was transporting a ticking time bomb I'd managed to keep from exploding.

A few weeks after my last Christmas at my parents' house, I started my journey of what became weekly therapy sessions with an incredible Christian counselor. After conversations with stakeholders in my life, I wanted to end this perennial duplicity. Ruthie did too. She felt ready to free her story from its cage.

While I would've gladly borne the weight of being that storyteller, Ruthie wanted me instead to stand nearby as she told her family and then mine. I still remember the various physical postures of those on the other end of the FaceTime calls I could see over Ruthie's shoulder. I can still see my mom wrestle with her tightly pressed lips as she looked out over Great Falls while Ruthie spoke. I will never forget how my dad leaned in like a boxer at that US-301 rest area. I can still hear his nasal voice blaming multiple other people for his actions. I continue to shake my head that he insisted that we misremembered things while also claiming that the potential of early onset dementia had affected his recall. I don't know if I kept his ink-jetted letter that followed. I do remember that he claimed to have attended a handful of counseling sessions and then stopped going, claiming to be healed and certified as such by his unnamed counselor.

It's been years now, and he has not yet voluntarily confessed his sexual sins. Despite Maryland's generous statute of limitations, Ruthie didn't press charges. She left my dad in the hands of the Impartial Judge. As far as we've been notified, my dad has yet to confess any of his pedophilia to the people on the short list I gave him in the tractor trailer lot of the Bay Country Rest Area.

Just as with thousands of other unsafe pastors who've committed atrocities against minors and women, the company line we were given for the discreetness was that revelation would hurt the Gospel. This case for secrecy came up in a follow-up conversation with my mom—to which I retorted, "Jesus didn't molest Ruthie. Dad did." The Jesus I knew was more concerned for his sheep than the wolves that hid amongst them.

Predators in the church twist the arms of their victims and anyone who learns about their perverse acts with this same call of Gospel protection. Clergymen conflate their reputation for God's. As self-appointed "men of

God," they convince the sheep in their care that sheep must protect the shepherd—not the other way around. In so doing, these wolves lurk in shepherd's clothing and avoid legal and professional consequences for their heinous behavior.

But even if you take Jesus' example and warnings out of the equation, this line of defense doesn't hold up. We don't distrust the entire banking industry when an employee of a local bank embezzles money. After he serves his time for his crime, that former banker can be many things. He's just not allowed to be a banker again. When a soldier commits treason, we don't hold the military industrial complex at fault. After the soldier faces the consequences of his crime, he can no longer serve in the military. If anything, his removal makes the collection of armed forces more trustworthy. If a teacher abuses a child, their justice includes never being allowed within five hundred feet of a school ever again. That makes children safer, not less safe. This occupational reality is true of doctors with intentional malpractice, attorneys who commit legal fraud, and police officers indicted for stealing or tampering with evidence.

So why is it that a minister can exploit and harm the very people he is called to serve and then be allowed to just slink over to another church and start over again?

In mainline and other hierarchical denominations, these predators use the system to get reassigned to different congregations. As in an illusionist's trick, well-practiced misdirection lifts the cup only after the ball is not where their parishioners are looking. In IFB churches, these debauched criminals get to hide in plain sight. Church services feel like my family Christmases did. Eventually, the victims who aren't gaslit leave for their own sanity. Out of sight, out of mind.

If the story does leak, one or more other IFB pastors circle the wagons with a session or two behind closed doors. Afterward, they walk out, wiping grease off their hands like an old mechanic, vouching for the perpetrator's healing. "See? All better now. Good as new!" With this declaration, there's now nothing constructive that can come of the story. The perpetrator and his accomplices will then warn parishioners not to retell the story. "That'd just be gossip."

While salacious stories can absolutely serve as fodder for gossip, they can also be leveraged for healing. When Jesus' little brother commanded early Christians to confess their sins one to another, he gave a holy purpose for confession: so the *confessor* could be healed.

Bringing our sin out into the sunlight doesn't make us a hypocrite; it shows the opposite. Revealing our sin doesn't mar the Gospel; it shows we can't earn heaven. When we take full responsibility for our depravity, we show why we are so dependent on Jesus. When we submit to the consequences of our actions, we give back some of the stolen agency of those we've hurt. The Father's sovereignty and omnipotence are plenty capable of redemption and even ministry out of our dysfunction.

But the story has to come from us.

We can't heal what we don't name. It's not enough for someone else to name it, especially if they're asked not to mention that name to anyone else. And there's a huge piece of the healing that requires our surrender—our proactive movement. The apostle James didn't call us simply to admit our faults to people who confronted us. His imperative was for us to initiate the process. We don't have to smear our mess on a billboard or in a public Facebook post. Wisdom must be leveraged in regard to the audience, timing, and content of our revelations.

But hiding isn't a holy option.

Hiding is a prison of our own making. To escape our cages, we must first free our stories.

As we tell our respective stories, they become easier to share. Shame loses its grip because it can use only diminishing fear to threaten our silence. The more we tell our stories, the more likely they'll reach people who need to hear them. Some of those hearers need to be prodded into their own confessions. Others need to feel the Father's embrace through camaraderie with people who hold similar pain.

In contrast, the IFB system in which I was reared encouraged bootstrap Christianity. Because our status in the church was determined by the collective perception of us having our lives together, we were incentivized to confess our faults and sins only to Jesus. In this framework, sin makes us lonely. We withdraw both from Jesus and from authenticity with our church peers. Just as God called Adam and Eve out of hiding, he still calls us into the light today.

In *What If Jesus Was Serious About Prayer?*, Skye Jethani captured this beneficial process well: "Confession is how we shatter our illusions about ourselves." He explained, "Confession is a vital means of growing us into God's likeness by first seeing and then admitting what is *unlike* God in our lives. It is a discipline that forces us to abandon the false image we'd prefer to believe so that we must gaze at our true self."

Hidden sin eats at us, gnawing from behind our ribs. As I've seen time and again, people will mold their theology around their sin and weakness. They grow into what Jesus called "whitewashed tombs." Silence loves legalism because legalism uses comparison of artificial criteria to claim spiritual health. To feel better about our private struggles, all we have to do is condemn others. In *The Truth about Us*, Brant Hansen captured this tendency well: "If we don't confess our sins, we'll confess someone else's sins."

But if we confess *our* sin, we contribute to God's story of unrelenting redemption. If we authentically share the distance between God's glory and our lack of it, we pull another bushel basket off his eternal light. An early church father declared that God's power works best in our weakness.[58] That would include stories of where our weakness led us.

In the dark hours of the morning today, I was thinking about how this truth has played out just in terms of the narrative that opens this chapter. See, both my dad and I abused Ruthie. Different ways and different severities, sure—I get that. But both of us brought her uninvited pain.

I started telling people the story of my regret soon after the incident, and I never asked Ruthie not to tell the story from her perspective. Unfortunately, this elementary student wasn't the only person I physically bullied. Several times, I resorted to misusing my strength on my sisters too.

Hurt people hurt people, though that was no excuse for my actions. Thankfully, that "get out of my room" incident was the second-to-last time I lashed out at a woman physically. (That last was during a driveway basketball game at my Aunt Sandi's house in which I intentionally kicked my oldest sister.) I'm embarrassed that physical abuse is part of my story; but as I've told that story more, it gets easier to tell. I told Crystal about my past before she was my wife because unforced candor builds trust. That trust has been rewarded with zero instances of physical violence in our marriage.

---

58 2 Corinthians 12:9 NLT

Over the next two decades, despite our significant age difference, Ruthie—that little girl in a romper who I kicked onto the landing at the top of the stairs—became a close friend. Not just my kid sister's friend. Mine too. She eventually named one of her sons after me. The word "FREE" is tattooed on Ruthie's wrist in my penmanship. When everything went down with my dad, I—as the son of her abuser—was the one she asked to go with her the first time, and the one to join her and her husband the second time. Telling my story (among other things) proved my repentance and my trustworthiness. I didn't sugarcoat my actions or blame someone else for my reactions. Taking responsibility for my sin against her and others has built trust not only from her but also from my sisters, my wife, and my daughter. I can't tell you how many times my heart has melted when my friends have invited me to carry their daughters while we play disc golf or when one of their toddlers wraps her hand around my index finger while we walk together. My little friend, Willow, races into my arms in our church parking lot, locks her arms around me, and blurts out, "I love you, Ryan!" Rarely in life do I feel as healed as in those moments.

Telling our stories doesn't shroud the Gospel, unless we're still proud of our sin. Confession shows the world we fully recognize the pain and damage our dysfunction has caused—the distance we've traveled from what Jesus intended. Inviting light into our darkness shows observers what Jesus has done in us since our defection from his way. That transformation makes the gospel more real, more practical, and more inviting. You can't be the hypocrite unchurched folks expect from Christians if you live authentically and talk candidly about when you blow it. Authenticity, especially in the church, is countercultural. People take notice.

It takes courage to treat our sin seriously, but as bestselling author Jon Acuff says: "Truth is kind in the long run." If it's God's kindness that leads us to repentance, why wouldn't he "desire integrity in the inner self"?[59]

This candor and vulnerability require expensive humility but repay us with contagious influence. When a faith leader has revealed his struggles in front of me, they have made it easier for me to share my failures with others. When I've gone first with confession around a fire or a table, others follow suit. I've been blown away with the confessions guys have entrusted

59 Psalm 51:6 CSB

to me—not after they discovered I had a Bible college degree or Christian books behind my name but after they saw how I trusted my heart in theirs and trusted God with it all. In other words, confession brings healing not only to us but also to the lives around us.

Apart from narcissists and the self-righteous, who wouldn't want to live in an ecosystem of health and healing, repair and growth? As vulnerability becomes a lifestyle, chains break and weights fall off our souls. A counterintuitive freedom grows into a contagious Gospel life. Jesus said there's no greater love than laying down our lives for our friends. When we lay down our pride and reputation in order to be healed, is it any wonder that love blossoms?

27 AN UNCONVENTIONAL REDEMPTION

Unsafe churches made me fear fatherhood and distrust my Father's heart, but Jesus has redeemed my pain against my will.

Before my dad was a fundamentalist or even a Baptist, he was an adventurer. He jumped off waterfalls and out of airplanes. According to him, the first time he ever drove a car, he put it up on two wheels. One night, he outran a cop and hid for hours in a stranger's doghouse. On a date with the woman who would become my mom, my dad was walking on a bridge when they came across a TV reporter documenting another guy who would be jumping off the bridge for the camera. My dad removed his shoes, tore off his shirt, handed it to my mom, told her he'd be right back, and then ran and jumped off the bridge.

I love these stories of my dad—and used to love telling them. I wanted to be like him when I grew up. I loved the times he taught me new, scary things. When he was an assistant pastor and Christian school teacher in an old Pennsylvania railroad town, he taught me how to jump a bike off a car ramp. Too big for my BMX, he got on his three-speed granny bike and jumped it—while wearing a sport jacket and tie. The flaps of that jacket flagged as he flew toward our mailbox. See, he gave that demonstration right before he drove down two dirt roads into the valley for door-to-door visitation. He had a cult to sell. But first, whimsy.

With a book like this, a lot of people I'll never meet could assume I hate my dad, that I hold grudges. There's an uncomfortable nuance to my relationship with him that makes my heart tight as I type this paragraph. But while the injustice of his abuse has left scars on my heart, I love my dad and wish more people could've experienced the version of him I admired so much as a kid.

I'm still blown away with how well he maximized coupons. I remember one time when he came home with more than twenty boxes of name-brand cereal—and either the store had paid him, or he had spent a mere dollar or two. I remember how he used to flip French toast over his shoulder all the way from the stove to the breakfast nook, where I'd try to catch the slices with my plate. Still the best French toast I've ever tasted.

My dad worked two full-time jobs. He dug, filled, and tamped ditches five days a week for an irrigation company. On nights and weekends, he pastored his church plant—the first IFB church on our island in the Chesapeake Bay. Kent Island held roughly thirty thousand homes at the time, and he or someone from his fledgling assembly stood at the front doors of almost all of them at one point or another. He genuinely wanted all those strangers to go to heaven, even if only through an IFB gate.

Before he was exposed as an abuser, my dad played the role of a defender of the innocent. After I left my third IFB day school for homeschool, I heard a rumor that the eighth-grade girl I had liked back at my old school had bruises seen only in her PE dressing room. I had a friend whose grotesque father mercilessly beat him, and I never told my dad about it because I didn't want to rock the boat. My buddy's mom taught English for seventh through twelfth grades, and I didn't know if reporting would take him or her or both away from our school and end our friendship. When it was the girl about whom I was writing poetry, though, I couldn't escape the possibilities behind those bruises. At that point, my dad hadn't gotten any more physical with me than a spanking; and that always came after a waiting period and a calm discussion of my offense. So, I trusted my dad with my heart. Seeing my tears and my earnestness, he comforted me and then made whatever phone calls eventuated in law enforcement officers showing up at the young lady's house in Delaware. The bruises were explained, and her parents were exonerated.

That's the dad I wish I could remember. Not the one who groomed and sexually molested teenage girls and then pulled out all of the stops to evade prosecution and punishment. Not the monster about whom Lisa's attorney told me, "Man. Your dad was slick." Not the dad who sent me out into a -30°F windchill, where I wrapped myself in old carpet padding to ward off the cold of exposure "discipline." Not the man who blamed others for his debauchery and still accuses his victims of fabricating their stories.

I now have some of the same longings that my dad had for his father.

My paternal grandfather disowned my dad mostly for leaving their previously shared Roman Catholic faith. It was 1985, and Grampa George's bevy of daily cigarettes had caught up with his lungs. He told nurses near his deathbed not to allow his thirty-three-year-old son into his Buffalo, New York, hospital room. My dad drove through the night from his Bible college in Chattanooga, Tennessee, to share his version of the Gospel with his father one last time. My dad pleaded with the nurses and convinced them to let him say goodbye to his father—only to hear his father dismiss him from the room and his life with "I'd rather die and go to hell as a Catholic than believe what you believe."

Crushing, right? Just a horrible way to leave your son. Then came my grandfather's will in which he left my dad one dollar, knowing there was a two-dollar fee to claim anything from the estate. When my dad told us or anyone these stories, he would add that the first Bible verse he found and memorized after becoming a fundamentalist was Psalm 27:10: "Even if my father and mother abandon me, the Lord will hold me close." (NLT)

And now, I'm the one claiming that verse. My dad would rather die with his beliefs than mine. A different cancer eats at him than devoured my grandfather's lungs, but it's stealing his life just the same.

Thankfully, multiple generations of physical and sexual abusers end with me. Redemptive beauty has flowered in the ashes of a relationship that burned to the ground. Sovereignty has sent multiple men into my life to pick up the different handles of fatherhood my dad dropped. I've had humble men who promptly and regularly confess their doubts, fears, and sins step into my life to take a place my dad could've held. I'm surrounded by guys who cherish their wives and put their kids' needs over their own desires. I'm encircled by dudes who come to the Bible with humility, asking Scripture to change them instead of to reinforce their self-righteousness—let alone to defend a salacious coverup. With the example and guidance of these Christ followers, I'm learning to make the choices my dad didn't.

In part because of that displacement, the concept of God the Father has changed for me, and my therapist has said she's noticed that some of my biggest breakthroughs in her office and in my life outside of it have come through the relatively recent process of becoming a dad.

A week before our final adoption hearing, our sweet-hearted attorney sat in our living room. She'd been working on our behalf for more than a year with an obtuse judge (who told us our adoption folder held more documents than any other he had ever seen). Sarah said she didn't know why the process of our slam dunk case had met so much resistance.

I replied, "I do. Jesus loves the irony of me fighting to be a dad after eighteen years of actively trying not to be one."

Eight hundred and ninety-three days before the adoption was approved, I was standup paddle-boarding in the Canadian Rockies on a helicopter expedition. When I got back to civilization, I read a text message from Crystal explaining that local law enforcement had placed our future daughter, D, in Crystal's protective care. A few days later, a Department of Social Services representative decided that my wife was the best option as D's caretaker. Two months after that, a judge awarded Crystal full custody of the youngest member of our household.

Crystal and I had not been pursuing adoption. We weren't certified for foster care, nor had we ever participated in the training or home studies that typically precede that kind of certification. Years earlier, I had taken biological kids off the table. When the urologist asked me which of the three surgical variations of a vasectomy I'd like, I told him, "All three."

I didn't want to be a dad.

My dad told me that he had to stop jumping out of airplanes when Mom got pregnant with me. What I heard was, "You can't have fun after you have kids." With his crooked index finger in my face he later told me that my birth ruined his marriage. I didn't want to give up my adrenaline rushes, my international travel, or the MINI Cooper my dad called a "yuppie car." I liked my autonomy, my freedom, and my disposable income. The way I'm wired, I run from pain and stress by stacking up trips, experiences, and releases of dopamine. I couldn't imagine not being able to escape my monsters.

I was scared to be a dad too. James Dobson (of Focus on the Family and "Donald Trump is a baby Christian" fame) told my parents that I was a "strong-willed child." Their Bible told them not to "spare the rod" in breaking my will. In a religious sect and a large family where conformity was valued more than individuality, I was a wild horse that had to be broken.

As my dad's violence compounded over time, I tried to fight back the only way I knew how. I threatened to call social services. The former poker shark dared me to do it—to blow up our family. "Say goodbye to your brother and sisters," he said through a smirk. I loved them too much to do that, and thankfully he spent all of his physical anger on me.

On several occasions, I perpetuated that bullying, channeling it into physical confrontations with others. After walking away from that shameful violence, I was so scared of what I could become. I told Crystal early in our marriage that if I ever touched her in anger, that I'd sign her divorce papers without contest. Thankfully, she's never had to invoke that promise.

Candidly, I was especially afraid to have a daughter. I was thirty-four years old when I first learned my dad had sexually molested Ruthie. Listening to my dad make excuses from a minivan driver's seat as Ruthie confronted him, I was left to wonder if I had it in me to make those same excuses.

After a victims-advocate podcast featured my father and described his grooming techniques, I realized he had used his tactics on girls as young as elementary school. Each new story of his debauched predation and his grooming of potential victims brought another wave of visceral anger. I've prayed so many times for forgiveness of the indignation that has clenched my fists. I've asked the Holy Spirit for supernatural help to forgive my abuser.

I didn't know of my father's serial predation until after I decided not to be a dad; but I knew that in the very least he had cheated on my mom with someone much younger than me. Both that reality and the ensuing revelations over the next two decades made me ask myself if I, as my father's son, had that darkness in me. *Do I have temptations like that? Could I do something like that?* Both the Bible and modern psychology tell us that addiction, malignant worldviews, and personality disorders often flow from one generation to the next. *Did I inherit predation from my dad? Will this someday be a temptation for me?* Thankfully, the answer to that introspection is that I'm breaking generational chains. All girls, women, and family members are safe around me—and hopefully feel safer when I'm nearby.

Having sensed that being D's dad was a sovereign calling, I've leaned into Sovereignty's assignment. If I was going to be a dad—her dad—I wanted D to know that she was safe, that she didn't need to earn love, and that Jesus redeems pain. And please know that those are the same truths that I hope readers and listeners of this book absorb. That intentionality with

D, and now with you, has forced me to wrestle with my wounds from the past and my misguided, inherited assumptions.

Throughout the adoption process, Jesus proved that his sovereign pursuit of my heart is gentle and patient but also relentless. While trying to convince my daughter that she is worth fighting for, the Holy Spirit and other trusted voices have quietly stated that so am I. That unconditional love is the underlying foundation of the Gospel—the good news that isn't tied to a denomination, to abusers, or to effort.

God wanted me to know what it's like to pursue a child and their adoption in order to get a glimpse of his heart for me. He wanted me to unlearn my doubts, my assumptions, and my self-imposed restrictions. Sovereignty sent voices into my life to correct perspectives influenced by trauma and cultish inculcation. Friends from my current faith communities supported me while so much of my life stretched with the growing pains of new fatherhood. My inner circle affirmed the big and small surrenders inherent in sacrificial parenting. Over the years, Crystal has explained contexts and offered counsel as we fast-forwarded through the adjustment process first to the care of a teenager and then to official parenthood. We're now learning together how to be parents of a college kid.

D staked a large, fenceless homestead in the open plains of my heart, where wild horses run free. And I'm freer than I've ever been from my dad's shadow, my dad's influence, and my dad's corrupted theology.

The fight *for* D was part of the sovereign gift *of* D. Jesus knew an easy adoption wouldn't have accomplished as much as a difficult one. The Father wanted me to experience an ironic and redemptive path to understanding more of his infinite heart. The Holy Spirit shaped the process so that my daughter could see that God, her mom, and I permanently love her. Incredibly, Jesus is redeeming the trauma and pain of both my youth and my daughter's childhood—at the same time and through our shared relationship. Sovereignty flexed so many of the aspects of God's character on our behalf that I am regularly left to worship in gratitude.

For decades I've been a child of God. But now I know better than ever why he wanted to be my dad. When you've seen the heart of your Creator, so many of the inane arguments about what he might have meant between the lines of what he actually said—well, they blur into the periphery. Over the past two decades of my life, I've been in a process described by Dante

Bowe in the Maverick City Music song "Real Thing." Its heart-wrecking lyrics include the line "I'm losing my religion to be loved like a child."

That beautiful reclamation is why I wrote this book. I survived wounding by a grievous church and its more-than-flawed systems. I love Jesus more than ever, and I pray you can experience your own version of healing and reconstruction. That hope finds sure footing not in anything I can take credit for, but in the inescapable pursuit to which I succumbed.

The thirteenth-century Persian poet Rumi wrote, "Through love all pain will turn to medicine." Eight centuries later, I've witnessed that alchemy of redemption in my life. Since a couple of naked people ate forbidden fruit in a garden we can no longer visit, every human being has suffered through pain. But pain has a million times over provided the contrast for the healing that an unfettered relationship with our Creator can do. I'm grateful to be writing to you from that place of healing.

Speaking of reclamation, ten weeks after our adoption was finalized, our adoption attorney told her salvation story on stage at our church right before getting baptized. At the podium, Sarah said working D's adoption was why she gave church and Jesus a second chance after being hurt by the church in her past. She didn't just get processed after a profession of faith. She's in a Bible study and serving in our assembly. And thirteen months after her baptism, Sarah's husband got baptized. Both have participated in my church's disciples-making-disciples training program. I believe Sarah still would've found the heart of Jesus without her interactions with Crystal; but I've cried in multiple public places while reflecting on this very sweet reward of embracing fatherhood.

It might surprise you that I don't wish I had a different childhood or an alternative backstory. Like anyone reading this book, I would like to have known in the different "thens" what I know now; but I accept that I was dealt the hands of my life for a reason, for an eternal purpose. Somebody reading this book might need to hear their story in the details of mine. Someone listening to my words might need to borrow some of my courage to say and do hard things. Someone taking in these pages might need to know that the healing I've experienced after church trauma is possible.

The recovery, redemption, and reclamation of my story doesn't have to be an exception to the rule. Your pain can find meaning. The lies you've been told can be rebutted. You can attune your radar to notice the malignant teachings that signal when a church is not safe. You can find safety in a God who hates abuse. You can connect to Eternal Life now and forever without legalism, superstition, or self-deception. You can fall in love with Jesus, even after people who bear his name mistreat you. If the abused son of a child-molesting preacher can watch orchids grow out of the religious manure and relational ashes of his life, so can you.

My friend Dave says, "People with wounds are looking for people with scars." This book bares my scars because I want wounded souls to know healing is possible. It might be too crazy to believe, but I believe wounds created in unsafe churches can be healed by safe faith communities. My counselor, Lindsey, reminds me often that trauma from relationship can be healed only in relationship—and not just in relationship with Jesus, though that helps.

In a 2018 blog post for the Center for Action and Contemplation, Father Richard Rohr encapsulated the redemptive journey I've been walking:

> All healthy religion shows you what to do with your pain, with the absurd, the tragic, the nonsensical, the unjust, and the undeserved—all of which eventually come into every lifetime. If only we could see these wounds as the way through, as Jesus did, then they would become sacred wounds rather than scars to deny, disguise, or project onto others. I am sorry to admit that I first see my wounds as an obstacle more than a gift. Healing is a long journey. If we cannot find a way to make our wounds into sacred wounds, we invariably become cynical, negative, or bitter. This is the storyline of many of the greatest novels, myths, and stories of every culture. If we do not transform our pain, we will most assuredly transmit it—usually to those closest to us: our family, our neighbors, our coworkers, and, invariably, the most vulnerable, our children.

What wounded me helped get me to a beautiful place that I hope you also find. This book was written because my life story was rewritten. I wrote it because your story can be rewritten too. In *Shadowlands*, William Nicholson's play about C.S. Lewis, the playwright wrote, "We read to know we are not alone."

I hope at this point in the book you know you aren't alone. You're not in too deep. You're not out too far. It's not too late. You might have to replace so much of your *Argo* that little wood remains from its maiden voyage. But I and this book exist to tell you one thing: it's worth it.

A fire burns in me to free people from abuse, from manipulation, and from ignorance. I don't care if escapees and longtime refugees attend a church that looks like mine. If there's any proselytization inherent in this effort, it isn't to a specific religion or partisanship—because I'm not an ambassador of a denomination or a fan of political parties. The red-hot boiler that powered the locomotion of this manuscript has been filled by the same fire you'll find in the lyrics sung by Abner Ramirez and Drew Holcomb: "Give back the pieces of my Jesus. Take your counterfeit to hell."

ACKNOWLEDGMENTS

Crystal, thank you for your patience during my recovery and also for your healing declaration: "You are not your dad."
真実はあなたを自由にしてくれるでしょう

Ruthie, thank you for trusting me to tell your story. It's FREE. And so are we.

Lisa, thank you for believing me and trusting my heart. Thank you more for telling your story. You emboldened me to tell mine.

Lindsey Perkins, thanks for helping me untangle all of this. Thank you for the gifts of both the shock on your face and the tears behind your glasses.

Joy Eggerichs Reed, thank you for recommending the story I needed to tell when I was enamored with others.

Robin Barnett, thank you for telling me my story was original and important. You lit a fire that lifted the balloon of this dream.

Ariel Curry, of all you contributed toward this book becoming a reality the most important may have been your moist eyes on the other end of a Zoom call when you told me I could be a protector of women I don't even know.

Jeremy Wilkinson, thank you for providing the filter through which to tell this story and for showing me the opposite of what is represented in this book's dangerous examples.

Timmay! Thank you for seeing the supervillain I didn't become. You inspire me to live life without a green screen.

Steve and Sandi Brundage, thank you for sacrificially keeping the lifeline close during the tumultuous years of my life. Your hearts have always and only been safe.

Doug Noffsinger, your questions about this book buoyed my spirit as gifts from a great friend.

Aaron Tice, thank you for making sure my integrity gap continues to shrink and that I live up to the standards I set online and in my public writing.

Nate and Bailey Brown, thank you for the gift of "Uncle Ryan." The affection of your family has been a salve to my soul. Your littles have convinced me of who I really am, which frees me to share that in print.

Logan Patton, thank you for stoking the fire of my curiosity during our Sanity Hikes® and wilderness adventures. I tried to channel your humble inquisitiveness and wry exasperation while writing this book.

Barry Napier and Matt Towles, thank you for treating me as an equal and for celebrating the various small wins along the way.

Don Pape, thank you for making an exception for me and for overlooking all the good reasons this book would be a hard sell.

Richard Brown, thank you for taking a chance on an unknown variable—for not needing me to be one of the popular kids.

Brianna McCabe, thanks for not murdering all of my darlings.

Amie Norris, thanks for teaching me tools in Microsoft Word I should've known and for never asking, "Is your writing degree from an *accredited* institution!?" (It is not. Shocker, I know.)

Kristen Orlando, your patience is as admirable as your attention to detail. Thank you for preempting future face palms.

Amelia Graves, you provided the relief of a professional net below the high-wire act of publishing. Thanks for being a reliable teammate.

Phyllis Rand, thank you for introducing me to personal essays. Sixteen weeks in your class changed how I process the world and led me to an ever-growing collection of discoveries.

Dave Kountz, thank you for asking the right questions, the tough questions—and for reliably having answers to questions I've not yet asked.

Daniel Gunter, thanks for the space you've given me to figure out all of this while we lead together—and your commiseration that I've absorbed as grace.

Deonnie Zagacia, thank you for changing my life forever. I love you. I'm proud of you. Being your dad has been the biggest adventure of my life.

HELPFUL RESOURCES

These books influenced my healing journey and spiritual reconstruction.

A Church Called Tov by Laura Barringer and Scot McNight
A Year of Biblical Womanhood by Rachel Held Evans
All My Knotted-Up Life by Beth Moore
American Idolatry by Andrew Whitehead
Analog Church by Jay Kim
Asking Better Questions of the Bible by Marty Solomon
Bad Faith by Randall Balmer
Better Decisions, Fewer Regrets by Andy Stanley
Better Together by Danielle Strickland
Beyond an Angry God by Steve McVey
Braving the Wilderness by Brené Brown
Bully Pulpit by Michael J. Kruger
Celebrities for Jesus by Katelyn Beaty
Counting the Cost by Jill Duggar, Derick Dillard, and Craig Borlase
Crying in H Mart by Michelle Zauner
Cultish by Amanda Montell
Emotionally Healthy Spirituality by Peter Scazzero
Everybody Always by Bob Goff
Everything Happens for a Reason by Kate Bowler
Extreme Ownership by Jocko Willink and Leif Babin
Finding God's Life for My Will by Mike Donehey
Forgiving What You Can't Forget by Lysa TerKeurst
Fortune by Lisa Sharon Harper
From Lost to Found by Nicole Zasowski
Gentle and Lowly by Dane Ortlund
Get Your Life Back by John Eldredge
Good Baggage by Ike Miller

Good Boundaries and Goodbyes by Lysa TerKeurst
Grace in the Gray by Mike Donehey
Help Thanks Wow by Anne Lamott
How the Bible Actually Works by Peter Enns
How to Heal Our Racial Divide by Derwin Gray
How to Hide an Empire by Daniel Immerwahr
How's Your Soul? by Judah Smith
I Guess I Haven't Learned That Yet by Shauna Niequist
I'm Still Here by Austin Channing Brown
Inspired by Rachel Held Evans
It Didn't Start with You by Mark Wolynn
Jesus and John Wayne by Kristin Kobes Du Mez
Lament for a Father by Marvin Olasky
Letters to the Church by Francis Chan
Live in Grace, Walk in Love by Bob Goff
Love Does by Bob Goff
Maybe You Should Talk to Someone by Lori Gottlieb
Misreading Scripture with Western Eyes by E. Randolph Richards and Brandon J. O'Brien
Necessary Endings by Henry Cloud
No Cure for Being Human by Kate Bowler
Not in It to Win It by Andy Stanley
Orphaned Believers by Sara Billups
PreachersNSneakers by Ben Kirby
Prey Tell by Tiffany Bluhm
Reading While Black by Esau McCaulley
Redeeming Power by Diane Langberg
Reorganized Religion by Bob Smietana
Sacred Pathways by Gary Thomas
Shrinking the Integrity Gap by Jeff Mattson and Terra Mattson
Something's Not Right by Wade Mullen
Soul Care to Save Your Life by Manda Carpenter
Tell Her Story by Nijay K Gupta
Testimony by Jon Ward
The Blue Parakeet by Scot McNight
The Cost of Control by Sharon Hodde Miller

The Deeply Formed Life by Rich Villodas
The Examined Life by Stephen Grosz
The Genius of Jesus by Erwin Raphael McManus
The Gift of Being Yourself by David G. Benner
The God Who Sees by Karen Gonzalez
The God-Shaped Brain by Timothy R. Jennings
The Great Sex Rescue by Sheila Wray Gregoire, Rebecca Gregoire Lindenbach, and Joanna Sawatsky
The Liturgy of Politics by Kaitlyn Schiess
The Making of Biblical Womanhood by Beth Allison Barr
The Men We Need by Brant Hansen
The Religion of American Greatness by Paul D. Miller
The Sin of Certainty by Peter Enns
The Thing Beneath the Thing by Steve Carter
The Truth about Us by Brant Hansen
The Very Worst Missionary by Jamie Wright
The World's Largest Man by Harrison Scott Key
Tribe by Sebastian Junger
Unoffendable by Brant Hansen
Unsettling Truths by Mark Charles and Soong-Chan Rah
Until Unity by Francis Chan
Untrustworthy by Bonnie Kristian
We the Fallen People by Robert Tracy McKenzie
What If Jesus Was Serious? by Skye Jethani
What If Jesus Was Serious about Prayer? by Skye Jethani
What If Jesus Was Serious about Heaven? by Skye Jethani
What Made Jesus Mad? by Tim Harlow
When Faith Fails by Dominic Done
When Narcissism Comes to Church by Chuck DeGroat
When Thoughts and Prayers Aren't Enough by Taylor S. Schumann
Where the Light Fell by Philip Yancey
White Fragility by Robin DiAngelo

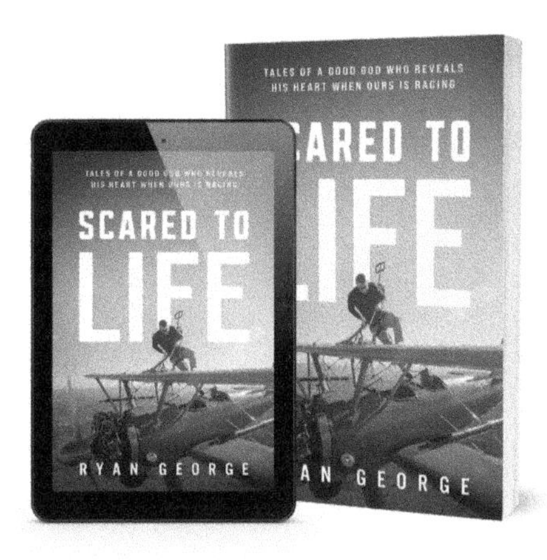

In *Scared to Life*, Ryan leverages tales of adventure to address our comparison culture, the ache we feel that the stories of our lives aren't enough, and the suspicion that there's more to the Christian journey than what we've experienced. In this book, Ryan offers practical suggestions for living an ordinary life in an extraordinary way. Scared to Life is available as a paperback, Kindle ebook, and audiobook. You can see all of Ryan's books at

www.booksbyryan.com

Ryan blogs about spiritual discoveries found during physical adventures at

www.explorience.org

Ryan interviews physical and spiritual adventurers on the Everyday Adventures podcast available wherever you listen to podcasts.

www.podcastfriends.com

biplane
productions

CONNECT WITH RYAN:

ryplane

Printed in the USA
CPSIA information can be obtained
at www.ICGtesting.com
CBHW040258240324
5746CB00010B/91

9 781955 051330